Mastering Knative
Comprehensive Strategies for Scalable Serverless Solutions on Kubernetes

Nova Trex

Published by Wang Press

For permissions and other inquiries, write to:
P.O. Box 3132, Framingham, MA 01701, USA

Contents

3

Introduction

The landscape of application development has undergone a monumental transformation in recent years, presenting both exciting opportunities and notable challenges for developers globally. As the quest for scalability, efficiency, and rapid deployment accelerates, serverless computing emerges as a formidable solution. This book, "Mastering Knative: Comprehensive Strategies for Scalable Serverless Solutions on Kubernetes," is meticulously crafted to provide developers with an in-depth understanding of Knative—a robust, open-source platform engineered to streamline serverless deployments on Kubernetes.

Knative epitomizes the evolution of cloud-native computing by abstracting the intricate complexities traditionally associated with managing application infrastructure. By focusing on code rather than the underlying operational tasks, developers can achieve accelerated deployment cycles and improved resource management. Knative melds the dependability and expansive capabilities of Kubernetes with the dynamic nature of serverless architectures, empowering developers to create applications that intelligently scale and adapt to fluctuating workloads.

Our journey begins by dissecting the foundational concepts that underpin serverless computing and Kubernetes. Readers will be equipped with essential insights into how Knative leverages these technologies to deliver unparalleled scalability, event-driven functionality, and seamless integration with a broad spectrum of cloud services.

Subsequent chapters are dedicated to the practical deployment and management of serverless applications utilizing Knative's extensive Serving and Eventing frameworks. Through meticulously detailed tutorials and meticulously curated real-world examples, readers will discover how to unlock the potential of Knative to forge applications characterized by enhanced scalability, resilience, and efficiency.

This volume also tackles crucial facets necessary for a seamless transition to serverless architectures, delving into monitoring, observability, and innovative approaches to security. The book emphasizes best practices for integrating Knative with continuous deployment workflows and offers an in-depth exploration of its symbiotic relationship with the wider Kubernetes ecosystem, making it an ideal choice for organizations keen on cloud-native technologies.

The concluding chapters illuminate real-world applications and success stories, illustrating Knative's adaptability across diverse industries and varied use cases. By the book's conclusion, developers will not only have fine-tuned their ability to deploy serverless applications using Knative but will also possess a robust strategic framework for leveraging this transformative technology to meet specific organizational objectives and challenges.

Whether you are a seasoned developer eager to delve into the world of serverless technology or a newcomer embarking on the exciting voyage of cloud-native development, "Mastering Knative" serves as an exhaustive resource for mastering the nuances of constructing and scaling serverless applications on Kubernetes. By enhancing your expertise with the insights contained herein, you will be better positioned to deliver cutting-edge applications that seamlessly address the dynamic technological demands of today's fast-paced digital era.

Chapter 1

Introduction to Knative and Serverless Concepts

This chapter lays the foundation by explaining the essentials of serverless architecture, highlighting its advantages over traditional computing models. It delves into the core components and objectives of Knative, illustrating its integration within the Kubernetes ecosystem. Key features of Knative, such as serving, eventing, and autoscaling, are discussed to showcase its capabilities. The chapter also examines how developers benefit from Knative by simplifying deployment and enhancing scalability, and it provides a comparison with other serverless platforms to underscore Knative's unique position in delivering serverless solutions within Kubernetes environments.

1.1   Understanding Serverless Architecture

Serverless architecture, or Function as a Service (FaaS), has emerged as a pivotal paradigm in modern cloud computing, fundamentally altering how developers design and deploy applications. Characterized by abstracting the server management away from the developers, it enables them to focus exclusively on deploying code. This section delves into the principles of serverless computing, its benefits, and how it deviates from traditional computing models.

Serverless architecture primarily revolves around executing functions in response to events, automating and scaling based upon demand, without the need for specific infrastructure management. This approach differs significantly from Infrastructure as a Service (IaaS) or Platform as a Service (PaaS) models, where developers must handle more extensive system configurations and maintenance.

In traditional models, systems are generally designed around the concept of dedicated servers. This involves provisioning and managing physical or virtual servers to handle runtime, often leading to over-provisioning issues for handling peak loads, resulting in underutilized resources during non-peak times. Serverless architecture, on the other hand, operates fundamentally differently by utilizing the cloud provider's capabilities to dynamically allocate resources only when needed.

```
# Example of deployable function in serverless environment
$ gcloud functions deploy helloWorld --runtime nodejs14 --trigger-http --allow-
    unauthenticated
```

Here, the command deploys a cloud function, 'helloWorld', with no dedicated server to manage, highlighting that functions execute in a stateless manner.

```
> Deployment completed.
> Function URL (helloWorld): https://REGION-PROJECT.cloudfunctions.net/helloWorld
```

The simplicity of this deployment showcases the core principle of serverless computing: ease of deployment, achieved by focusing solely on code and logic, while abstracting server infrastructure. Moreover, it accentuates a cost-efficient model where billing is strictly usage-based—charging for exact compute time and resources utilized, rather than a flat rate for server uptime.

Within serverless architectures, the central component, often referred to simply as a "function", executes in response to specific events. These events can be HTTP requests, file uploads, database updates, and more. With such fine-grained scalability, serverless platforms automatically ensure high availability and fault tolerance by managing multiple deployments and geographical distributions.

The benefits of serverless computing are manifold:

- **Efficient Scaling**: The platform automatically and dynamically scales functions based on the incoming workload. There are no manual configurations for scaling policies or load balancers.

- **Cost Management**: As costs are proportional to the number of requests and execution time, it avoids paying for idle server time and improves cost-efficiency.

- **Focus on Development**: Developers concentrate on writing application logic with pre-built services for database management, authentication, cloud storage, etc., significantly accelerating development time.

When contrasting serverless with traditional models, it is imperative to understand the notion of statelessness in functions. Statelessness implies that each invocation receives no memory of previous executions. To maintain session information or share common state, supplementary services like databases or cache layers (e.g., Redis, DynamoDB) must be leveraged.

In serverless platforms, messaging queues (e.g., Amazon SQS, Google Pub/Sub) often play a crucial role, predominantly in event-driven architectures. By decoupling the invocation events from the consuming functions, they help in coordinating various computational tasks within a cloud-based application.

To illustrate a typical serverless application workflow, consider this scenario: A user uploads an image to a cloud service, triggering a sequence of automated functions:

- An image upload event is detected.

- A function is invoked to process and categorize the image.

- Another function may store metadata in a database.

- Finally, the categorization result triggers further notifications.

Each component operates independently and scales automatically based on the demand for each individual function, illustrating the versatility of serverless solutions.

Serverless architecture's immediate advantages are palpable in scenarios demanding rapid scaling, diverse functionality, and extensive integration with third-party APIs. Streaming data processes and real-time applications often adopt serverless models to alleviate the complexity inherent in managing continuously running services.

Consider the following example demonstrating an architecture using AWS Lambda, a serverless computing service from Amazon Web Services:

```python
import json

def lambda_handler(event, context):
    # Extract the 'message' attribute from the event data
    message = event.get('message', 'Hello, World')

    # Respond with a simple JSON output
    return {
        "statusCode": 200,
        "body": json.dumps({
            "message": f"Received message: {message}"
        }),
    }
```

The above function listens for incoming events, responding with a simple message transformation as an HTTP response. The robust integration capabilities of serverless platforms also allow this handler to integrate with APIs, feeding data into machine learning models, or even orchestrating complex workflows through AWS Step Functions.

While serverless presents compelling advantages, understanding its inherent trade-offs is vital for informed decision-making. Potential downsides may include:

- **Cold Start Latency**: Due to the nature of serverless technology, an initial request to a function can experience latency while resources are provisioned. Optimizing these cold starts often involves keeping minimal resources warm but may introduce nominal cost implications.

- **Limited Runtime and Execution Time**: Serverless functions typically run in constrained environments with strict limits on execution duration and available resources (memory, storage).

- **Complexity in Debugging**: Debugging distributed serverless functions can be arduous due to the stateless nature and decentralized execution across different infrastructure services.

- **Platform Specific Constraints**: Vendor lock-in and platform-specific configurations may hinder portability of serverless configurations across different cloud providers.

To contend with these complexities, serverless applications are often architected with robust logging (e.g., AWS CloudWatch), monitoring services, and extensive use of API gateways for interfacing between disparate features. Proper design patterns and efficient use of cloud-native tools ensure reliability and system resilience.

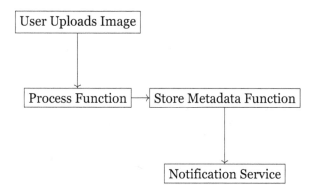

With overall comprehension, serverless architecture invariably influences contemporary software design by promoting modularity, fostering innovation through reduced operational burdens, and maximizing developer productivity. Its evolutionary progression substantiates its role in enabling rapid digital transformations, accommodating novel user experiences, and encouraging business model optimization.

1.2   Overview of Knative

Knative is a comprehensive Kubernetes-based platform designed to provide the necessary components to build, deploy, and manage modern serverless applications. As the landscape of serverless computing evolves, Knative stands out by integrating these capabilities tightly into the Kubernetes ecosystem, providing developers with a robust framework for deploying cloud-native applications with enhanced agile delivery and management features.

Knative's architecture is built around two core components: *Serving* and *Eventing*, each facilitating different aspects of building serverless applications. By leveraging Kubernetes' orchestration prowess, Knative aims to simplify managing the lifecycle of applications while embracing Kubernetes' flexibility and scalability.

Knative Serving focuses on deploying and managing serverless workloads, making it easy to run services on demand, handle HTTP requests, and autoscale based on necessity. It extends Kubernetes capabilities by providing a higher level of abstraction, focusing on revisions, configurations, and routes.

A basic Knative Serving deployment workflow involves the following elements:

- **Service**: A Knative Service object describes the details of a serverless application. Each service comprises configurations and routes, ensuring correct request routing.

- **Route**: Routes handle incoming requests, mapping them to specific revisions or services, enabling users to control traffic splitting and rollbacks efficiently.

- **Configuration**: This specifies the desired state of the application, defining environmental variables, images, and more.

14

- **Revision**: Each change to the configuration results in a new revision—a snapshot of the code and configuration state, facilitating version control and canary deployments.

Deploying a Knative Service involves creating a manifest that declares application properties, akin to Kubernetes Deployment manifests, facilitating smooth integrations with existing tools.

```yaml
apiVersion: serving.knative.dev/v1
kind: Service
metadata:
  name: helloworld-go
spec:
  template:
    spec:
      containers:
      - image: gcr.io/knative-samples/helloworld-go
        env:
        - name: TARGET
          value: "Go Sample v1"
```

This YAML manifest describes a Knative Service called 'helloworld-go', specifying the container image and environment variables. The declarative nature aligns with Kubernetes principles, providing a seamless deployment experience.

Upon deploying, Knative creates a route to automatically expose the service over HTTP, assigning a unique URL. Its automated traffic management capabilities allow developers to direct traffic between revisions, affording precise control over application updates.

Knative Serving's autoscaling mechanisms are deeply integrated, automatically adjusting the number of pods based on request throughput. This aids in cost management by allocating resources only when demand necessitates it.

Moving to **Knative Eventing**, this component addresses the need for event-driven architectures, empowering developers to build and integrate applications that respond to cloud events from various sources, processing them in a loosely coupled, scalable manner.

Knative Eventing framework sees the use of several critical resources:

- **Source**: Event sources generate events, effectively bridging external services with Knative-compliant components.

- **Broker**: A central hub for receiving events, managing event distribution without requiring direct connections between producing and consuming applications.

- **Trigger**: Defines the event routing rules, specifying how events are dispatched from brokers to services.

- **Channel and Subscription**: Channels serve as event dispatching medium, while subscriptions attach consumers to channels, managing message flow.

A fundamental eventing setup in Knative might involve defining a broker and triggering an event-driven service when a specific event occurs. Consider the following Knative Eventing configuration:

```yaml
apiVersion: eventing.knative.dev/v1
kind: Broker
metadata:
  name: default

---

apiVersion: eventing.knative.dev/v1
kind: Trigger
metadata:
  name: demo-trigger
spec:
  broker: default
  filter:
    attributes:
      type: dev.knative.sample
  subscriber:
    ref:
      apiVersion: serving.knative.dev/v1
      kind: Service
      name: event-display
```

This setup introduces a 'Broker' named 'default', alongside a 'Trigger' that listens for events of type 'dev.knative.sample', directing them to a Knative Service 'event-display'. The decoupled nature of the eventing model enhances flexibility and abstraction, allowing scalable applications that easily react to environmental changes or external inputs.

Central to Knative's architecture is the Kubernetes ecosystem, leveraging Kubernetes Custom Resource Definitions (CRDs) to extend Kubernetes into a serverless platform. This integration provides several advantages:

16

- **1. Uniform Tooling**: Existing Kubernetes tools and practices, such as kubectl and helm charts, seamlessly manage Knative components, diminishing the learning curve for Kubernetes-savvy developers.

- **2. Scalability**: Kubernetes' inherently scalable architecture ensures that Knative Services and Events operate efficiently regardless of load, encapsulating infrastructure-level concerns.

- **3. Portability**: Being built on Kubernetes ensures that Knative services can run easily across on-premise and any cloud environments that support Kubernetes, promoting a hybrid and multi-cloud strategy.

- **4. Flexibility**: Developers retain control over lower-level Kubernetes resources, tuning performance and behavior to suit specific application needs.

Knative's ecosystem not only standardizes serverless workloads on Kubernetes but also establishes a strong foundation for community collaboration and innovation. It supports a variety of extensions through its pluggable architecture, allowing for the integration of different networking layers, observability tools, and authentication mechanisms.

The flexibility inherent to Knative encourages the development of complex workflows using its components, streamlining orchestration processes. Developers can build comprehensive serverless applications by combining Knative Serving and Eventing, seen in real-time data streaming applications, responsive microservices, or event-driven machine learning pipelines.

Knative provides seamless integration capabilities with other cloud-native utilities, such as Istio for advanced network scenarios, Prometheus for metrics collection, and OpenTracing for distributed application tracing. These integrations enable fine-grained monitoring and troubleshooting across multiple deployments, ensuring optimal application performance and developer productivity.

For practical applications, consider a use case where a Kubernetes-native containerized application requires reactive scaling. By employing Knative Services, developers can effortlessly define their 'Deployment' logic, facilitating rapid upscaling in response to HTTP load

17

changes without manual interventions, demonstrated in a configuration below:

```
apiVersion: autoscaling.knative.dev/v1alpha1
kind: Metric
metadata:
  name: concurrency
  namespace: default
spec:
  thresholds:
    target: 10
```

The aforementioned YAML manifests set criteria for Knative to autoscale pods based on concurrent requests, emphasizing an immediate infrastructure response aligned with incoming traffic patterns, thus optimizing performance and cost-effectiveness.

Through this architectural overview, the compelling position of Knative within the serverless ecosystem becomes apparent. Its enhancements over traditional serverless approaches, together with native Kubernetes integration, provide developers with unprecedented control and adaptability in cloud-native application management. Knative not only strengthens Kubernetes-centric workloads but also paves the way for scalable, event-driven application development poised for future technological innovations.

1.3   Key Features of Knative

Knative is a cutting-edge open-source platform deployed on Kubernetes that provides essential building blocks for developers to create, deploy, and manage serverless applications. Its feature set empowers developers to efficiently handle demanding workloads while leveraging Kubernetes' scalable architecture. This section elaborates on the key features of Knative, including *Serving*, *Eventing*, and *Autoscaling*, each optimizing the serverless experience within the Kubernetes ecosystem.

1. Knative Serving is a core component that manages stateless services, streamlining the deployment and management of serverless containers. It introduces the following key concepts and features:

Revisions: Knative facilitates immutable deployment entities called re-

18

visions, snapshots of code and configuration state. Each configuration change leads to a new revision, allowing developers to revert to earlier versions effortlessly, thus enabling traffic splitting and canaries for testing updates without penalty.

Traffic Routing: By defining intricate traffic distribution, Knative permits developers to direct specific percentages of traffic to different service revisions seamlessly. This is particularly useful for gradual rollouts (canary deployments) or blue-green deployments. Traffic splitting can be specified as follows:

```
apiVersion: serving.knative.dev/v1
kind: Service
metadata:
  name: myservice
spec:
  traffic:
  - revisionName: myservice-00001
    percent: 50
  - revisionName: myservice-00002
    percent: 50
```

This configuration sends equal percentages of incoming traffic to two different revisions, allowing simultaneous testing and production stability.

Configuration: This includes container image specifications, environment variables, scaling configurations, and more, abstracting complexities otherwise managed through Kubernetes Deployment.

Networking Integration: Integrated seamlessly with network layers like Istio or Contour, Knative provides advanced networking features like request-based load balancing, mTLS (mutual Transport Layer Security), and seamless connectivity for secure service-to-service communication.

2. Knative Eventing offers an event-driven architecture following the design principles of flexibility, extensibility, and developer empowerment. It provides:

Decoupled Event Producers and Consumers: Through channels and brokers, Knative introduces an event mesh that decouples sources from consumers, providing a flexible, pluggable approach to handling events from diverse sources.

Choice in Messaging Layers: Knative Eventing supports various underlying messaging infrastructures, ensuring compatibility and adaptability. RabbitMQ, Kafka, and Google Pub/Sub are popular examples that developers can swap as per infrastructure preference.

To create an eventing mechanism:

```
apiVersion: messaging.knative.dev/v1
kind: Channel
metadata:
  name: my-channel

---

apiVersion: eventing.knative.dev/v1
kind: Subscription
metadata:
  name: my-subscription
spec:
  channel:
    apiVersion: messaging.knative.dev/v1
    kind: Channel
    name: my-channel
  subscriber:
    ref:
      apiVersion: serving.knative.dev/v1
      kind: Service
      name: my-service
```

This setup sends messages from events through 'my-channel' to the service 'my-service', illustrating an efficient flow of information encapsulated within channels and subscriptions.

Event Filtering and Triggers: Developers can apply filters to route specific events to targeted consumers, allowing sophisticated workflows and dynamic service invocation.

3. Autoscaling (KPA and HPA): One of Knative's most renowned features is its ability to efficiently manage loads by scaling services automatically, adapting to incoming pressures via two main patterns:

Knative Pod Autoscaler (KPA): Primarily focuses on request-based metrics for autoscaling, managing upscaling and downscaling based upon the number of concurrent requests, ensuring resources align closely with demand.

Horizontal Pod Autoscaler (HPA): Utilizes Kubernetes' built-in autoscaling capabilities by analyzing CPU utilization or custom metrics. It defines resource-based scaling policies easily integrated with existing Kubernetes clusters.

Here's a sample autoscaling policy defined within a Knative Service:

```
apiVersion: serving.knative.dev/v1
kind: Service
metadata:
  name: scalable-service
spec:
  template:
    metadata:
      annotations:
        autoscaling.knative.dev/target: "100"
    spec:
      containers:
      - image: gcr.io/myproject/scalable-app
```

The specification uses annotations to define target concurrency for scaling. Knative ensures seamless pod scaling up or down, maintaining consistent application performance.

4. Pluggability and Extensibility: Knative's architecture caters to highly configurable extensions. Pluggability enables developers to easily integrate purpose-fit components, such as custom networking, monitoring, or messaging solutions without modifying core Knative constructs. This flexibility fosters growth and encourages innovative solutions tailored to specialized needs.

5. Developer Productivity and CI/CD Integration: Knative inherently improves developer workflows by embracing CI/CD pipelines, facilitating shorter development cycles through automated testing and deploying capabilities. It integrates robustly with CI/CD tools like Tekton Pipelines and Jenkins. This seamless integration cuts toolchain complexity, allowing developers to focus on feature delivery and refinement efficiently.

Developers can implement automated deployment pipelines using the Tekton Pipeline principles with Knative for easy CI/CD as exemplified below:

```
apiVersion: tekton.dev/v1alpha1
kind: Task
metadata:
  name: build-and-deploy
spec:
  steps:
  - name: build
    image: gcr.io/cloud-builders/docker
    ...
  - name: deploy
    image: knative.dev/client/cmd/kn
```

21

```
...
```

This process defines tasks for building and deploying applications, ensuring a cohesive, automated, and repeatable approach to application lifecycle management.

Through these features, Knative solidifies itself as a formidable platform for crafting serverless applications. Its careful orchestration brings substantial benefits to various categories of cloud-native applications by enhancing maintainability and scalability. It offers unparalleled deployment speed, agility, and scalability, propelling application efficiency and robustness in diverse cloud environments.

Knative encourages modularity and clean separation of concern in application architecture, linking services and functions via well-defined interfaces and patterns. It leverages extensive open-source community support, ensuring continuous improvements and innovations. Developers gain tightly integrated tools to enhance resilience, observability, and security across deployed serverless solutions.

The success of Knative hinges upon holistic precept compatibility with Kubernetes, delivering scalability, operational consistency, and resource management accuracy. Knative's designed abstractions elevate serverless deployment on Kubernetes not only to meet present demands but also to reach new horizons in cloud-native computing evolution.

1.4   Benefits of Using Knative for Developers

Knative is an open-source initiative designed to streamline the development of serverless applications, building on top of Kubernetes. For developers, Knative presents a suite of advantages that markedly improve efficiency, reduce operational burdens, and facilitate the effective management of cloud-native applications. In this section, we analyze the tangible benefits that Knative offers developers, alongside practical insights and coding examples to underscore its utility.

Accelerated Development Cycle: Knative abstracts much of the complexity inherent in managing cloud infrastructure, enabling developers to concentrate on writing business logic rather than managing servers or networking configurations. By utilizing Knative's built-in components, developers can implement agile development methodologies, reducing time-to-market and accelerating the iteration cycle for applications.

With Knative Serving, deploying updated code versions becomes a streamlined process with built-in revision management. Consider deploying application updates using Knative's YAML configuration:

```
apiVersion: serving.knative.dev/v1
kind: Service
metadata:
  name: myapp-v2
spec:
  template:
    spec:
      containers:
      - image: gcr.io/myproject/myapp:v2
```

This configuration allows seamless updating to a new version of the application container with minimal downtime and without worrying about underlying infrastructure changes.

Scalability and Resource Optimization: Knative's automatic scaling features ensure that applications can handle traffic spikes effortlessly without manual intervention. This dynamic scaling provides a crucial advantage regarding resource utilization: applications automatically scale in and out in response to load, reducing costs and optimizing performance.

Developers can configure autoscaling policies directly in their service manifests, tuning application scalability to align with business needs. Autoscaling based on concurrent request load can be specified as follows:

```
apiVersion: serving.knative.dev/v1
kind: Service
metadata:
  name: autoscale-svc
spec:
  template:
    metadata:
      annotations:
        autoscaling.knative.dev/minScale: "1"
        autoscaling.knative.dev/maxScale: "10"
    spec:
```

```
containers:
- image: gcr.io/myproject/autoscale-app
```

Here, the configuration sets limits on the minimum and maximum pod instances, ensuring controlled and predictable scaling behavior without requiring developers to modify Kubernetes resources directly.

Cost Efficiency: The introduction of serverless architecture facilitated by Knative brings a pay-per-use pricing model, which often translates to direct cost savings. Developers benefit by deploying applications that consume resources only when called, reducing idle capacity costs.

Knative allows granular control over computing resources, optimizing for cost reduction—vital for startups and organizations focused on minimizing operational expenditures while scaling digital solutions.

Seamless CI/CD Integration: Knative is built to work effectively alongside modern CI/CD tools, such as Jenkins, Tekton, and GitLab CI/CD, which automates the building and deploying of applications. This seamless integration ensures that new changes are continuously deployed, minimizing manual steps in the development pipeline and reinforcing rapid iteration and efficiency.

Developers can implement Tekton tasks specifically tailored for Knative to ensure continuous delivery excellence, as demonstrated in the following code snippet:

```
apiVersion: tekton.dev/v1beta1
kind: Task
metadata:
  name: build-deploy-knative
spec:
  steps:
  - name: building
    image: gcr.io/cloud-builders/kaniko-project/executor
    command: ["--context=/workspace/source", "--destination=gcr.io/myproject/
        myapp"]
  - name: deploy
    image: gcr.io/knative-releases/kn
    script: |
      kn service apply myapp --image=gcr.io/myproject/myapp
```

The above task automates the build and deployment of a Knative service myapp, highlighting the integration capabilities of Knative within continuous delivery workflows.

Improved Developer Productivity: By removing the operational overhead associated with managing server environments, Knative frees developers to focus on application features and innovations. The abstractions eliminate repetitive tasks such as configuring load balancers, writing complex deployment scripts, and ensuring scalability through dedicated hardware or VM management.

Developers benefit from deploying applications with simplicity and ease, using Knative's intuitive command-line interface (kn) to interact with resources efficiently:

```
# Create and expose a new service
$ kn service create myapp --image=gcr.io/myproject/myapp

# Update the service to a new image
$ kn service update myapp --image=gcr.io/myproject/myapp:v2
```

This command-line interaction showcases the streamlined deployment and management that Knative offers, also reflecting cloud-native computing principles with Kubernetes.

Robust Event Handling: Knative's Eventing capabilities equip developers to build applications that act on event triggers, enforcing modern event-driven paradigms central to microservices frameworks and complex applications. This open eventing model ensures comprehensive event routing, filtering, and transformation, promoting flexibility and modular design principles.

Consider a scenario using Knative Eventing to send notifications when an event is triggered:

```
apiVersion: eventing.knative.dev/v1
kind: Broker
metadata:
  name: default

---

apiVersion: eventing.knative.dev/v1
kind: Trigger
metadata:
  name: notify-trigger
spec:
  broker: default
  filter:
    attributes:
      type: dev.knative.demo
  subscriber:
    ref:
```

25

```
apiVersion: serving.knative.dev/v1
kind: Service
name: notification-service
```

This setup enables an event sent with type dev.knative.demo to be dispatched to the notification-service, a typical pattern for dispatching notifications or triggering subsequent workflows in event-router models.

Enhanced Flexibility and Extensibility: Built on Kubernetes, Knative consistently aligns with cloud-native design, affording developers significant flexibility and extensibility. Integrating open standards, pluggable components for messaging or networking, and custom resources caters to varied development requirements. This ensures that developers can adapt Knative to fit specific use-case requirements, bolstering innovation.

Robust Support and Ecosystem Integration: Being an open-source project with substantial industry backing, Knative guarantees developers a well-supported environment. With continuous contributions from leading cloud providers and an active community, developers gain access to a wide spectrum of support resources, updates, and ecosystem tools.

Compatibility with Istio and additional networking layers ensures advanced traffic management capabilities. By supporting industry standards, Knative interplays flawlessly with existing system components and tooling, emphasizing interoperability and enhancing system reliability.

Security and Observability: Knative's architecture delivers built-in security mechanisms and robust observability features. Integration with monitoring systems such as Prometheus and observability tools like Grafana provides insights into service behavior, performance metrics, and infrastructure access logs, empowering developers to maintain and optimize services effectively.

Security layers include mutual Transport Layer Security (mTLS) and the ability to define tightly controlled network policies, further extending application security layers by following Kubernetes security best practices.

Cloud-Agnostic Development: Knative offers an unprecedented level of portability across cloud providers and on-premise

26

deployments, ensuring applications are not tightly coupled to specific environments. Developers can deploy Knative on any Kubernetes-compatible system, providing significant management flexibility and supporting multi-cloud strategies without vendor lock-in constraints.

Knative materials' easy reproducibility assures that applications can migrate across cloud ecosystems, leading to ideal resource optimization and cost effectiveness. This approach facilitates strategic deployment decisions based on performance needs, geographical proximity considerations, or organizational policy requirements.

Knative provides developers a potent platform combining ease of use, cost efficiency, scalability, compatibility, and flexibility. By encapsulating the principles of modern serverless architecture with the proven infrastructure management of Kubernetes, Knative not only enhances the serverless and cloud-native development experience but also fuels the seamless transformation of organizational technological landscapes. It enables developers to harness cutting-edge cloud architectures, ensuring they remain at the forefront of deploying and maintaining sophisticated and adaptable software solutions.

1.5 Comparing Knative with Other Serverless Platforms

The serverless computing landscape has been fundamentally transformed by the introduction of platforms tailored to abstract infrastructure management and streamline application deployments. Among these platforms, Knative stands out due to its Kubernetes-native design, contrasting significantly with other prominent serverless offerings such as AWS Lambda, Azure Functions, and Google Cloud Functions. This section provides an in-depth comparative analysis of Knative relative to these services, emphasizing its unique benefits within Kubernetes environments alongside insightful discussions on implementation and operational paradigms.

Serverless platforms primarily aim for agility, scalability, and reduced operational overhead, yet they diverge in their architectural constructs, features, and user experiences. Understanding these nuances is cru-

27

cial for organizations seeking the optimal serverless solution tailored to their specific needs.

- **1. Kubernetes-Native Architecture:** Knative is inherently designed to operate within Kubernetes clusters, leveraging existing Kubernetes resources such as pods, deployments, and services. This alignment with Kubernetes empowers users with unparalleled control over their serverless deployments, allowing complete customization and integration with Kubernetes-based workflows.

- Contrastingly, platforms like AWS Lambda and Azure Functions are tightly integrated with their respective cloud provider ecosystems. These are inherently closed systems that abstract the lower-level details and offer less direct control over the underlying execution environment. Developers on AWS Lambda, for example, are limited to a set runtime environment without the flexibility to customize beyond the provided configurations.

- In Knative, developers can leverage Kubernetes Custom Resource Definitions (CRDs) to define serverless functionalities, integrating naturally with Kubernetes management tools and enabling complex deployment scenarios:

```
apiVersion: serving.knative.dev/v1
kind: Service
metadata:
  name: custom-runtime-service
spec:
  template:
    spec:
      containers:
      - image: custom/knative-app:latest
        env:
        - name: CONFIG
          value: "production"
```

This configuration showcases the seamless deployment of custom runtime applications within a Kubernetes ecosystem, an inherent advantage of Knative over pre-defined environments seen in AWS Lambda or Google Cloud Functions.

- **2. Eventing Capabilities:** Knative Eventing provides a flexible, extensible event-driven architecture where developers can

28

build powerful event processing systems without being tied to proprietary formats or protocols. It supports various sources and sinks using a decoupled architecture, enabling sophisticated event orchestration.

- Alternatively, AWS Lambda excels at event-driven computing but tends to lock users into the AWS ecosystem, especially when integrating with AWS-specific services such as S3, SNS, or DynamoDB. Azure Functions and Google Cloud Functions similarly encourage users to leverage their proprietary event and data services.

- Knative's open model allows for integration with any event source or messaging protocol through its pluggable architecture. Developers enjoy the freedom to utilize existing enterprise messaging systems, forming event chains or workflows:

```
apiVersion: messaging.knative.dev/v1
kind: Channel
metadata:
  name: rabbitmq-channel

---

apiVersion: eventing.knative.dev/v1
kind: Subscription
metadata:
  name: rabbitmq-subscription
spec:
  channel:
    apiVersion: messaging.knative.dev/v1
    kind: Channel
    name: rabbitmq-channel
  subscriber:
    ref:
      apiVersion: serving.knative.dev/v1
      kind: Service
      name: process-service
```

Here, Knative channels integrate seamlessly with RabbitMQ, providing advanced event routing capabilities compatible with various backend systems.

- **3. Scalability and Performance:** The robustness of Knative in handling scale lies in its tight integration with Kubernetes. It benefits from Kubernetes' inherent scalability, managing pod lifecycles efficiently to respond to variable loads. Knative's scaling is highly configurable through annotations, offering greater flexibility to meet specific workload characteristics.

- In contrast, AWS Lambda and Google Cloud Functions abstract the scaling capability, automatically managing instances based on real-time demand. This approach simplifies the user experience but at the cost of reduced visibility and influence over runtime scaling mechanics.

- Knative users have the advantage of configuring detailed scaling properties driven by concurrent requests or custom signals:

```
apiVersion: autoscaling.knative.dev/v1alpha1
kind: Metric
metadata:
  name: custom-metric
  namespace: production
spec:
  thresholds:
    target: 50
```

This capability allows Knative users to tailor their autoscaling strategies based on precise business metrics, maintaining efficiency and cost-effectiveness across dynamic workloads.

- **4. Cost Structures and Pricing Models:** Adopting Knative, running on self-managed Kubernetes clusters, affords greater predictability and control over resource utilization, allowing organizations to tailor cloud spend according to operational needs and traffic patterns.

- Serverless functions on AWS Lambda or Azure Functions often incur varied charges based on executions, runtime durations, and allocated resources, leading to variable and often less predictable costs. These platforms' serverless pricing models may become costly for high-throughput applications depending on function call frequencies and execution durations.

- Knative's approach aligns with Kubernetes cost management, leveraging existing allocation-based models, and developers can optimize cluster resources, offering developers insight and control over operational budgets.

- **5. Integration and Extensibility:** Knative's design focuses on flexibility, allowing seamless integration with existing Kubernetes components and services. The interoperability with Kubernetes-native tools enable developers to harness Helm Charts, kubectl, and Prometheus for monitoring and management without additional investments in proprietary solutions.

- In contrast, adopting AWS Lambda or Google Cloud Functions often necessitates investment in corresponding tools offered by the provider, within a proprietary ecosystem. Integrating non-native tools involves increased complexity and additional cloud service costs.

- Developers implementing complex workflows may use Tekton Pipelines alongside Knative to form robust continuous delivery systems:

```
apiVersion: tekton.dev/v1beta1
kind: PipelineRun
metadata:
  name: knative-deploy-pipeline-run
spec:
  pipelineRef:
    name: knative-deploy-pipeline
  resources:
  - name: app-source
    resourceRef:
      name: source-repo
```

Knative's pluggable components ensure effective synergy with new technologies, promoting organizational agility without cultural or architectural disruption.

- **6. Vendor Independence and Portability:** The vendor-agnostic nature of Knative ensures compatibility with multiple cloud providers, supporting hybrid and multi-cloud strategies critical for modern enterprises. By avoiding vendor lock-ins, Knative facilitates seamless migration across environments, enabling organizations to diversify their cloud investments to meet strategic objectives.

- Other platforms, particularly AWS Lambda, Azure Functions, and Google Cloud Functions, often bind developers to specific service models or cloud ecosystems, limiting the flexibility to re-deploy functions on different clouds.

- Such deployments ensure optimal economic deployment models, maximizing business performance while enabling strategic agility within cloud-native computing realms.

- **7. Security and Compliance:** Knative benefits significantly from Kubernetes' mature security features, incorporating container orchestration best practices, as well as role-based access control (RBAC) and network security policies, to keep serverless deployments secure across various domains.

- Furthermore, by operating on Kubernetes, Knative adheres to open source best practices, enabling organizations to leverage global community contributions to enhance security postures and ensure compliance with industry standards.

- In comparison, Google Cloud Functions and AWS Lambda offer proprietary security implementations which, while often robust, could impose constraints for organizations with unique compliance or regulatory requirements.

While each serverless platform presents its own strengths and unique offerings, Knative differentiates itself by providing an expansive, adaptable, and intuitive solution engineered for Kubernetes. Its modular architecture, coupled with flexibility and extensibility, positions it as a leading choice for developers and organizations seeking to harness serverless computing paradigms while maintaining control and visibility over their cloud infrastructure. Knative allows developers to connect diverse solutions, scale effortlessly, and integrate seamlessly with existing technologies and toolsets, proving its relevance and utility in today's rapidly evolving technological landscape.

Chapter 2

Getting Started with Kubernetes

This chapter offers a comprehensive overview of Kubernetes, beginning with its fundamental concepts, including pods, nodes, clusters, and namespaces. It provides step-by-step guidance on installing Kubernetes across various environments, both locally and in the cloud. The architectural design of Kubernetes is examined, explaining how its components collaborate to manage applications effectively. Key kubectl commands are introduced for resource management and cluster interaction. Practical insights into deploying applications, understanding networking models, and managing storage solutions within Kubernetes are also covered, equipping readers with the necessary tools to effectively navigate this robust platform.

2.1   Core Concepts of Kubernetes

Kubernetes, often abbreviated as K8s, is a robust container orchestration platform that facilitates the deployment, scaling, and operation of application containers across clusters of hosts. To effectively harness the capabilities of Kubernetes, a foundational understanding of its core concepts such as pods, nodes, clusters, and namespaces is essential.

At the heart of Kubernetes lies the concept of a **pod**, the smallest and simplest Kubernetes object. A pod encapsulates one or more containers that share the same storage resources, network identity, and specification for how to run the containers. When multiple containers are co-located in a pod, they can communicate with each other using the local host network stack. This design allows for tightly coupled application components, such as a helper container that shares data volume with the main application.

```
{
  "apiVersion": "v1",
  "kind": "Pod",
  "metadata": {
    "name": "simple-webapp"
  },
  "spec": {
    "containers": [
      {
        "name": "webapp",
        "image": "nginx",
        "ports": [
          {
            "containerPort": 80
          }
        ]
      }
    ]
  }
}
```

This JSON structure defines a simple pod with a single container running the Nginx web server. The containerPort specified is exposed to communicate with other pods or services.

Moving up from pods, a **node** is the next fundamental building block. Nodes are the worker machines in a Kubernetes cluster and can be either virtual or physical. Each node contains the necessary services to run pods and is controlled by the master components present in the control plane. A node contains the kubelet, a kube-proxy, and a container runtime, such as Docker.

- kubelet

- kube-proxy

34

- Container runtime (e.g., Docker)

The **cluster** is the aggregation of nodes that Kubernetes manages as a unit. Clusters handle scheduled workloads on nodes and manage resources dynamically. The control plane orchestrates processes across the cluster, ensuring the desired operational state is maintained. Among its key responsibilities, the control plane performs:

- Scheduling decisions: determining which nodes will run pending workloads.

- Monitoring and maintaining the desired state through reconciliation loops.

The concept of **namespaces** provides a mechanism for isolating resources within a single Kubernetes cluster. Namespaces allow users to divide cluster resources between multiple users. By default, Kubernetes has namespaces like default, kube-system, and kube-public.

```
kubectl get namespaces
```

Namespaces are particularly useful in environments with multiple teams or projects, offering logical separation and permitting the reuse of named resources.

Resource allocation, implicit security boundaries, and logical separation of concerns make namespaces a beneficial tool for organizing systems effectively. The Kubernetes API allows for operations, such as listing all pods in a specific namespace or even creating new namespaces using the following command line commands:

```
kubectl create namespace development
```

A pivotal part of Kubernetes' design philosophy is **declarative management**. As opposed to imperative commands, you describe the desired state of infrastructure using manifests, and Kubernetes ensures the cluster reaches the prescribed state. This declarative approach simplifies complex operations such as scaling, upgrading, and rollback through configurations rather than scripted operations.

In addition to these core concepts, understanding Kubernetes requires knowledge of controllers and services which enhance its predictability and resilience. Services create a stable interface for pods running variable lifespans due to scaling or updates.

```
{
  "apiVersion": "v1",
  "kind": "Service",
  "metadata": {
    "name": "web-service"
  },
  "spec": {
    "selector": {
      "app": "simple-webapp"
    },
    "ports": [
      {
        "protocol": "TCP",
        "port": 80,
        "targetPort": 80
      }
    ],
    "type": "ClusterIP"
  }
}
```

This service definition encapsulates a stable network endpoint for applications. The selector identifies the pods that form endpoints of this service.

Understanding these elements in conjunction offers the ability to define repeatable applications and infrastructure, fostering predictability. Kubernetes abstracts the complexity of orchestrating distributed applications across varied environments, facilitating portability and longevity of services.

Kubernetes' robust model encourages the engineering of reliable, microservices-based architectures that can handle fluctuating loads proficiently. The knowledge of its core concepts serves as an essential stepping stone toward mastering its comprehensive capabilities, further empowering teams to construct sophisticated, cloud-native solutions that are both resilient and scalable.

2.2 Installing Kubernetes

The installation of Kubernetes can be achieved through a variety of methodologies, depending on whether one wishes to deploy it locally for development and testing purposes, or in a cloud environment for production-grade applications. Understanding the installation process is crucial, as it lays the foundation for subsequent interactions with the Kubernetes cluster. In this section, we will provide a detailed exploration of installing Kubernetes on local machines and cloud environments, covering tools such as Minikube, kubeadm, and managed Kubernetes services like Google Kubernetes Engine (GKE).

For local installations, Minikube provides an ideal environment to run a single-node Kubernetes cluster locally, offering a minimal yet fully functional cluster setup. Minikube is particularly useful for developers who wish to prototype applications without deploying them to a full-scale cluster. It supports various container runtimes and hypervisors, such as VirtualBox and Hypervisor.framework.

```
# Install Minikube using a package manager
brew install minikube

# Start a local Kubernetes cluster
minikube start
```

Once Minikube is installed and running, interacting with the cluster can be done using kubectl, Kubernetes' command-line interface. Minikube automatically configures kubectl to connect to the local cluster.

```
# Check the status of the Minikube cluster
minikube status

# Get the current context used by kubectl
kubectl config current-context
```

Transparency in configurations is an important factor while using Minikube, as it allows experimenting with Kubernetes components such as deployments, services, and volumes.

For those looking to install Kubernetes on virtual or physical machines, either on-premises or in a cloud environment, **kubeadm** offers a reliable and more production-ready method. Kubeadm handles the complexity of bootstrapping a new cluster, focusing on setting configurations consistently and correctly.

Before installing Kubernetes through kubeadm, it is crucial to meet system prerequisites, including compatible Linux distributions and pre-installed Docker containers. The installation begins with setting up each node, beginning with the control plane.

37

```
# Update the package index and install packages needed
sudo apt-get update && sudo apt-get install -y apt-transport-https curl

# Download Google's public signing key
curl -s https://packages.cloud.google.com/apt/doc/apt-key.gpg | sudo apt-key add -

# Add Kubernetes to the list of package sources
cat <<EOF | sudo tee /etc/apt/sources.list.d/kubernetes.list
deb https://apt.kubernetes.io/ kubernetes-xenial main
EOF

# Install kubelet, kubeadm, and kubectl
sudo apt-get update
sudo apt-get install -y kubelet kubeadm kubectl
```

After installing necessary packages, initialization of the control plane is executed on a master node using:

```
sudo kubeadm init --pod-network-cidr=192.168.0.0/16
```

Upon initializing kubeadm, the output provides instructions on how to set up local machine access to the new Kubernetes cluster by copying credentials to the home directory:

```
# Copy kubeadm configuration to the user's home directory
mkdir -p $HOME/.kube
sudo cp -i /etc/kubernetes/admin.conf $HOME/.kube/config
sudo chown $(id -u):$(id -g) $HOME/.kube/config
```

Next, deploying a pod network is essential for enabling pod communication, wherein the Calico or Flannel network add-ons can be integrated as follows:

```
kubectl apply -f https://docs.projectcalico.org/v3.14/manifests/calico.yaml
```

Once the control plane is operational, adding worker nodes involves joining these nodes to the cluster using tokens and discovery information emitted by kubeadm. This join command is executed on each worker node:

```
sudo kubeadm join <master-node-ip>:6443 --token <token> --discovery-token-ca-cert-
    hash sha256:<hash>
```

The reliability and scalability of kubeadm make it indispensable for medium to large-scale Kubernetes deployments, emphasizing cluster configuration accuracy and automated certificate management.

38

Deploying Kubernetes in the cloud has been simplified with managed services such as Google Kubernetes Engine (GKE), Amazon Kubernetes Service (EKS), and Azure Kubernetes Service (AKS). These services eliminate the heavy lifting involved in managing the Kubernetes control plane, focusing instead on scaling, updates, and integration within their respective cloud ecosystems.

Using Google Kubernetes Engine (GKE) as an example, deploying a Kubernetes cluster involves interactions within the Google Cloud console and the gcloud command-line tool. This workflow involves setting up a new project, enabling the Kubernetes Engine API, and creating a cluster:

```
# Set the Google Cloud project
gcloud config set project <project-id>

# Enable the Kubernetes Engine API
gcloud services enable container.googleapis.com

# Create a Kubernetes cluster on GKE
gcloud container clusters create cluster-name --zone=<zone>
```

After the cluster is provisioned, access is established through the downloading of cluster credentials:

```
gcloud container clusters get-credentials cluster-name --zone=<zone>
```

Managed Kubernetes services offer advantages such as automatic management of master components, easy upgrades, integrated logging, and monitoring services. These services cater to teams that target accelerated deployment cycles and higher service availability without investing heavily in infrastructure management.

Throughout installing Kubernetes, aligning infrastructure and application needs with the deployment type is essential. Local environments foster development and testing, while scalable, robust installations in cloud environments suit production needs. These installation methods built on solid foundations yield rich environments for deploying reliable and scalable applications using Kubernetes.

2.3   Kubernetes Architecture

Kubernetes architecture is a robust, modular framework designed to manage distributed applications in a scalable and automated fashion. Understanding its architecture is paramount for developers and system administrators seeking to fully leverage its potential. The architecture is comprised of control plane components, node components, and networking aspects that together form a cohesive and dynamic system for orchestrating containerized workloads.

Control Plane Components

The control plane is the central management entity responsible for maintaining the desired state of the cluster. It includes several key components:

1. **API Server (kube-apiserver)**: The API server is the heart of the Kubernetes control plane, serving as the hub through which all other components communicate. It exposes the Kubernetes API, enabling interaction with cluster resources using kubectl, client libraries, and other API consumers. API server operations involve handling, authenticating, validating, and serving RESTful API requests.

2. **Etcd**: This is a distributed key-value store used to persist all cluster data and state management, including configuration data, secrets, and the resource state. etcd ensures consistency and high availability of the critical data through distributed consensus algorithms like Raft, embodying the consistent storage backend for cluster operations.

3. **Controller Manager (kube-controller-manager)**: The controller manager runs various controllers that regulate the cluster state by observing the state of cluster objects and attempting to modify them to meet the intended state. These controllers include the ReplicaSet controller, Job controller, Node controller, and others, facilitating operability and automation.

4. **Scheduler (kube-scheduler)**: The scheduler assigns new pods to suitable nodes. It identifies non-assigned pods and determines optimal placement by considering constraints such as resource availability, affinity, anti-affinity, and node capacity.

40

The inter-component communication within the control plane is typically secured using TLS encryption, ensuring the integrity and confidentiality of the data in transit.

```
# Check the logs of kube-apiserver to debug issues
kubectl logs -n kube-system kube-apiserver-<node-name>

# View the status of all control plane components
kubectl get componentstatuses
```

Node Components

Node components are essential for managing pods and maintaining the desired state defined by the control plane:

1. **Kubelet**: The kubelet is an agent running on each node, tasked with ensuring that containers are running in a pod. It communicates with the API server to receive pod specifications and uses the container runtime on the node to execute containers according to the defined configurations. The kubelet also reports resource utilization and events back to the control plane.

2. **Kube-proxy**: This network proxy implements part of the Kubernetes Service abstraction and maintains network rules on nodes, handling request forwarding either within the node or to external networks. It provides service discovery and load balancing for network traffic intended for pods.

3. **Container Runtime**: The container runtime executes containers on a node. While Docker has been the most prevalent, Kubernetes now supports diverse container runtimes through the Container Runtime Interface (CRI), such as containerd and CRI-O, ensuring flexible integration options.

```
# Inspect the kubelet configuration of a node
kubectl describe node <node-name>

# Display all kube-proxy logs on a specific node
kubectl logs -n kube-system kube-proxy-<node-name>
```

41

Networking Aspects

Networking in Kubernetes abstracts and simplifies direct host-to-host communication challenges. It involves several key concepts, ensuring seamless and secure communication:

- **Pod-to-Pod Communication**: All pods in a Kubernetes cluster communicate with each other without requiring network address translation (NAT). The flat network model ensures that every node's IP address is uniformly addressable across the entire cluster.

- **Service Networking**: Services in Kubernetes provide stable endpoints to access a dynamic set of pods. Kubernetes supports service types like ClusterIP, NodePort, or LoadBalancer, each facilitating different levels of access.

```
{
  "apiVersion": "v1",
  "kind": "Service",
  "metadata": {
    "name": "webapp-service"
  },
  "spec": {
    "type": "LoadBalancer",
    "selector": {
      "app": "simple-webapp"
    },
    "ports": [
      {
        "protocol": "TCP",
        "port": 80,
        "targetPort": 80
      }
    ]
  }
}
```

- **Ingress**: Ingress resources manage external access to services within a cluster, usually HTTP, offering configurations for load balancing, SSL termination, and name-based virtual hosting.

- **Network Policies**: These provide fine-grained control over inbound and outbound traffic flow to pods within a cluster. By default, Kubernetes allows unrestricted communication; network policies enforce constraints as per specified rules.

```
apiVersion: networking.k8s.io/v1
kind: NetworkPolicy
metadata:
```

```
  name: allow-web-traffic
spec:
  podSelector:
    matchLabels:
      role: web
  ingress:
    - from:
      - ipBlock:
          cidr: 172.17.0.0/16
```

Inter-Component Interactions

The architecture's success is attributable to the constant reconciliation and interactions among components. For example, controllers continue to check on object statuses, scheduling decisions repeat periodically, and node health checks stream ongoing results to the control plane.

Moreover, Kubernetes integrates gracefully with various system and application frameworks, facilitating extension through custom resources, webhooks, and add-on controllers. Its design fosters adaptability and extensibility, allowing novel abstractions like custom controllers and operators.

```json
{
  "apiVersion": "apiextensions.k8s.io/v1",
  "kind": "CustomResourceDefinition",
  "metadata": {
    "name": "foos.samplecontroller.k8s.io"
  },
  "spec": {
    "group": "samplecontroller.k8s.io",
    "versions": [
      {
        "name": "v1alpha1",
        "served": true,
        "storage": true
      }
    ],
    "scope": "Namespaced",
    "names": {
      "plural": "foos",
      "singular": "foo",
      "kind": "Foo",
      "shortNames": ["f"]
    }
  }
}
```

The comprehensive Kubernetes architecture is key to understanding the orchestration of containerized workloads. It provides a robust, scalable framework that adapts to varied environments, from localized development settings to extensive multi-cloud strategies. The architectural principles laid in Kubernetes foster innovation and provide a stable platform that abstracts away infrastructure complexity, allowing teams to focus on delivering resilient, scalable applications.

2.4 Basic kubectl Commands

The kubectl command-line tool is an indispensable utility in the Kubernetes ecosystem, serving as the primary method for interacting with Kubernetes clusters and resources. This tool offers an extensive set of commands that allow users to manage cluster applications, obtain diagnostic information, and orchestrate cluster operations efficiently. The sophistication and versatility of kubectl stem from its integration with the Kubernetes API, enabling seamless access to cluster objects and operations across varied environments. In this section, we offer an in-depth examination of fundamental kubectl commands, their usage, and practical examples that facilitate efficient cluster management.

Effective use of kubectl begins with proper configuration. Configuration context holds details about clusters, users, and namespaces, encapsulated in a kubeconfig file, usually located at $HOME/.kube/config. Users can switch between different cluster configurations by manipulating this file.

```
# Display the current context
kubectl config current-context

# List all available contexts in the kubeconfig
kubectl config get-contexts
```

Switching contexts involves setting an active context, which determines the cluster and user for API operations:

```
kubectl config use-context <context-name>
```

By configuring context parameters explicitly, users can reduce repetitive command line options and ensure consistent interactions across different environments.

44

Basic kubectl commands allow users to gather detailed information about the running state of the Kubernetes control plane and nodes. This is typically the first step in assessing cluster health or diagnosing issues:

```
# List all nodes in the cluster with their status
kubectl get nodes

# Access detailed status and conditions of each node
kubectl describe nodes
```

Additionally, the following command provides an overview of essential component health:

```
kubectl get componentstatuses
```

These commands help administrators obtain insights into the operational status and resource availability within the cluster.

Pods form the backbone of Kubernetes workloads, and kubectl provides extensive capabilities for their management. Users can list, describe, and troubleshoot issues with pods using the following commands:

```
# List all pods within the default namespace
kubectl get pods

# Retrieve detailed information about a specific pod
kubectl describe pod <pod-name>
```

To troubleshoot pod issues, logs are invaluable. The kubectl logs command retrieves output from the containers within a pod, aiding in diagnosis:

```
# View logs for a specific pod
kubectl logs <pod-name>

# Display logs for a particular container in a multi-container pod
kubectl logs <pod-name> -c <container-name>
```

Deployments in Kubernetes automate the creation and management of pod replicas, ensuring applications are always available:

```
# Update the image version for a deployment
kubectl set image deployment/<deployment-name> <container-name>=<new-image>

# Check the rollout status for ongoing deployments
kubectl rollout status deployment/<deployment-name>
```

Rollback actions are equally straightforward, facilitating recovery and version management:

```
kubectl rollout undo deployment/<deployment-name>
```

kubectl is essential in managing Kubernetes services that expose pods to internal and external networks. Service discovery and updates are simplified through command-line interactions:

```
# View all services in a specific namespace
kubectl get services -n <namespace>

# Add an external IP to an existing service
kubectl patch svc <service-name> -p '{"spec": {"externalIPs": ["192.168.1.100"]}}'
```

Modifying network policies involves straightforward command structures, aiding in the governance of traffic within a Kubernetes cluster.

Kubernetes' configuration management, including ConfigMaps and Secrets, is managed using kubectl to ensure consistency across environments. ConfigMaps manage configuration data in key-value pairs, while Secrets handle sensitive information:

```
# Create a ConfigMap from a literal key-value pair
kubectl create configmap <configmap-name> --from-literal=key=value

# Describe ConfigMap contents
kubectl describe configmap <configmap-name>
```

Similarly, secret management is crucial for securing sensitive application information:

```
# Create a secret from a file containing sensitive data
kubectl create secret generic <secret-name> --from-file=path/to/secretfile

# Specify base64-encoded values when creating a secret through manifest
kubectl apply -f secret-definition.yaml
```

Kubernetes access control, management capabilities, and security alignments are driven by kubectl through Role-Based Access Control (RBAC). Modifying role bindings and examining resource permissions enhances cluster security:

```
# List current role bindings
kubectl get rolebindings -n <namespace>

# Bind a cluster role to a user
kubectl create clusterrolebinding <binding-name> --clusterrole=cluster-admin --user
    =<username>
```

46

Tools such as kube-capacity and kubectl-exec assist with deeper investigations into namespace-specific metrics, while offloading infrequent tasks like backups:

```
# Access an interactive shell within a container
kubectl exec -it <pod-name> -c <container-name> -- /bin/bash
```

Scripting kubectl interactions can automate complex and repetitive tasks, leveraging shell scripts and CI/CD pipelines. Consider the following illustrative example of a script to clean up completed jobs:

```
#!/bin/bash

kubectl get jobs --field-selector=status.successful=1 --no-headers | \
  awk '{print $1}' | \
  xargs kubectl delete jobs
```

The example above finds jobs with successful completions and deletes them, maintaining an uncluttered cluster state.

By grasping the functionalities underlying kubectl, administrators and developers can unlock the full potential of Kubernetes. The rich command-set promotes transparency, engagement, and efficient management of cluster resources, enabling initiatives that contribute to robust, fault-tolerant, and scalable application architectures.

2.5 Deploying Applications on Kubernetes

Deploying applications on Kubernetes allows developers to take full advantage of the platform's capabilities in orchestrating cloud-native applications. Kubernetes provides potent abstractions for deployment, scaling, and management, enabling developers to deliver applications with improved reliability and agility. This section delves into deploying applications on Kubernetes, emphasizing deployment files, deployment strategies, and best practices.

Understanding deployment files is crucial for utilizing Kubernetes effectively. Kubernetes employs declarative YAML or JSON configu-

47

ration files to manage application deployments, ensuring that applications are deployed consistently across environments. Deployment files specify the application's desired state, including container images, replicas, networking, and volumes, allowing Kubernetes to maintain this state through its reconciliation loops.

A typical deployment file includes metadata, a spec section specifying pod configurations, and strategy instructions for update handling. Below is an example of a basic deployment YAML manifest:

```
apiVersion: apps/v1
kind: Deployment
metadata:
  name: webapp-deployment
spec:
  replicas: 3
  selector:
    matchLabels:
      app: webapp
  template:
    metadata:
      labels:
        app: webapp
    spec:
      containers:
        - name: webapp
          image: nginx:1.19
          ports:
            - containerPort: 80
```

The above file defines a Kubernetes Deployment for running three replicas of an Nginx web server. The selector aids in identifying Pods managed by the Deployment through label matching.

To deploy an application using these manifests, kubectl apply is the preferred method. This command accepts a filename or a directory, updating or creating objects as needed:

```
kubectl apply -f webapp-deployment.yaml
```

Upon executing this command, Kubernetes creates the deployment and the associated replicaset, initializing pods accordingly. Observing the deployment's progress and ensuring it reaches the desired state can be achieved with:

```
kubectl rollout status deployment/webapp-deployment
```

To facilitate communication with deployed applications, Kubernetes services provide a stable endpoint. A service definition exposes back-end pod workloads, utilizing selectors to define endpoints dynamically:

```
apiVersion: v1
kind: Service
metadata:
  name: webapp-service
spec:
  selector:
    app: webapp
  ports:
    - protocol: TCP
      port: 80
      targetPort: 80
  type: LoadBalancer
```

Creating the service from this manifest establishes load balancing across pods:

```
kubectl apply -f webapp-service.yaml
```

Network routing rules facilitate true horizontal scaling, implicitly offering resilience to node failures.

Kubernetes facilitates several deployment strategies, each suited to specific application requirements and contexts:

- **Recreate**: This simple approach involves terminating old versions before spinning up new ones. While straightforward, it introduces downtime and is suitable for environments that can tolerate brief unavailability.

- **Rolling Update**: This default strategy gradually replaces old instances with newer ones, ensuring minimal disruption through a controlled, gradual shift. Rolling updates are configured with parameters for batch size and wait time, balancing speed and stability.

```
strategy:
  type: RollingUpdate
  rollingUpdate:
    maxUnavailable: 1
    maxSurge: 1
```

- **Canary Deployment**: Entrepreneurs seeking progressive exposure can utilize canary deployments to roll out changes to a

49

subset of users. This strategy integrates seamlessly with service meshes and ingress controllers.

- **Blue-Green Deployments**: This offers a fallback mechanism by deploying in parallel, redirecting traffic to the updated version contingent on successful validation.

Each strategy requires meticulous configuration to maximize efficiency. Automated tools like Helm can simplify deployment templating, enhancing portability through reusable charts.

Deploying applications often requires configuration management, accomplished through Configuration Maps and Secrets. These enable externalization of service properties, maintaining environment consistency without hardcoding sensitive data.

To create a ConfigMap from literal values:

```
kubectl create configmap app-config --from-literal=API_KEY=12345
```

Incorporating these configurations within deployments involves environment variable injections or mounting as files:

```
env:
 - name: API_KEY
   valueFrom:
     configMapKeyRef:
       name: app-config
       key: API_KEY
```

Secrets follow a comparable pattern, though they necessitate base64 encoding due to their sensitive nature, requiring appropriate role-based access controls.

Kubernetes' elastic scaling capabilities simplify resource optimizations by adjusting replica numbers based on demand. Autoscaling aligns containers with workloads through criteria like CPU usage:

```
kubectl autoscale deployment webapp-deployment --cpu-percent=50 --min=1 --max=10
```

This command dynamically adjusts replica counts, reducing infrastructure costs and maximizing availability during peak loads. Oversubscription policies achieve optimal constraint management by utilizing existing node capabilities.

Observability aligns closely with satisfactory deployment outcomes,

50

mandating comprehensive monitoring and diagnostic tool integration. Tools like Prometheus and Grafana visualize key performance indicators, permitting real-time metric assessments.

Logging solutions like Fluentd capture container and cluster logs, aided by Elasticsearch and Kibana for indexing and visualization:

```
# Retrieve logs for diagnosing pod behaviors
kubectl logs webapp-deployment-<pod-id>
```

Combining metric analysis with structured logging furnishes in-depth insights into environment states—accelerating response times to anomalies.

To ensure efficient Kubernetes deployments, adhere to these best practices:

- **Declarative Management**: Employ configuration files over imperative commands, supporting consistency and rollback options.

- **Robust Security**: Harden your deployment with comprehensive Role-Based Access Control (RBAC), network policies, and regular vulnerability assessments.

- **Immutability of Containers**: Build immutable containers for rapid rollbacks and precise testing phases, underpinned by continuous integration pipelines.

- **Environment Segmentation**: Isolate sensitive workloads through namespace policies and separate data planes, maximizing operational security.

By embracing the principles elucidated above, developers can effectuate efficient, reliable, and scalable Kubernetes deployments, molding robust applications that adeptly adapt to dynamic cloud-native paradigms.

2.6 Kubernetes Networking

Kubernetes networking is a fundamental aspect of container orchestration, enabling seamless communication within and outside the cluster. Understanding the networking model is critical for deploying applications in Kubernetes that require robust, scalable, and secure communication. This section provides a comprehensive exploration of Kubernetes networking, covering pods, services, ingress controllers, network policies, and underlying networking models.

Pod Networking Model

In Kubernetes, each pod is assigned a unique IP address within the cluster's virtual network, allowing for seamless pod-to-pod communication without the need for Network Address Translation (NAT). The flat networking model ensures that all pods in the cluster can communicate with each other directly.

To facilitate this, Kubernetes relies on a network plugin via the Container Network Interface (CNI) standard. Popular network plugins such as Flannel, Calico, and Weave Net are used to provide the necessary networking layer:

```
kubectl apply -f https://docs.projectcalico.org/v3.14/manifests/calico.yaml
```

These plugins create overlay networks or manipulate routing tables to handle traffic between pods, enabling the native Kubernetes networking model across various infrastructures.

Network Namespaces and Isolation

Kubernetes clusters are divided into namespaces to logically isolate resources. Network policies define rules about how pods can communicate with one another and with external services, facilitating secure communication.

Creating a network policy involves specifying ingress and egress rules. The following YAML configuration restricts the traffic allowed to a pod:

```
apiVersion: networking.k8s.io/v1
kind: NetworkPolicy
metadata:
  name: deny-all
spec:
  podSelector: {}
```

```
policyTypes:
 - Ingress
 - Egress
```

The above policy effectively denies all incoming and outgoing traffic for the selected pods. Modifying policies to allow select traffic involves defining selectors and specifying permissible IP blocks or specific pod labels.

Service Abstraction

Services in Kubernetes abstract pod networking, providing a stable endpoint that presides over a dynamic group of pod replicas. Service types dictate the visibility of IP addresses within or outside of the cluster:

- **ClusterIP**: Exposes a service within the cluster. Other apps in the cluster can access the service.

- **NodePort**: Allocates a common port on each node to facilitate external traffic routed to the service.

- **LoadBalancer**: Provisions an external load balancer with public IPs, facilitating internet-facing services.

- **ExternalName**: Used to alias services outside the cluster without exposing an endpoint.

Kubernetes service definitions encapsulate configuration details for each service type:

```
apiVersion: v1
kind: Service
metadata:
  name: internal-service
spec:
  selector:
    app: webapp
  ports:
    - protocol: TCP
      port: 80
      targetPort: 8080
```

This file defines a ClusterIP service, facilitating in-cluster communication on port 80 while routing traffic to port 8080.

Service Discovery

Beyond simple load balancing, Kubernetes provides an integrated service discovery mechanism through the built-in dnsPolicy and clusterDNS options. CoreDNS, a highly configurable DNS service, typically facilitates service discovery:

```
# CoreDNS config in corefile
.:53 {
    errors
    kubernetes cluster.local in-addr.arpa ip6.arpa {
        pods verified
        fallthrough in-addr.arpa
    }
}
```

Service discovery translates service names into IP addresses automatically, enabling pods to discover services dynamically using the service's DNS name rather than hardcoded IPs.

Ingress Resources

Ingress resources provide HTTP and HTTPS routing to services within a Kubernetes cluster, serving as a powerful alternative to the LoadBalancer type for managing external access. An ingress controller must be deployed in the cluster to interpret Ingress resources.

Below is an example specifying rules, host configurations, and TLS for a service:

```yaml
apiVersion: networking.k8s.io/v1
kind: Ingress
metadata:
  name: webapp-ingress
spec:
  tls:
  - hosts:
    - example.com
    secretName: webapp-secret
  rules:
  - host: example.com
    http:
      paths:
      - path: /
        pathType: Prefix
        backend:
          service:
            name: webapp-service
            port:
              number: 80
```

This ingress definition routes traffic directed to example.com to the webapp-service, specifying TLS termination with a secret.

Ingress controllers like Nginx or Traefik are often employed for managing ingress configurations, providing flexible routing logic, SSL termination, and advanced capabilities like circuit breaking and request throttling.

Network Policies

Network policies are dynamically crafted to define permissible traffic paths, controlling pod ingress and egress based on labels and select criteria. This granularity fosters micro-segmentation, limiting attack surfaces by allowing only necessary communication paths.

Here's an example that permits traffic only from certain pods:

```
apiVersion: networking.k8s.io/v1
kind: NetworkPolicy
metadata:
  name: access-nginx
spec:
  podSelector:
    matchLabels:
      app: nginx
  policyTypes:
  - Ingress
  ingress:
  - from:
    - podSelector:
        matchLabels:
          access: true
```

This policy restricts traffic to only permit clients marked with a label access:true, securing the nginx application.

Challenges and Best Practices

While Kubernetes simplifies networking, challenges persist due to the varying nature of underlying infrastructures and network deployments:

- **Latency and Bandwidth Optimization**: Efficient pod placement and service-level optimizations are critical in high-throughput systems, and optimizing the Service networking can enhance performance.

- **Security and Compliance**: Implementing best practices for network security, including comprehensive network policies and auditing ingress and service configurations, ensures robust security.

- **Monitoring and Troubleshooting**: Leveraging Kubernetes-native monitoring tools and third-party integrations aids in visualizing network health and diagnosing issues efficiently. Tools like Prometheus, Grafana, and Istio can provide deep insights into network performance and service communication patterns.

- **Efficient Resource Utilization**: Right-sizing services, limiting pod replicas, and managing vertical and horizontal scaling strategies ensure an optimal balance between performance and cost.

Kubernetes networking, with its robust platform abstractions and flexibility via the CNI model, provides a framework for building scalable, performant, and secure applications. These networking capabilities also extend to hybrid and multi-cloud architectures, making Kubernetes a universal solution for modern cloud-native application deployments. Understanding and mastering these components is vital for any team looking to harness the power of Kubernetes fully.

2.7 Managing Storage in Kubernetes

Effective storage management in Kubernetes is integral to harnessing the full capabilities of container orchestration, particularly for stateful applications that require persistent data storage. Kubernetes abstracts and manages storage resources through several concepts, including Volumes, PersistentVolumes, PersistentVolumeClaims, StorageClasses, and dynamic provisioning. Understanding these storage abstractions is essential for deploying resilient applications that maintain data continuity across cluster operations.

Volumes

Kubernetes volumes are directories accessible to containers within a pod, utilized to store temporary files, share data between containers, or persist data throughout the lifecycle of a pod. Despite being tied to a pod's lifecycle, several volume types exist for various use cases, such as:

- emptyDir: A simple volume type created when a pod is launched and deleted when the pod terminates. It is well-suited for ephemeral data.

```
apiVersion: v1
kind: Pod
metadata:
  name: emptydir-example
spec:
  containers:
  - name: busybox
    image: busybox
    command: ["sh", "-c", "echo Hello from busybox > /data/hello.txt && sleep
        3600"]
    volumeMounts:
    - mountPath: /data
      name: example-volume
  volumes:
  - name: example-volume
    emptyDir: {}
```

- hostPath: Mounts a directory or file on the host node's filesystem. This volume type allows access to specific host files, yet it risks compromising portability due to dependencies on host configurations.

```
apiVersion: v1
kind: Pod
metadata:
  name: hostpath-example
spec:
  containers:
  - name: busybox
    image: busybox
    command: ["sh", "-c", "while true; do sleep 3600; done"]
    volumeMounts:
    - mountPath: /host
      name: host-volume
  volumes:
  - name: host-volume
    hostPath:
      path: /etc
      type: Directory
```

The broad array of volume types, including NFS, CephFS, AWS EBS, and GCE Persistent Disks, supports diverse storage requirements and interconnectivity options, aligning application needs with infrastructure capabilities.

Persistent Volumes and Claims

Persistent Volumes (PV) and Persistent Volume Claims (PVC) abstract storage provision and requests. Persistent Volumes represent physical disks or network shares, retaining data beyond individual pod lifetimes. They are created administratively or dynamically, based on Storage-Class configurations.

A Persistent Volume Claim specifier defines storage requirements such as size and access mode. Kubernetes binds claims to available Persistent Volumes, bridging the user's storage requirements with the underlying infrastructure offerings:

```
apiVersion: v1
kind: PersistentVolume
metadata:
  name: pv-example
spec:
  capacity:
    storage: 10Gi
  accessModes:
   - ReadWriteOnce
  hostPath:
    path: /data/pv-example
```

```
apiVersion: v1
kind: PersistentVolumeClaim
metadata:
  name: pvc-example
spec:
  accessModes:
   - ReadWriteOnce
  resources:
    requests:
      storage: 10Gi
```

The synergy between PV and PVC permits consistent management of container-agnostic storage resources, transparently interacting with storage providers across multiple clouds and local clusters.

Storage Classes and Dynamic Provisioning

Kubernetes extends storage capabilities through StorageClasses, simplifying storage provisioning by abstracting provider-specific configurations and enabling dynamic provisioning.

Dynamic provisioning requires configuration through provisioners, enabling Kubernetes to automatically manage volumes through APIs provided by cloud providers or storage solutions:

```
apiVersion: storage.k8s.io/v1
kind: StorageClass
metadata:
  name: fast
provisioner: kubernetes.io/aws-ebs
parameters:
  type: gp2
```

This declarative approach automates volume creation, letting users instantiate persistent volumes through PVCs based on the defined StorageClass, refining the deployment pipeline for rapid placement and compliance.

StatefulSets for Stateful Applications

Kubernetes promotes the use of StatefulSets for applications where persistence and predictable networking are pivotal, such as databases and distributed systems. Unlike Deployments, StatefulSets maintain ordered deployment and scaling, stable identifiers, and persistent storage guarantees:

```
apiVersion: apps/v1
kind: StatefulSet
metadata:
  name: app
spec:
  serviceName: "nginx"
  replicas: 3
  selector:
    matchLabels:
      app: nginx
  template:
    metadata:
      labels:
        app: nginx
    spec:
      containers:
      - name: nginx
        image: nginx
        ports:
        - containerPort: 80
        volumeMounts:
        - name: html
          mountPath: /usr/share/nginx/html
  volumeClaimTemplates:
  - metadata:
      name: html
    spec:
```

59

```
accessModes: [ "ReadWriteOnce" ]
resources:
  requests:
    storage: 1Gi
```

This example showcases how persistent volume claims are integral to StatefulSets, dynamically provisioning storage for each replica, adhering to access modes and resource constraints.

Best Practices for Managing Storage

Kubernetes efficiently decouples storage management from application logic, yet optimal operations hinge on prudent practice and careful strategy:

- **Capacity Planning**: Align storage with application demands, computing current and future data needs within dynamic scaling paradigms.

- **Access Mode Appropriation**: Choose access modes wisely based on use cases. The ReadWriteOnce, ReadOnlyMany, and ReadWriteMany parameters determine the accessibility scope via pods and cluster topology.

- **Data Lifecycle Management**: Establish robust data retention strategies, recognizing that self-managed volume deletion capability requires thoughtful policy assessment to minimize data loss risk unintentionally.

- **Security and Compliance**: Ensure that PersistentVolumes are governed by strict security protocols. Integrate encryption, Role-Based Access Control (RBAC), and vigilant compliance assessments into storage management workflows.

- **Monitoring and Auto-scaling**: Leverage tools like Prometheus and Grafana to monitor usage metrics, scaling policies, and storage health, implementing alert systems for efficient preemptive infrastructure adjustments.

- **Backup and Recovery**: Develop and test reliable backup and disaster recovery processes. Employ utility programs like Velero for cluster-level backup solutions or provider-specific tools, ensuring uninterrupted data availability.

By embracing these strategic insights, Kubernetes environments transcend traditional confines, offering a resilient and adaptable framework for data continuity across versatile operational landscapes. This approach facilitates a diversified, scalable infrastructure empowered by innovative, container-aware storage paradigms.

Chapter 3

Knative Serving: Deploying Serverless Applications

This chapter explores the architecture of Knative Serving, emphasizing its significant role in deploying and managing serverless applications. It provides a detailed guide for setting up Knative Serving on Kubernetes, followed by the steps to deploy a serverless application, focusing on the creation of services and revisions. Key concepts such as traffic splitting and versioning are discussed for efficient application updates and testing. The chapter also covers networking essentials, including domain mapping, and delves into the autoscaling capabilities that optimize resource allocation. Configuration and secrets management within Knative environments are also highlighted, ensuring secure and efficient application deployment.

3.1   Understanding Knative Serving

Knative Serving is a pivotal component within the Knative ecosystem, designed to facilitate the deployment and management of serverless applications. Leveraging Kubernetes as the underlying platform, Knative Serving abstracts the complexities traditionally associated with deployment, scaling, and management of applications in a cloud-native environment. This section delves into the architectural nuances and operational dynamics of Knative Serving, elucidating its pivotal role in the seamless orchestration of serverless workloads.

Central to Knative Serving is its enhancement of the traditional Kubernetes capabilities, extending them to support serverless paradigms. Unlike traditional server management, serverless introduces a model where the infrastructure is abstracted away, allowing developers to focus solely on writing code without managing the underlying compute resources. Knative Serving achieves this by implementing a set of Kubernetes Custom Resource Definitions (CRDs) that introduce concepts such as Service, Route, Configuration, and Revision. These CRDs form the backbone of Knative's serverless capabilities, orchestrating the lifecycle of serverless applications from deployment to scaling and beyond.

A cornerstone of Knative Serving's architecture is its reliance on a request-driven model. The system autonomously scales the underlying compute resources based on incoming requests, ensuring optimal resource utilization. This auto-scaling behavior is achieved through integration with the Kubernetes Horizontal Pod Autoscaler (HPA), whilst also introducing additional auto-scaler types, such as the Knative Pod Autoscaler (KPA), which enables scaling down to zero pods when there is no incoming traffic. The following elucidates the core components of Knative Serving:

- **Service**: In Knative Serving, a Service is the abstraction that encapsulates the user-facing concept of your application or microservice. The Service object defines a desired state for a customer-facing application, thus serving as an entry point for external traffic. When a Knative Service is deployed, the system automatically creates several underlying Kubernetes resources including Revisions, Configuration, and Route.

- **Route:** Routes in Knative are responsible for mapping traffic to different Revisions of a Service. It defines how incoming HTTP requests are routed to one or more Revisions. This capability facilitates advanced traffic management features such as traffic splitting and blue-green deployments.

- **Configuration:** Configuration captures the desired state of the application posed as a template for new Revisions. Whenever a Configuration is modified, a new Revision is automatically created to represent the change in the application's state. This reflects the immutable nature of Revisions where each change results in a new snapshot.

- **Revision:** Revisions are immutable snapshots of the application code and configuration. Each time the source code or environment configuration is altered, a new Revision is created. This enables rollback capabilities and version management, key features of a robust CI/CD pipeline.

```
apiVersion: serving.knative.dev/v1
kind: Service
metadata:
  name: helloworld-go
  namespace: default
spec:
  template:
    spec:
      containers:
        - image: gcr.io/knative-samples/helloworld-go
          env:
            - name: TARGET
              value: "Go Sample v1"
```

In the example provided above, the creation of a Knative Service named 'helloworld-go' is depicted. This example specifies a single container image that constitutes the service. Once applied to the cluster, Knative provides an endpoint where this service can be accessed. The Kubernetes resources that Knative creates underneath manage routing, configuration, and scaling of this service.

Deploying serverless applications with Knative Serving offers numerous advantages over traditional deployment models, particularly in terms of resource efficiency, deployment simplicity, and operational flexibility. By abstracting infrastructure management, developers can focus more on application logic, enhancing productivity and innovation.

The architecture of Knative Serving is also designed to be extensible, integrating with various build systems and continuous integration/continuous deployment (CI/CD) pipelines. This extensibility is realized through the Knative Build component, although external systems like Jenkins and Tekton can augment this functionality.

A significant aspect of understanding Knative Serving's architecture involves recognizing how it leverages Istio for routing and ingress, although recent adaptations allow the integration of other ingress solutions such as Kourier or Contour. The ingress layer is crucial as it manages external access to services, enabling functionalities such as custom domains, protocol support, and advanced routing capabilities.

```
apiVersion: serving.knative.dev/v1alpha1
kind: Route
metadata:
  name: blue-green-route
  namespace: default
spec:
  traffic:
  - revisionName: blue-revision
    percent: 50
  - revisionName: green-revision
    percent: 50
```

The snippet above demonstrates how Knative Serving facilitates traffic management via a Route. By splitting traffic between two Revisions, this configuration enables implementation of progressive delivery strategies such as canary releases and A/B tests. This fine-grained traffic control is indispensable for modern software delivery pipelines focusing on rapid iteration and customer feedback.

Understanding the operational flow when a service request is made sheds light on Knative Serving's efficiency:

- **Request Handling**: When a request is received, Knative Serving dynamically schedules compute resources (pods) based on the underlying configuration data specified by the service's Revision.

- **Scaling**: The Knative Pod Autoscaler adjusts the number of running pods based on real-time demand. If traffic falls, resources gradually scale back, potentially down to zero, conserving energy and cost without sacrificing responsiveness.

- **Execution**: Pods process the requests, ensuring the application scales seamlessly with imposed workload.

- **Resource Teardown**: As requests dwindle, the autoscaler reduces active pods, effectively releasing resources.

Knative Serving also incorporates observability through integration with tools like Prometheus, Grafana, and OpenCensus. This facilitates comprehensive monitoring, logging, and tracing capabilities, essential for maintaining operational excellence.

Despite its many strengths, Knative Serving is not without its challenges. The integration with Kubernetes means that its operational complexity mirrors that of Kubernetes itself. Additionally, achieving optimal performance requires a balance between configuring Knative and leveraging technologies and tools such as networking layers and deployment strategies.

The ecosystem around Knative Serving is evolving rapidly, with an active community contributing to its development. Recent iterations have introduced enhancements aimed at improving its usability, performance, and interoperability with other cloud-native technologies.

Knative Serving's serverless deployment model is poised to redefine modern application development, providing organizations a robust platform to innovate while enhancing operational efficiencies. By providing mechanisms for versioning, traffic management, and autoscaling, it empowers developers to focus on delivering value rather than managing infrastructure, thus embracing the transformative potential of cloud-native paradigms.

3.2 Setting Up Knative Serving

Installing and configuring Knative Serving on a Kubernetes cluster is an essential step towards deploying and managing serverless applications. This section provides a comprehensive guide to setting up Knative Serving, emphasizing each stage of the process to ensure an optimized and functional deployment environment. The setup procedure can vary slightly depending on the Kubernetes provider, but the fundamental steps remain the same.

The prerequisites for installing Knative Serving include having a functional Kubernetes cluster with sufficient resources. It is recommended that this cluster supports at least Kubernetes version 1.21 or higher to ensure compatibility with Knative's dependencies. Additionally, kubectl, a command-line tool for interacting with Kubernetes clusters, should be installed and configured to interact with the target cluster.

A typical setup includes the following stages: preparing the cluster, installing the networking layer, deploying Knative Serving, and verifying the installation.

- Before installing Knative Serving, ensure your Kubernetes environment meets specific requirements. This includes ensuring the cluster is running and accessible, with necessary command-line tools like kubectl configured for access.

- Furthermore, check that your cluster's nodes have sufficient computational resources (CPU, memory) and network configurations. Knative typically requires at least four CPUs and 16 GB of memory to function fluidly in a development environment. Production environments might require more significant resources based on expected workloads and traffic.

- Ensure that the cluster has LoadBalancer capability, either facilitated by your cloud provider or through alternative solutions such as MetalLB in on-premises setups. These capabilities are critical for exposing services to external traffic.

Knative Serving relies on a robust networking layer to handle ingress and routing of HTTP requests. Originally, Istio was the default networking layer for Knative, but alternatives such as Kourier, Contour, and Ambassador are now often used for their lighter resource footprint and ease of configuration.

The following YAML snippet exemplifies installing Kourier, a lightweight alternative, as the ingress layer:

```
# Install Kourier
```

68

```
kubectl apply -f https://github.com/knative/net-kourier/releases/download/<version
    >/kourier.yaml

# Configure Knative Serving to use Kourier
kubectl patch configmap/config-network \
    --namespace knative-serving \
    --type merge \
    --patch '{"data":{"ingress.class":"kourier.ingress.networking.knative.dev"}}'
```

This setup initializes Kourier within the cluster and configures Knative to use it instead of other available options. Ensure that the '<version>' is replaced with the correct version number matching your Kubernetes and Knative Serving setups.

Once the networking layer is in place, deploy Knative Serving onto the Kubernetes cluster. This involves applying a series of YAML manifests that set up the various components of Knative Serving.

Download the current Knative Serving release YAML and apply it using kubectl:

```
# Download and apply Knative Serving YAML
kubectl apply -f https://github.com/knative/serving/releases/download/<version>/
    serving-core.yaml
kubectl apply -f https://github.com/knative/serving/releases/download/<version>/
    serving-default-domain.yaml
```

These commands initiate the deployment of Knative Serving components such as the controller, webhooks, autoscaler, and other key controllers. The separate default-domain manifest configures Knative for service access under a default domain configuration.

Verify the installation by checking that all the Knative Serving components are up and operational. This can be achieved through the following command:

```
# Verify Knative Serving Installation
kubectl get pods -n knative-serving
```

The expected output should indicate that all the pods in the 'knative-serving' namespace are running. Any errors or pending statuses would require further investigation into resource allocations or configuration settings.

After installing Knative Serving, the next step is to configure DNS and expose the services. If using services like Google Kubernetes Engine (GKE) or Amazon EKS, these might provide automatic HTTP/S routing and DNS management. For a manual setup, the following example provides insight into using external DNS:

```
# Configure external DNS for Knative
kubectl apply -f https://github.com/knative/serving/releases/download/<version>/
    serving-cert-manager.yaml
kubectl apply -f https://github.com/knative/serving/releases/download/<version>/
    cert-manager.yaml
kubectl apply -f https://github.com/knative/serving/releases/download/<version>/
    serving-custom-domain.yaml
```

This configuration presumes having Cert-Manager installed for managing HTTPS certificates. It simplifies DNS management, especially when handling multiple managed or custom domains for varied Knative Services.

With Knative Serving and its networking layer installed, validate the setup by deploying a sample serverless application. Use the following manifest to create a "Hello World" service:

```
apiVersion: serving.knative.dev/v1
kind: Service
metadata:
  name: helloworld-python
  namespace: default
spec:
  template:
    spec:
      containers:
      - image: gcr.io/knative-samples/helloworld-python
        env:
        - name: TARGET
          value: "Knative Servicing"
```

Apply this configuration using:

```
kubectl apply -f helloworld-python.yaml
```

After deployment, Knative should automatically provide a URL to access the service, which can be found in the created Route's status. Test this URL using curl or a web browser to ensure that Knative Serving is routing requests to the newly deployed service efficiently.

Setting up Knative Serving involves several steps that can seem complex initially, but once mastered, they equip developers with the tools to manage serverless applications efficiently. By understanding and optimizing each stage of the setup, teams can significantly reduce development friction, enhancing application deployment and management experiences within cloud-native environments.

3.3 Deploying a Serverless Application

Deploying a serverless application on Knative Serving is a transformative process that empowers developers to deliver applications with minimal operational overhead. Knative Serving acts as a bridge between the developer and the complex intricacies of Kubernetes management, enabling seamless application deployments. This section outlines the process of deploying a serverless application using Knative Serving, encompassing the preparation of code, containerization, crafting of Kubernetes manifests, and the intricacies of the deployment workflow.

At the heart of deploying serverless applications with Knative is the containerization of applications. Knative leverages containers to abstract and standardize deployment, offering reproducibility, consistency, and portability across different environments. This container-centric approach simplifies the transition from development to production, mitigating issues related to environment discrepancies.

Preparing Application Code

The initial step in deploying a serverless application with Knative is preparing the application code. Applications destined for serverless deployment should be able to handle start and stop requests efficiently because Knative dynamically adjusts resources based on demand. Efficient resource handling ensures shorter start-up times and better performance under varying load conditions.

Consider a Python-based application designed to return a simple "Hello World" message:

```
from flask import Flask
import os

app = Flask(__name__)

@app.route('/')
def hello_world():
    target = os.environ.get('TARGET', 'World')
    return f'Hello {target} from Knative!'

if __name__ == '__main__':
    app.run(host='0.0.0.0', port=8080)
```

71

This example illustrates a basic web application using Flask, a lightweight web framework for Python. The deployment of this application will involve creating a container from this code.

Containerizing the Application

Containerizing the application is a process whereby the application code, dependencies, configuration, and operating environment are captured into an immutable artifact – a container image. Docker is commonly used for this purpose.

A Dockerfile is essential for creating a Docker image:

```
# Start with the official Python image
FROM python:3.9-slim

# Set the working directory
WORKDIR /app

# Copy the current directory contents into the container
COPY . .

# Install any needed packages specified in requirements.txt
RUN pip install --no-cache-dir -r requirements.txt

# Make port 8080 available to the world outside this container
EXPOSE 8080

# Define environment variable
ENV NAME Knative

# Run app.py when the container launches
CMD ["python", "app.py"]
```

This Dockerfile describes the steps to construct the image: it starts from a base Python image, sets the working directory, copies application code, installs dependencies, exposes port 8080, and specifies the command to run the application.

Build the Docker container with:

```
# Build Docker image
docker build -t gcr.io/[your-project-id]/helloworld-python .
```

Replace '[your-project-id]' with your Google Cloud project ID if using Google Container Registry, or adapt for your respective container registry.

Pushing the Container to a Registry

Once the application is containerized, the image needs to be stored in a container registry accessible by the Kubernetes nodes in the cluster. Here is an example with Google Container Registry:

```
# Authenticate with Google Cloud and push image
gcloud auth configure-docker
docker push gcr.io/[your-project-id]/helloworld-python
```

The image's URL ('gcr.io/[your-project-id]/helloworld-python') becomes a crucial part of the Kubernetes manifest, allowing for uniform application deployment across various environments.

Crafting the Kubernetes Manifest for Knative

A Kubernetes manifest is necessary to deploy a service using Knative Serving. Knative manifests are typically written in YAML format and describe the components of your application and its configuration. Below is a manifest for deploying the 'helloworld-python':

```
apiVersion: serving.knative.dev/v1
kind: Service
metadata:
  name: helloworld-python
  namespace: default
spec:
  template:
    spec:
      containers:
      - image: gcr.io/[your-project-id]/helloworld-python
        ports:
        - containerPort: 8080
        env:
        - name: TARGET
          value: "Knative users"
```

This manifest defines a Knative Service named 'helloworld-python', using the container image built earlier. The environment variable 'TARGET' can be configured to customize the message.

Deploying the Application

Deploy the Knative service by applying the created manifest to your Kubernetes cluster:

```
kubectl apply -f helloworld-python-service.yaml
```

This command triggers the Kubernetes API to process the manifest and initiate the deployment. Knative Serving handles creating or updating resources, managing scaling, and configuration endpoints.

73

Routing and Accessing the Service

Upon successful deployment, Knative Serving automatically assigns a URL to the service, ensuring it is accessible over the internet. To retrieve this URL, execute:

```
kubectl get ksvc helloworld-python \
  --output=custom-columns=NAME:.metadata.name,URL:.status.url
```

Test the service by accessing this URL through 'curl' or a web browser. This test ensures that the application deployment is functioning as expected in the Knative environment.

Versioning and Revisions

One of Knative's standout features is its native support for application versioning. Each change in the application configuration or container image results in a new Revision. These immutable snapshots allow for easy rollbacks and traffic splitting between different application versions.

To deploy a new version of your application, modify the container image or configuration within the manifest and reapply it. Knative will automatically manage the creation of a new Revision and route traffic accordingly.

Understanding traffic splitting mechanisms in Knative is essential for executing blue-green or canary deployments. This involves configuring traffic percentages to direct a set amount to specific Revisions, facilitating controlled rollouts or A/B testing.

Traffic management can be accomplished through the Route resource, which enables detailed traffic distribution and adjustment without impacting existing service availability.

Deploying serverless applications with Knative Serving simplifies many traditional complexities associated with application deployment over Kubernetes. By utilizing containerization, standardized manifests, and automated routing and scaling, developers can focus on writing clean, efficient code while Knative handles the operational overhead. As the community evolves and Knative continues to incorporate advanced features, its promise as a serverless deployment framework within Kubernetes environments further solidifies, driving the next generation of cloud-native applications.

74

3.4 Traffic Splitting and Versioning

Traffic splitting and versioning in Knative Serving provide powerful methodologies to manage application versions and implement advanced deployment strategies. These features are crucial for continuous delivery, particularly for enabling seamless updates, A/B testing, and canary deployments in a production environment. This section delves into the mechanisms, strategies, and practical applications of traffic splitting and versioning within Knative Serving.

Versioning in Knative is inherently linked to the concept of *Revisions*. Each configuration change, whether that be alterations in the environment variables, container image update, or resource constraint adjustments, leads to the creation of a new Revision. Every Revision is immutable and serves as a self-contained snapshot of the function or application at a certain point in time, allowing easy rollbacks or scale operations.

Understanding Knative Revisions

A Revision in Knative is automatically generated whenever a configuration change is applied to a Service. This feature streamlines version control of applications, allowing developers to experiment with new features or optimizations without disrupting the current production version. Each Revision maintains its complete environment, including runtime, dependencies, and environment variables.

The lifecycle of a Revision involves several stages:

- **Creation**: Triggered by changes to Service or Configuration objects, leading to the automatic instantiation of a new Revision.

- **Deployment**: The Revision is deployed and can receive traffic if configured as such.

- **Scaling**: Like any other Knative resource, Revisions are subject to auto-scaling behavior.

- **Obsolescence**: Older Revisions, no longer receiving traffic, eventually become inactive but remain available for reactivation or rollback if needed.

Consider the following YAML configurations to illustrate Revisions within a Knative Service:

```
apiVersion: serving.knative.dev/v1
kind: Service
metadata:
  name: my-service
  namespace: default
spec:
  template:
    metadata:
      annotations:
        autoscaling.knative.dev/maxScale: "10"
    spec:
      containers:
      - image: gcr.io/[project-id]/my-app:v1
        env:
        - name: FEATURE_FLAG
          value: "enabled"
```

In this configuration, altering any part of the 'containers' array, such as changing 'my-app:v1' to 'my-app:v2', leads to a new Revision. This allows stable and controlled experimentation by deploying multiple versions of an application and directing traffic selectively.

Traffic Splitting Fundamentals

Traffic splitting in Knative is achieved through the *Route* resource, which dictates how incoming requests are apportioned across different Revisions. Traffic can be distributed across multiple Revisions with defined percentages, enabling flexible application delivery strategies.

For instance, a route might send 90% of traffic to the stable version and 10% to the new version. This traffic split can verify the performance or test new features without fully committing to the new version, thus significantly mitigating risk.

Here's how traffic split can be configured:

```
apiVersion: serving.knative.dev/v1
kind: Route
metadata:
  name: my-service
  namespace: default
spec:
  traffic:
  - revisionName: my-service-v1
    percent: 50
  - revisionName: my-service-v2
    percent: 50
```

76

In this scenario, half of the incoming traffic is handled by 'my-service-v1' and the other half by 'my-service-v2'. This kind of configuration is pivotal for executing safe deployment rollouts such as blue-green deployments and canary releases.

Strategies for Traffic Management

Several deployment strategies are supported by Knative's traffic management features, most notably canary deployments, blue-green deployments, and A/B testing.

- **Canary Deployments**: In this gradual deployment strategy, a small portion of traffic is initially routed to the new version. If performance metrics validate the change, traffic allocation is progressively increased.

- **Blue-Green Deployments**: This strategy involves running two environments, one active (blue) and one staging (green). Traffic can be fully switched to the green environment once it is validated, ensuring zero downtime deployment.

- **A/B Testing**: Knative allows fine-tuned control over traffic routing, vital for A/B testing scenarios where different application variants are exposed to different user sets.

Practical Considerations

Traffic splitting and versioning feature prominently in many continuous integration/continuous deployment (CI/CD) pipelines. Automation of these tasks involves integrating Knative's routing capabilities into larger orchestration frameworks, such as Jenkins, Tekton, or GitLab CI. Webhooks within these systems trigger deployments, configure traffic splits, and handle automated rollbacks in case of performance regression or failures.

Moreover, observability is integral to successful implementation. Utilize tools such as Prometheus, Grafana, or Kiali for monitoring and visualizing traffic patterns across your Revisions. These tools provide insights into application behavior and enable rapid troubleshooting and optimization.

Logging is equally crucial, with systems like Fluentd or Loki offering robust logging solutions that extend visibility into revision-specific issues. Real-time log analytics support proactive performance management and alerting, essential for maintaining service reliability.

Example of Implementing Canary Deployment

Below is a workflow example showcasing how to automate a canary deployment in Knative:

- **Deploy initial version** with 100% traffic allocation:

```
apiVersion: serving.knative.dev/v1
kind: Route
metadata:
  name: my-service
  namespace: default
spec:
  traffic:
  - revisionName: my-service-v1
    percent: 100
```

- **Introduce new version** and allocate a small traffic portion:

```
apiVersion: serving.knative.dev/v1
kind: Route
metadata:
  name: my-service
  namespace: default
spec:
  traffic:
  - revisionName: my-service-v1
    percent: 90
  - revisionName: my-service-v2
    percent: 10
```

- **Monitor metrics**: Utilize observability tools to assess the performance and stability of the new version.

- **Adjust traffic allocation** based on observed metrics, increasing traffic to the new version once stability is verified.

- **Finalize deployment**:

```
apiVersion: serving.knative.dev/v1
kind: Route
metadata:
  name: my-service
  namespace: default
spec:
  traffic:
  - revisionName: my-service-v2
    percent: 100
```

- **Rollback if needed**: Revert traffic allocation to the previous version if issues arise.

Traffic splitting and versioning in Knative Serving augment the deployment process by providing a controlled environment for application testing, iteration, and scaling. By deeply understanding these features, developers and operations teams can leverage the robust capabilities of Knative to deliver high-quality applications with minimal disruption to production services, ensuring agile and fail-safe deployment pipelines. The seamless integration of these features into overarching architectural strategies emphasizes Knative's role in modern software development, fostering innovation while maintaining operational stability.

3.5 Networking and Domain Mapping

Networking and domain mapping are foundational aspects of deploying serverless applications using Knative Serving. These components ensure that applications are accessible, isolated, and routable according to specific organizational and security requirements. This section explores the configuration and management of networking in Knative, the inner workings of domain management, and the impact of ingress choices on application exposure.

Knative Serving abstracts the complexity of networking on Kubernetes by integrating with various ingress controllers to route traffic to services. Updated capabilities allow the integration of lighter alternatives to Istio, such as Kourier, Contour, and Ambassador, enhancing performance and simplifying configuration. Domain mapping, on the other hand, offers crucial support for assigning human-friendly URLs to Knative services, providing flexibility and ease of use for end-users.

Networking in Knative revolves around the concept of routing external HTTP requests to the respective Knative services deployed in the cluster. This process entails configuring ingress controllers and leveraging Kubernetes' native service networking capabilities to manage traffic flow.

Ingress solutions in Knative allow for the dynamic routing of HTTP(S) traffic. Here's a brief outline of popular ingress controllers used with

Knative:

- **Istio**: Originally the default for Knative, Istio provides extensive features around traffic routing, retry logic, load balancing, and A/B testing. Despite its robust features, it's often critiqued for its complexity and resource consumption.

- **Kourier**: A lighter alternative suitable for Knative, Kourier simplifies the ingress setup and reduces the footprint on the cluster without sacrificing essential routing capabilities.

- **Contour**: Designed for dynamic HTTP proxying, Contour utilizes Envoy as a data plane, offering quick setups and simple operations compared to Istio.

```
# Install Kourier on the cluster
kubectl apply -f https://github.com/knative/net-kourier/releases/download/<version
    >/kourier.yaml

# Set Kourier as the ingress for Knative
kubectl patch configmap/config-network --namespace knative-serving --type merge --
    patch '{"data":{"ingress.class":"kourier.ingress.networking.knative.dev"}}'
```

In this script, the installation of Kourier as an ingress controller allows Knative Serving to route and manage traffic while offering a more streamlined operation compared to heavier alternatives.

Once the networking is configured correctly with a chosen ingress, associating services with human-readable domain names is the next step. Domain mapping enables users to access applications via custom URLs rather than cryptic, auto-generated subdomains.

The DNS setup for Knative involves:

- **Subdomain Configuration**: Typically managed through a Cloud DNS provider or internal DNS service. Automating DNS or using wildcard domains ensures that all Knative services under a specific namespace are dynamically accessible.

- **Cert-Manager Configuration**: Issuing of TLS/SSL certificates to ensure secure HTTPS access via Let's Encrypt or other certificate services.

Using Kubernetes Custom Resources for domain mapping can efficiently bind multiple domains to services or abstract this integration if utilizing the 'serving-domainmapping' controller package.

For instance, to configure a simple domain mapping:

```
apiVersion: serving.knative.dev/v1alpha1
kind: DomainMapping
metadata:
  name: example.com
  namespace: default
spec:
  ref:
    apiVersion: serving.knative.dev/v1
    kind: Service
    name: my-service
  tls:
    secretName: example-tls-secret
```

This YAML configures a domain mapping resource associating 'example.com' to 'my-service', securing communication using a TLS certificate.

Custom domain mappings can augment security paradigms by enforcing HTTPS connections for all incoming traffic. The automated issuance and renewal of SSL certificates via integrated certificate managers bolster security and ease the operational load of managing certificates manually.

Moreover, domain mapping overlays Knative Serving's inherent support for multitenancy. Administrators can define logical boundaries within the cluster, using namespaces and domain prefixes for multi-user environments. This modular separation permits tenants to customize their domain mappings independently, maintaining isolated operational states.

Custom domains and tenant isolation can be configured to align with organizational policies and compliance needs. Tools like OPA (Open Policy Agent) can further enforce these intentions by ensuring that deployed resources conform to expected configurations across development, testing, and production environments.

Knative assists in advanced traffic management by integrating various policies around load balancing, traffic splitting, and request routing. In complex applications, splitting traffic among revisions (covered in prior sections), enforcing geographic restrictions through ad-

81

vanced networking setups, or balancing load effectively according to QoS (Quality of Service) policies are crucial:

- **Load Balancing**: By default, Knative inherits Kubernetes' round-robin load balancing but can be extended through the ingress controller to achieve more sophisticated balancing methodologies.

- **Geographic Routing**: Networking layers like Istio can enforce rules to direct traffic based on geographic locale, optimizing content delivery and reducing latency.

In production, managing ingress security is as important as routing requests correctly. Set control policies to restrict which clients, CIDR blocks, or network sources can access Knative services. Integrated Network Policies or Ingress object rules refine the security posture by filtering requests, controlling rates, and providing fallback logic.

For example, to restrict traffic to whitelisted IP ranges:

```
apiVersion: networking.k8s.io/v1
kind: NetworkPolicy
metadata:
  name: allow-specific-ips
  namespace: default
spec:
  podSelector:
    matchLabels:
      app: my-service
  ingress:
  - from:
    - ipBlock:
        cidr: 192.168.0.0/16
    - ipBlock:
        cidr: 173.194.55.0/24
```

This policy allows only specific IP ranges to interact with 'my-service', ensuring unwanted traffic is filtered out.

Finally, centralized observability tools significantly enhance understanding and responsiveness to networking anomalies. Leveraging tools like Prometheus, Grafana, and Jaeger can provide deep insights into HTTP request flows, latencies, and request failure rates. Default time-series data collection in combination with outlier and anomaly detection enables proactive management of robust and reliable serverless applications.

82

Networking and domain mapping constitute integral components of successful Knative Serving deployments, determining how services are exposed, accessed, and managed within the cloud-native ecosystem. By thoughtfully configuring ingress controllers and domain strategies, organizations can design resilient, scalable, and secure serverless systems, capable of supporting diverse user bases and high-throughput demands while adhering to modern application delivery practices. Networking overlies the operational excellence enhancements provided by Knative Serving, empowering developers and administrators in the swift delivery of cloud-native applications.

3.6 Scaling Applications in Knative

Scaling is a critical component of cloud-native applications, enabling systems to handle varying loads efficiently while optimizing resource utilization. Knative Serving provides robust scaling capabilities, automating the complex processes behind traditional scalability practices and offering fine-grained control over application responsiveness. This section describes the core concepts, mechanisms, and configurations required to scale applications effectively in Knative.

Knative Serving leverages the power of Kubernetes to achieve elastic scaling, allowing applications to automatically adjust the number of serving instances based on real-time demand. This elasticity encompasses both horizontal scaling – adjusting the number of container instances – and vertical scaling to some extent, managed indirectly through resource requests and limits.

At the heart of Knative's scaling capabilities are key system components:

- **Knative Pod Autoscaler (KPA)**: This default autoscaler adjusts the number of pods based on incoming requests, allowing services to scale to zero when they are not in use. KPA is ideal for latency-sensitive workloads, dynamically reacting to fluctuating demand.

- **Horizontal Pod Autoscaler (HPA)**: In scenarios where CPU and memory utilization metrics drive scaling, HPA can

83

be leveraged to complement the KPA. This is suitable for compute-intensive applications where resource peaks should trigger scaling events.

- **Cluster Autoscaler**: Extending beyond Knative, the Kubernetes Cluster Autoscaler can adjust node counts based on cluster-wide demand, offering foundational support for surviving extensive load spikes by ensuring pods find available resources across the cluster.

The KPA is a primary scaling mechanism in Knative, specifically developed to accommodate the serverless nature of applications by managing scale-to-zero scenarios. Configuration of the KPA is encapsulated within the Knative Service manifests using explicit annotations to control behavior:

```
apiVersion: serving.knative.dev/v1
kind: Service
metadata:
  name: autoscaled-service
  namespace: default
spec:
  template:
    metadata:
      annotations:
        autoscaling.knative.dev/minScale: "1"
        autoscaling.knative.dev/maxScale: "10"
        autoscaling.knative.dev/target: "100"
    spec:
      containers:
      - image: gcr.io/[project-id]/autoscaled-app
```

In this configuration:

- minScale defines the minimum number of pods to maintain, preventing the scale-to-zero behavior if persistent presence is necessary.

- maxScale sets a threshold to avoid resource exhaustion, safeguarding against over-scalation during high-demand periods.

- target specifies the average number of in-flight requests each pod aims to manage, influencing scaling decisions based on current request load.

84

Knative's KPA allows for advanced application deployment strategies that require different scaling behaviors:

- **Scale to Zero**: Automatically deallocates resources when inactive, reducing costs significantly. Ideal for services with irregular traffic patterns where 24/7 uptime is unnecessary.

- **Burstable Scaling**: Quickly reacts to spikes, maintaining QoS by provisioning new pods as requests surge.

- **Stable Scaling**: Ensures a consistent behavioral deployment by finely tuning min/max scaling annotations, offering reliability over pure elasticity.

The HPA extends Knative's scaling abilities, especially when pod CPU and memory utilization are the primary scaling triggers. HPA works alongside Cluster Autoscaler, adjusting computing resources across cluster nodes.

An HPA configuration includes:

```
apiVersion: autoscaling/v2beta2
kind: HorizontalPodAutoscaler
metadata:
  name: hpa-autoscaled-service
  namespace: default
spec:
  scaleTargetRef:
    apiVersion: apps/v1
    kind: Deployment
    name: autoscaled-service
  minReplicas: 1
  maxReplicas: 20
  metrics:
  - type: Resource
    resource:
      name: cpu
      target:
        type: Utilization
        averageUtilization: 70
```

In this example, the HPA adjusts pod replicas for autoscaled-service based on CPU utilization, enabling responsive adjustments to real-time operating needs.

Deciding on KPA versus HPA depends on the specific use-case requirements:

- **KPA and Scale to Zero**: Best for cost-efficient, sporadic workloads typical of functions-as-a-service.

- **HPA**: Necessary for loads defined by resource consumption, where guaranteeing specific CPU or memory performance is critical.

A hybrid strategy may often apply, where KPA manages elasticity around requests while HPA fine-tunes scaling for CPU/memory constraints.

Observable metrics support informed scaling decisions and verification of autoscaler configurations. Prometheus, Grafana, and custom metrics integration offer deep insights into auto-scaling dynamics:

- **Request Counts**: Offers visibility into current load, indicating autoscaler responsiveness.

- **Pod Lifecycle Metrics**: Reveals insights into pod startup times, helping tweak target concurrency effectively.

- **Resource Utilization**: Monitors average and peak usage, validating HPA thresholds for effective resource planning.

For applications with complex scaling needs, Knative integrates with external systems to empower sophisticated scaling solutions. Custom metrics offer the ability to fine-tune autoscaler decisions based on parameters beyond standard metrics:

- **Business-Oriented Metrics**: Use business drivers such as transaction counts or user sessions per pod.

- **Predictive Scaling**: Techniques such as machine learning models help anticipate scaling needs ahead of time, ensuring pods are ready as demand predictably grows.

- **Multi-dimensional Strategies**: Combine various metrics, e.g., concurrent requests and CPU utilization, to yield a comprehensive perspective on scaling needs.

Adopting best practices maximizes the efficiency and reliability of scaling implementations:

- **Scale Testing**: Conduct load tests to simulate real-world conditions, validating the autoscaler's preparedness under projected workloads.

- **Refinement of Resources**: Regularly reassess pod resource requests/limits for optimal scaling behavior.

- **Balancing Cost with Performance**: Weigh the benefit of scale-to-zero and burst scaling against any latency costs or resource availability trade-off.

- **Security Posture**: Pair scaling behaviors with robust security policies, ensuring that any influx of scaling events doesn't expose vulnerabilities such as resource exhaustion attacks.

Scaling applications with Knative Serving promotes agility and robustness, enabling cloud-native architectures to thrive amid fluctuating demands. Knative empowers enterprises to manage infrastructure costs tightly while ensuring consistent application responsiveness through its autoscaling capabilities. Continuous observation and adjustment cement a proactive scaling strategy, facilitating innovation without barriers as serverless paradigms evolve and grow.

3.7 Managing Configuration and Secrets

In serverless applications, managing configuration and secrets securely is pivotal for maintaining application integrity and security. Knative Serving streamlines this process by integrating seamlessly with Kubernetes' configuration management capabilities, providing a robust framework for securely handling sensitive information. This section explores methods for managing configuration data and secrets in Knative Serving, illuminating best practices and advanced strategies for safeguarding application data.

Configuration management in Kubernetes, and by extension Knative, revolves around the use of ConfigMaps and Secrets. These Kubernetes resources allow developers to decouple application configuration from code, fostering a more dynamic and adaptable application environment. This approach not only separates concerns but also facilitates automated deployments and greater operational agility.

- **Managing Configuration with ConfigMaps**

ConfigMaps enable developers to store configuration data as key-value pairs that can be easily consumed by applications within the cluster. They offer a flexible and central repository for configuration parameters, enhancing the application's ability to adapt to change without necessitating a rebuild of the application image.

Consider the following YAML manifest to create a ConfigMap in Kubernetes:

```
apiVersion: v1
kind: ConfigMap
metadata:
  name: app-config
  namespace: default
data:
  database_url: jdbc:mysql://db.example.com:3306/mydb
  feature_flag_enabled: "true"
```

In this example, a ConfigMap named 'app-config' is created, housing configuration data such as a database URL and a feature flag. Applications can mount this ConfigMap via volumes or environmental variables, promoting seamless consumption of configuration data.

To mount a ConfigMap in a Knative Service, one would adjust the service manifest as follows:

```
apiVersion: serving.knative.dev/v1
kind: Service
metadata:
  name: my-service
  namespace: default
spec:
  template:
    spec:
      containers:
      - image: gcr.io/[project-id]/my-service
        envFrom:
          - configMapRef:
              name: app-config
```

- **Securing Sensitive Information with Secrets**

While ConfigMaps are suitable for non-sensitive configuration data, Secrets are crucial for managing sensitive configuration data, such as credentials, tokens, or SSH keys. Secrets are base64 encoded and stored securely within the cluster, only accessible by authorized users and applications.

Creating a Secret in Kubernetes involves encoding your sensitive information:

```
# Encode username and password
echo -n "myusername" | base64
echo -n "mypassword" | base64
```

The output from these commands serves as input for the Kubernetes Secret:

```
apiVersion: v1
kind: Secret
metadata:
  name: db-credentials
  namespace: default
type: Opaque
data:
  username: bXllc2VybmFtZQ==
  password: bXlwYXNzd29yZA==
```

This Secret can now be injected into a Knative Service, allowing controlled access to the stored credentials:

```
apiVersion: serving.knative.dev/v1
kind: Service
metadata:
  name: credentialed-service
  namespace: default
spec:
  template:
    spec:
      containers:
      - image: gcr.io/[project-id]/secure-service
        env:
        - name: DB_USERNAME
          valueFrom:
            secretKeyRef:
              name: db-credentials
              key: username
        - name: DB_PASSWORD
          valueFrom:
            secretKeyRef:
              name: db-credentials
              key: password
```

In this configuration, 'credentialed-service' consumes the 'db-credentials' Secret, enabling safe handling of sensitive information.

- **Insights and Best Practices in Configuration and Se-**

89

crets Management

When managing configuration and secrets within a Knative environment, adhering to best practices ensures both security and operational efficacy:

- Separation of Concerns: Decouple configuration from application code, minimizing hard-coded configurations. Separate sensitive data using Secrets to enforce stricter access controls.

- Regular Rotation: Implement routine rotation policies for secrets (e.g., passwords, certificates) which bolster security posture by minimizing exposure risk.

- Audit and Access Control: Regularly audit access to ConfigMaps and Secrets. Utilize Kubernetes' Role-Based Access Control (RBAC) to ensure that only authorized personnel and applications have access to these resources.

- Encryption at Rest: Configure Kubernetes to encrypt Secrets at rest to protect sensitive information effectively. This can involve using Kubernetes providers' encryption features or third-party solutions that integrate with cloud-native environments.

- Using External Secret Managers: Adopt external secret management systems such as HashiCorp Vault, AWS Secrets Manager, or Azure Key Vault to seamlessly synchronize secrets into Kubernetes, leveraging robust traffic encryption and secret lifecycle management features these systems provide.

- **Integrating Configuration and Secrets into CI/CD Pipelines**

For teams employing CI/CD pipelines, automated configuration and secret management are vital for maintaining secure and consistent deployments across environments:

- Environment-Specific Variables: Store environment-specific configurations in separate ConfigMaps and Secrets, parameterizing these at build-time based on the target environment within the pipeline.

- Automated Secret Injection: Leverage CI/CD systems to inject secrets programmatically, ensuring sensitive data is securely available to applications at deployment without manual intervention.

- Continuous Configuration Updates: Integrate sources of configuration changes (e.g., Git repositories, API calls) into pipelines to automatically update application configurations and trigger deployments as necessary.

- **Advanced Techniques for Configuration Management**

Advanced scenarios involve dynamic configuration and secret management with evolving applications:

- Feature Flags and Rollouts: Utilize feature flags stored in ConfigMaps for progressive rollouts and canary tests, toggling new features in real-time based on API responses or service health.

- Dynamic Secrets: Employ dynamic secrets that provide short-lived credentials to applications. Implementing systems like Vault allows for issuing temporary access tokens, enhancing security by reducing the window of opportunity in case of a breach.

- Cloud Provider Integrations: Leverage cloud-native integrations for secrets management, allowing applications running within Knative to interact with native Secret Managers efficiently.

Managing configurations and secrets securely is a cornerstone of modern application delivery, and Knative provides extensive tooling to do so within Kubernetes environments. By utilizing Kubernetes' native resources alongside best practices, leveraging external systems for enhanced secret management, and integrating configuration management naturally into development pipelines, organizations can maintain a secure, responsive, and adaptable serverless application framework.

Chapter 4

Knative Eventing: Building Event-Driven Architectures

This chapter investigates the principles of event-driven architecture, focusing on its benefits for building scalable applications. It explains the architecture and components of Knative Eventing, including sources, brokers, triggers, and sinks. Readers are guided through the installation and configuration process for Knative Eventing on Kubernetes. The chapter also details the creation and management of event sources and the setup of brokers and triggers to route events efficiently. A comprehensive approach to building event-driven applications using Knative Eventing is provided, along with strategies for integrating external services and event sources for a robust, event-driven system.

4.1 Principles of Event-Driven Architecture

Event-driven architecture (EDA) is a design paradigm in computer science that stands central to modern software application design, especially in the context of building scalable and efficient systems. At its core, EDA relies on event producers and consumers working asynchronously, where the system's behavior is primarily driven by occurrences, or "events," that indicate a system state change or a condition that may be of interest. This section delves into the essential principles of event-driven architecture and elucidates how these principles can be harnessed to construct robust, scalable applications.

An event is any significant change in the state of a system or an object within a system, describing an action or occurrence that might trigger additional processing. In EDA, events are the core notion upon which the architecture revolves. These events can originate from various sources, including user actions, sensor outputs, message services, or system state changes. The primary components of EDA are typically divided into event producers, event consumers, and an optional event manager or broker that enables the communication between producers and consumers.

The primary principle governing EDA is decoupling. In traditional architectures, components often rely on direct communication pathways, resulting in tight coupling that can hinder system scalability and flexibility. By contrast, EDA emphasizes the autonomy of components. An event producer need not be aware of which components consume its events or how these events are processed. Similarly, event consumers do not require knowledge of the events' origins. This autonomy allows systems to adapt to changes more rapidly and efficiently.

One of the critical advantages of EDA is its inherent scalability. As systems expand and the number of events increases, EDA allows the addition of new event producers and consumers dynamically, without significant architectural modifications. This capability is central to addressing the demands of modern cloud-native applications that require elastically scaling resources to accommodate varying loads.

Furthermore, EDA promotes enhanced responsiveness and resilience.

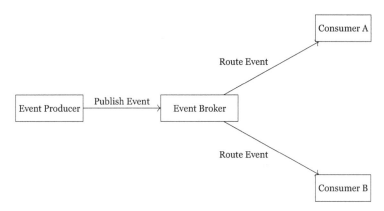

Figure 4.1: Basic Components of Event-Driven Architecture

Event-driven systems can quickly react to events, executing related logic as soon as an event occurs. This immediacy contrasts with traditional request-response models, where latency may result from waiting for explicit requests. Resilience in EDA is facilitated through redundant, distributed event consumers that can handle failures gracefully. Furthermore, the event store, often built on a publish-subscribe pattern, ensures that events are durable, thus enhancing the system's fault tolerance.

- **Event Types and Event Representation:**

  Events in EDA are typically categorized into two primary types: discrete and continuous. Discrete events represent explicit occurrences, like user actions. Continuous events capture ongoing state changes, such as data stream updates from IoT devices. These events are often encapsulated in structured formats like JSON, XML, or Avro for unambiguous communication between producers and consumers.

- **Event Producers and Consumers:**

  - **Event Producers:** Responsible for generating and transmitting events. Examples include user interfaces, IoT devices, or system processes where a change or activity must be logged or acted upon.

95

- **Event Consumers:** Responsible for receiving and acting upon events. These can be diverse in function, ranging from updating databases to launching computations or engaging with external APIs.

• **Event Routers and Brokers:**

Event routing is handled by intermediaries such as message brokers or event buses. Frameworks like Apache Kafka and RabbitMQ are prevalent choices. The broker's role is to ensure the correct routing of events to appropriate consumers based on predefined criteria, using patterns like "publish-subscribe," "fan-out," or "topic-based" routing.

• **Event Patterns and Processing Models:**

- **Publish-Subscribe Pattern:** Facilitates decoupled interactions where producers publish events without needing knowledge of consumers, and consumers subscribe to events of interest, triggered upon reception.

- **Event Sourcing Pattern:** Redefines state persistence. Rather than storing the resultant states, all events leading to a change in state are stored to allow reconstructing any state by replaying events.

- **Complex Event Processing (CEP):** Deals with identifying meaningful patterns of events. CEP engines process multiple event streams in near real-time to detect complex scenarios, using algorithms and rules to derive insights or trigger actions.

• **Implementing Event-Driven Architecture in Practice:**

Effective implementation of EDA necessitates understanding and leveraging several key technologies and considerations. Below, we delve into some practices and technologies used in deploying EDA systems.

```
import json
import pika

def send_event(event_data):
```

96

```
connection = pika.BlockingConnection(pika.ConnectionParameters('localhost'))
channel = connection.channel()
channel.exchange_declare(exchange='logs', exchange_type='fanout')

event_message = json.dumps(event_data)
channel.basic_publish(exchange='logs', routing_key='', body=event_message)

print(" [x] Event sent: %r" % event_message)
connection.close()

event_data = {'user': 'Alice', 'action': 'login', 'timestamp': '2023-10-02T15:00:00'}
send_event(event_data)
```

The example above shows an event producer implemented in Python, using a message queue library, 'pika', to send events to a RabbitMQ broker. It highlights the simplicity of publishing events and the flexibility in choosing different brokers, depending on the system requirements.

- **Consideration of Event Consistency and Idempotency:**

  Given the asynchronous nature of EDA, ensuring event consistency is paramount. Idempotency is a crucial concept, ensuring that the processing of an event multiple times results in the same system state. Consumers should be designed to handle repeated events gracefully, without side effects that yield inconsistent results. Systems may use unique identifiers with events to detect duplicates.

- **Scalability and Resilience with Distributed Systems:**

  Distributed systems inherently support scalability but introduce complexities such as network latency and partial failures. Ensuring reliable communication, maintaining schema versions for backward compatibility, and implementing patterns like circuit breakers and bulkheads can mitigate these issues.

- **Monitoring and Observability:**

  Monitoring EDA systems requires capturing metrics on event flow and processing times, consumer lag, and processing errors. Observability tools like Prometheus and Grafana can visualize these metrics, offering insights and alerting capabilities to maintain system health.

```
{
    "event_type": "UserAction",
```

97

```
"event_timestamp": "2023-10-02T15:00:00",
"user": "Alice",
"action": "login",
"details": {
    "location": "NY",
    "device": "mobile"
  }
}
```

This JSON is structured to show a comprehensive event payload encompassing various event characteristics, including metadata like 'event_timestamp', aiding future retrieval and processing tasks.

Finally, EDA is continuing to evolve, underpinned by innovations in technology and consumer expectations. With growing advances in distributed streaming platforms, edge computing, and serverless solutions, event-driven systems are better equipped than ever to handle data-intensive tasks. As organizational data requirements evolve, understanding the principles of EDA and effectively applying them remains crucial to developing responsive, next-generation applications.

4.2   Overview of Knative Eventing

Knative Eventing is an integral component of the Knative project, which provides Kubernetes-based platforms with higher-level abstractions for building, deploying, and managing modern serverless workloads. It is specifically designed to offer event-driven, serverless architecture capabilities in a cloud-native environment, thus enabling applications to scalably react to changes and respond to events in real-time without heavy infrastructure management.

Knative Eventing is built upon the foundational concepts of event-driven architectures and extends Kubernetes' capabilities to handle eventing effectively. By leveraging container orchestration, Knative Eventing delivers a robust mechanism to connect and channel events through various ecosystem components, including sources, brokers, triggers, and sinks, while allowing developers to deploy event-driven functions effortlessly.

- **Event Sources:**

Event sources are pivotal to Knative Eventing, acting as the initial producers of events. They capture external occurrences in a system, such as HTTP requests, messages from a queue, or file uploads, and translate them into a specific event format that the Knative Eventing system can process. Knative includes support for numerous event sources, including:

- **Webhook Sources** for HTTP-based events.

- **CloudPubSub Sources** for Google Cloud Pub/Sub.

- **Kafka Sources** for Apache Kafka streams.

- **CronJob Sources** triggering events at specific time intervals.

The primary role of event sources is to provide a seamless interface for converting various real-world interactions into structured, dispatchable events within the Kubernetes ecosystem.

For instance, an event source can be configured to listen to a specific Kafka topic and continuously stream messages as events to Knative:

```
apiVersion: sources.knative.dev/v1beta1
kind: KafkaSource
metadata:
  name: my-kafka-source
spec:
  consumerGroup: knative-group
  bootstrapServers:
  - kafka-broker:9092
  topics:
  - my-topic
  sink:
    ref:
      apiVersion: serving.knative.dev/v1
      kind: Service
      name: event-display
```

The configuration above ensures that messages from the 'my-topic' will be translated into events and forwarded to the Knative Service 'event-display'.

- **Brokers:**

Brokers serve as the event ingress and delivery mechanisms within Knative Eventing, implementing the publish-subscribe mechanism.

They function as the conduit for routing events from producers to interested consumers. Events are published to a broker, which then routes them based on certain filtering criteria or configuration set through triggers. Broker implementations can vary, facilitating different quality-of-service levels and scaling parameters.

Knative typically includes a default broker, enabling rudimentary event-routing setups using Kubernetes' internal messaging capabilities. Advanced use cases might incorporate custom-configured brokers tied to specific messaging backbones like Kafka or more specialized event meshes.

- **Triggers:**

Triggers are pivotal in Knative Eventing setups as they connect brokers to event consumers, specifying which events a consumer is interested in based on attributes or conditional filters. A trigger effectively binds a broker to a specific service that will receive and act on events. It is essential for defining the rules and criteria by which events are selected and dispatched to services.

In configuring a trigger, users can set filters that define which events a consumer should receive, based on metadata within the event messages:

```
apiVersion: eventing.knative.dev/v1
kind: Trigger
metadata:
  name: log-trigger
spec:
  broker: default
  filter:
    attributes:
      type: dev.knative.eventing.logging
  subscriber:
    ref:
      apiVersion: serving.knative.dev/v1
      kind: Service
      name: log-service
```

This YAML configuration ensures that only events related to 'dev.knative.eventing.logging' are routed to the 'log-service', demonstrating the specificity and power of triggers within Knative Eventing configurations.

- **Sinks:**

In Knative Eventing, sinks act as the ultimate consumers of events where the business logic is executed. A sink could be a Knative service, a Kubernetes job, or another process configured to respond to and process the events it receives. Sinks are responsible for implementing the functionality that is triggered by an event, which might include tasks like logging information, transforming data, or interacting with external systems.

- **Architecture and Working of Knative Eventing:**

Knative Eventing is built on top of Kubernetes, inheriting its resilience and scalability. The architecture primarily employs existing Kubernetes objects (e.g., Services, Deployments) while extending them with custom resources defined for eventing purposes. These custom resources ensure users can set up and manage complex event-driven workflows akin to serverless systems, without dealing directly with the underlying infrastructure.

- **Decoupling Production and Consumption:**

Knative Eventing inherently decouples event producers from consumers, facilitating a loose coupling model. Events produced by sources do not have a predetermined path or association with consumers, enabling easy reconfiguration, replacement, and expansion of event topologies without significant disruption.

- **Dynamic Scalability:**

Whenever there is a spike in event production, Knative Eventing uses Kubernetes' auto-scaling mechanisms to effortlessly scale consumer services to handle increased load. Conversely, events that diminish in frequency allow consumers to scale back down, ensuring efficient use of computational resources.

- **Event Provisioners:**

Knative Eventing supports event provisioners, which serve as runtime components to facilitate broker functionality across various platforms and infrastructures. These provisioners implement interfaces required to deliver events reliably and in order, maintaining quality-of-service stipulations across diverse operational setups.

- **Event Delivery Guarantees:**

Knative Eventing provides several levels of delivery guarantees, ranging from "at-most-once" to "at-least-once" mechanisms, depending on configuration. This degree of flexibility helps cater to diverse use cases, economic considerations, and application criticality, by allowing architects to choose suitable service levels.

- **Observability and Event Logging:**

Knative Eventing integrates with mainstream observability solutions such as Prometheus and Grafana, ensuring event flows can be monitored, visualized, and analyzed effectively. This integration is crucial for debugging, tuning performance, and maintaining transparency over event-driven workflows.

- **Knative Eventing in Practice:**

Knative Eventing's flexibility is compounded with robust developer tools and ecosystems designed to integrate seamlessly into CI/CD pipelines and DevOps tasks. Here is an example:

```python
from flask import Flask, request, jsonify

app = Flask(__name__)

@app.route('/process_event', methods=['POST'])
def process_event():
    event = request.json
    if event is not None:
        print(f"Processing event: {event}")
        # Implement business logic here
        return jsonify(status='Processed'), 200
    else:
        return jsonify(status='No Event'), 400

if __name__ == '__main__':
    app.run(host='0.0.0.0', port=8080)
```

The service defined above demonstrates how events can be consumed in a Python-based Knative service, executing business logic upon receipt.

Knative Eventing extends the capabilities of Kubernetes by combining the principles of event-driven architecture with serverless deployment models. Developers can leverage Knative Eventing to build applications that respond dynamically to real-time events with minimal manual intervention, fewer resource constraints, and superior operational efficiencies. By incorporating and extending industry-standard protocols and interfaces, Knative Eventing remains a versatile choice for modern cloud-native developers seeking scalable, flexible event processing paradigms.

4.3 Setting Up Knative Eventing

Setting up Knative Eventing involves a series of steps that ensure your Kubernetes cluster is primed to handle event-driven workflows efficiently. It involves selecting appropriate configurations, installing necessary components, and verifying the setup's functionality. This section details the process of deploying Knative Eventing on a Kubernetes cluster, focusing on achieving a seamless and robust event-driven system ready to scale with your application needs.

Prerequisites for Installation

Before installing Knative Eventing, ensure that the following requirements are met:

1. **Kubernetes Cluster:**

A properly functioning Kubernetes cluster is a prerequisite. Knative Eventing is compatible with multiple Kubernetes distributions, including Minikube, Google Kubernetes Engine (GKE), Amazon EKS, and Azure AKS. A cluster running version 1.19 or later is generally recommended to leverage the newest Kubernetes features and security updates. The cluster should be configured with adequate resources, typically a minimum of 4 CPU cores and 8 GB of RAM.

2. **kubectl Command Line Interface:**

The 'kubectl' command-line utility, which facilitates interaction with the Kubernetes API server, must be installed and configured. It is crucial for applying configuration files and managing cluster resources.

3. **Istio or Other Ingress Controller:**

An ingress controller is required to route external traffic to the Knative Services. Istio is often recommended due to its advanced service mesh capabilities; however, simpler ingress options like Contour or Kourier may be used depending on system needs.

Installing Knative Eventing

The installation process consists of deploying the correct release versions and configuring the cluster components to establish a functional event-driven environment.

1. **Install Knative Serving (Optional):**

While not strictly necessary for Eventing, Knative Serving can provide a robust runtime environment for handling events. It dynamically manages the lifecycle of serverless workloads, providing scaling to zero capabilities.

Deploy Knative Serving by executing:

```
kubectl apply -f https://github.com/knative/serving/releases/download/knative-
    vVERSION/serving-crds.yaml
kubectl apply -f https://github.com/knative/serving/releases/download/knative-
    vVERSION/serving-core.yaml
```

Replace 'VERSION' with the desired Knative release version.

2. **Deploy an Ingress Controller:**

Deploy the desired ingress controller to manage traffic:

```
kubectl apply -f https://github.com/knative/net-kourier/releases/download/knative-
    vVERSION/kourier.yaml
kubectl patch configmap/config-network --namespace knative-serving --type merge --
    patch '{"data":{"ingress.class":"kourier.ingress.networking.knative.dev"}}'
```

3. **Install Knative Eventing:**

Knative Eventing is comprised of custom resource definitions (CRDs) and core components which facilitate event routing and processing. For installation, the following steps are necessary:

```
kubectl apply -f https://github.com/knative/eventing/releases/download/knative-
    vVERSION/eventing-crds.yaml
```

Follow this by installing core eventing components:

```
kubectl apply -f https://github.com/knative/eventing/releases/download/knative-
    vVERSION/eventing-core.yaml
```

The above commands deploy essential components such as brokers, triggers, and default event sources onto the cluster.

4. **Configure an Event Broker:**

The default broker is typically set up during installation; however, configurations may need adjustment depending on specific performance criteria or external message system integrations.

Verifying Installation

Before deploying applications, ensure that the components of Knative Eventing are running correctly:

1. **Inspect Knative Components:**

Use 'kubectl' to verify that the Knative Eventing components are operational:

```
kubectl get pods -n knative-eventing
```

All pods associated with Eventing should be in 'Running' state. Moreover, services and deployments should also reflect a healthy status, viewable via:

```
kubectl get deployments -n knative-eventing
kubectl get services -n knative-eventing
```

2. **Testing Event Flow with Sample Applications:**

Deploy a simple application to validate event delivery:

```
kubectl apply -f https://knative.dev/docs/eventing/samples/simple-api.yaml
```

Send a test event via an event source, observing logs on both source and service to ensure receipt and processing.

Configuration and Optimization Considerations

When configuring Knative Eventing, several factors should be considered to optimize and tailor the event-driven experience:

1. **Broker and Trigger Customization:**

Brokers and triggers can be fine-tuned based on service-level agreements (SLAs), required message durability, delivery guarantees, and concurrency limits. Custom brokers may be configured to use Kafka or NATs for handling higher throughput with stringent latency and reliability requirements.

2. **Resource Limits and Autoscaling:**

Assign appropriate resource limits for event consumers based on anticipated workload demands. Knative Serving's autoscaling capabilities should complement Eventing by scaling services up and down responsively according to event load.

3. **Security Configuration:**

Enable authenticated access controls, particularly for HTTP event sources. Integrating with tools like Istio or Gloo can enhance security with mTLS or OAuth2 policies.

4. **Observability and Logging:**

Ensure an observability solution is in place. Hook into the Kubernetes logging infrastructure and link to centralized logging services like Elasticsearch or Splunk. Implement traces for deep analysis using tools like Jaeger, ensuring comprehensive visibility across event flow and service interactions.

5. **Resilience Tactics:**

Design services to gracefully handle failed message delivery, incorporating patterns like dead-letter queues or retry with exponential backoff policies. A robust failure handling helps mitigate adverse impacts of partial outages or stalls.

Advanced Topics in Knative Eventing Setup

Here are some advanced aspects and techniques for setting up and managing Knative Eventing deployments on Kubernetes:

1. **Custom Event Sources:**

Develop custom event sources by extending the Knative platform to meet domain-specific needs. Implement stream adapters for proprietary protocols or legacy systems ensuring they integrate within existing workflows.

2. **Cluster-Wide Event Bus Configuration:**

Transform your Knative installation into a ubiquitous event bus with custom developer conventions and default event routing configurations. This setup simplifies cross-service event integration across microservice architectures.

3. **Federated Deployment Configurations:**

In multi-cluster environments, handle inter-cluster event propagation via federated eventing configurations, employing shared brokers and synchronized event consumption patterns.

Programming with Knative Eventing

Understanding the practical aspects of working with Knative Eventing significantly increases a developer's productivity. Here is a concise example of a Knative service that interprets incoming HTTP events:

```
package main

import (
    "encoding/json"
    "fmt"
    "net/http"
    "os"
)

type Event struct {
    ID string 'json:"id"'
    Type string 'json:"type"'
    Source string 'json:"source"'
    Data string 'json:"data"'
}

func main() {
```

107

```
http.HandleFunc("/process", func(w http.ResponseWriter, r *http.Request) {
    var event Event
    err := json.NewDecoder(r.Body).Decode(&event)
    if err != nil {
        http.Error(w, "Unable to decode JSON", http.StatusBadRequest)
        return
    }
    fmt.Printf("Event received: %+v\n", event)
})

port := os.Getenv("PORT")
if port == "" {
    port = "8080"
}
fmt.Printf("Listening on port %s\n", port)
http.ListenAndServe(":"+port, nil)
}
```

This Go application serves HTTP requests, decoding event data, and can run within a Knative Service deployment to handle incoming events routed through brokers.

Setting up Knative Eventing requires meticulous planning, understanding of system requirements, and thorough configuration testing. Leveraging Knative Eventing within Kubernetes environments enables developers to create efficient, scalable, and resilient cloud-native applications by simplifying event processing within heterogeneous and distributed ecosystems. The overarching goal of reducing manual infrastructure management attains new heights with practical implementation, observability mechanisms, and focused pattern utilization.

4.4 Creating and Managing Event Sources

Event sources are foundational to the functionality of Knative Eventing, bridging external systems with event-driven services within a Kubernetes environment. They are the producers of events and serve as connectors that ingest continuous streams or discrete occurrences from varied origins, processing them into events that Knative can consume. Effectively managing event sources involves understanding their configuration, deployment, and lifecycle within a Kubernetes cluster. This section focuses on various principles, components, and configurations required for creating and managing event sources in Knative, providing an intricate understanding aimed at optimizing system architecture.

Understanding Event Sources in Knative Eventing

Event sources in Knative are custom resources that bridge event production with consumption, encapsulating the logic to process incoming data into events received by Knative's eventing infrastructure. They interact with cloud storage, messaging services, HTTP endpoints, custom systems, and much more, translating these inputs into CloudEvents, a standardized event data format that benefits inter-service communication and interoperability.

- **Event Source Lifecycle:**

    - **Creation and Configuration:** Event sources are defined using YAML files specifying the necessary source type, configurations, and target sink for event dispatch.

    - **Deployment:** Upon deployment, Knative event sources operate as Kubernetes controllers, monitoring external systems and generating events.

    - **Management and Scaling:** Event sources can scale to meet performance needs, either manually or automatically, responding to load variations.

    - **Termination and Cleanup:** Managed effectively through Kubernetes' garbage collection and resource finalizers, ensuring no resources are drained without appropriate shutdown procedures.

- **Types of Event Sources:**

    - **HTTP-Based Sources:** Capture and produce events from HTTP requests, suitable for RESTful APIs.

    - **Messaging Sources:** Integrate with messaging systems like Apache Kafka, Google Pub/Sub, or RabbitMQ.

    - **Time-Driven Sources:** The CronJob source, triggering events at specific intervals or schedules.

    - **Change Data Capture Sources:** Transmit database change streams by packaging transactional logs into events.

- **Custom Sources:** Developers may extend the event source catalog by implementing custom sources for specialized use cases.

Deploying and Managing Event Sources

- **HTTP Event Source:**

The HTTP event source is commonly used due to its straightforward configuration and broad applicability across different scenarios. It operates by translating HTTP requests into events for Knative:

```
apiVersion: sources.knative.dev/v1beta1
kind: ApiServerSource
metadata:
  name: my-http-source
spec:
  mode: Resource
  resources:
    - apiVersion: v1
      kind: Event
  sink:
    ref:
      apiVersion: serving.knative.dev/v1
      kind: Service
      name: event-display
```

This configuration allows an API server to route HTTP-generated events into a Knative service named event-display.

- **Apache Kafka Source:**

The Kafka source ingests streaming data from Kafka topics and routes them within the cluster. Configuration involves setting Kafka consumer properties:

```
apiVersion: sources.knative.dev/v1beta1
kind: KafkaSource
metadata:
  name: kafka-source
spec:
  consumerGroup: knative-sources-group
  bootstrapServers:
    - kafka-server:9092
  topics:
    - test-topic
  sink:
    ref:
      apiVersion: serving.knative.dev/v1
      kind: Service
```

```
name: log-service
```

KafkaSource integrates well within a Knative cluster, providing high-throughput event streaming aligned with cloud-native application attributes.

- **CronJob Source:**

  Time-triggered events are often necessitated by business logic requiring scheduled tasks. CronJob sources enable precise timing for event dispatch:

```
apiVersion: sources.knative.dev/v1beta1
kind: CronJobSource
metadata:
  name: heartbeat
spec:
  schedule: "*/5 * * * *" # Every 5 minutes
  data: '{"message": "Heartbeat Check"}'
  sink:
    ref:
      apiVersion: serving.knative.dev/v1
      kind: Service
      name: health-check
```

Evaluating the above setup shows a simple CronJob source that emits a "Heartbeat Check" message every 5 minutes to a health-check service.

Operational Considerations for Knative Event Sources

- **Performance Scaling:**

  Proper scaling ensures that event sources can handle increased loads without compromising delivery speed or data fidelity. Use Kubernetes Horizontal Pod Autoscaler (HPA) to scale event source controllers depending on CPU utilization or custom metrics.

- **Reliability and Durability:**

  Implement fault-tolerant patterns and retrial mechanisms for transient failures in event sources. Ensure message durability by employing message stores or adopting persistent configurations in event highways.

- **Security:**

  Secure event sources by enabling authentication mechanisms where applicable. Use network policies in Kubernetes to restrict traffic via ingress and egress, controlling data security across the cluster boundaries.

- **Monitoring and Observability:**

  Integrate with monitoring solutions such as Prometheus and visualize event source metrics in Grafana to track performance patterns. Employ centralized logging to capture and analyze event failures or anomalies promptly.

Developing Custom Event Sources

With flexibility in design objectives, custom event sources provide end-users control over special-use cases demanding proprietary event processing:

- **Creating a Custom Source:**

  Develop a custom source controller leveraging Kubernetes Controller Runtime, adopting CloudEvent standards for communication:

```
package main

import (
    "context"
    "github.com/cloudevents/sdk-go/v2"
    knapis "knative.dev/eventing/pkg/apis/sources/v1alpha1"
)

func main() {
    source := knapis.Source{
        Spec: knapis.SourceSpec{
            Sink: knapis.Sink{
                URI: "http://example-sink",
            },
        },
    }

    client, err := cloudevents.NewClientHTTP()
    if err != nil {
        panic("Failed to create client: " + err.Error())
    }

    err = client.StartReceiver(context.Background(), func(ctx context.
        Context, event cloudevents.Event) {
```

```
        // Custom event logic
    })
    if err != nil {
        panic("Failed to receive events: " + err.Error())
    }
}
```

This Go language skeleton shows the construction of a custom event source, primed with integrations for handling diverse data formats and types.

- **Deploying Custom Event Sources:**

  Package your controller using a Docker image, deploy to your Kubernetes cluster, and define a corresponding Custom Resource Definition (CRD) tailored to your application logic and system architecture.

Using Managed Event Sources as a Service

Cloud providers often extend their services to offer managed event sources, abstracting complexities and infrastructure concerns that bare-metal configurations entail. Leveraging these solutions can offer the following benefits:

- **Reduced Operational Overhead:**

  By using cloud-managed event sources like Google Pub/Sub or AWS SQS, organizations circumvent maintenance headaches related to patching, scaling, or security updates.

- **Seamless Integration:**

  You benefit from pre-built integration SDKs and APIs that expedite development, harmonizing with other services in the ecosystem such as databases, analytics, or CI/CD pipelines.

- **Scalability:**

  Provider solutions ensure robust scaling that autonomously aligns with demand surges, minimizing latency issues typical in high-volume event sources.

- **Billing and Cost Management:**

Usage-based billing models afford better cost visibility and predictability, facilitating effective budget allocation and resource utilization tracking.

Creating and managing event sources in Knative Eventing provides a fundamental backbone for event-driven systems in cloud-native environments. By understanding these components' principles and configurations, developers can effectively harness event sources' potential to craft enduring, responsive architectures that stand the test of evolving application demands. Ensuring a seamless connection between event production and consumption opens avenues for systems to achieve exceptional agility, maximizing the benefits of Knative Eventing frameworks within Kubernetes.

4.5   Configuring Event Brokers and Triggers

Configuring event brokers and triggers is pivotal in orchestrating event routing within the Knative Eventing ecosystem. Brokers and triggers facilitate the movement and filtering of events throughout the system, allowing developers to build robust, event-driven applications that intelligently respond to dynamics in real-time. This section explores the intricacies of setting up brokers and triggers, detailing the methodologies, considerations, and best practices involved in their configuration.

Understanding Event Brokers

An event broker is a central hub in the Knative Eventing system responsible for receiving and managing event flow from producers to consumers. It implements the publish-subscribe pattern, enabling events to be published to the broker by sources and consumed by subscribers efficiently. By abstracting the routing logic, brokers ensure loose coupling between producers and consumers.

Default vs. Custom Brokers

- **Default Broker:**
  Knative provides a default broker configuration that is typically sufficient for simple use cases or development environments.

This standard broker automatically routes events according to default settings, leveraging in-built resources to manage basic event processing requirements.

Configuration of a default broker is achieved by labeling a namespace:

```
kubectl label namespace default knative-eventing-injection=enabled
```

This command introduces a default-broker in the specified namespace, relying on the internal messaging layer for routing.

- **Custom Broker:**

  Custom brokers permit finer control of configuration parameters such as event retention, specific transport protocols, and third-party integrations like Apache Kafka or NATS. They cater to specialized use cases needing enhanced throughput, reliability, or global scale.

  Creating a custom broker involves selecting a particular broker class and defining its unique properties:

```
apiVersion: eventing.knative.dev/v1
kind: Broker
metadata:
  name: custom-broker
  namespace: custom-namespace
spec:
  config:
    apiVersion: v1
    kind: ConfigMap
    name: custom-config
```

This YAML configuration initializes a broker with parameters sourced from custom-config, empowering users to tailor transport protocols or QoS settings.

Understanding Triggers

Triggers connect event brokers with consumers, defining rules that specify how and which events should be dispatched to particular services. They employ powerful filtering mechanisms to streamline event delivery based on attributes such as type, source, or custom data fields within events.

Configuring Triggers

115

- **Trigger Definitions:**

  Define triggers using YAML, specifying filters and subscriber details:

  ```yaml
  apiVersion: eventing.knative.dev/v1
  kind: Trigger
  metadata:
    name: example-trigger
  spec:
    broker: custom-broker
    filter:
      attributes:
        type: dev.knative.example.event
    subscriber:
      ref:
        apiVersion: serving.knative.dev/v1
        kind: Service
        name: event-consumer
  ```

  In this configuration, the trigger binds the custom-broker to event-consumer service, filtering for events with type dev.knative.example.event.

- **Advanced Trigger Filters:**

  Filters can be fine-tuned through complex criteria, accommodating various conditional logics:

  ```yaml
  apiVersion: eventing.knative.dev/v1
  kind: Trigger
  metadata:
    name: advanced-trigger
  spec:
    broker: advanced-broker
    filter:
      attributes:
        type: dev.knative.advanced.event
        source: example-source
    subscriber:
      ref:
        apiVersion: serving.knative.dev/v1
        kind: Service
        name: advanced-consumer
  ```

  Here, events filtered are contingent upon both their type and originating source, highlighting the precision in event filtering.

Effective Broker and Trigger Management

- **Scaling and Load Balancing:**

116

Brokers and triggers should be augmented to dynamically respond to system loads. Utilize the Horizontal Pod Autoscaler (HPA) to scale broker infrastructure according to real-time demands, ensuring consistent event-flow performance.

- **Security Considerations:**

  Implement stringent authorization mechanisms for brokers and triggers across the cluster. Enforce policies using Kubernetes Role-Based Access Control (RBAC) to limit unauthorized operations on critical eventing components.

- **Observability and Debugging:**

  Monitoring tools such as Prometheus, Grafana, or Kiali can be leveraged to oversee broker performance, subscriber latency, and trigger filtering efficiency. Enable request logs and event traces via Jaeger to assist in debugging event flows, network bottlenecks, or unexpected application behaviors.

Building Fault Tolerant Eventing Pipelines

- **Handling Event Failures:**

  Implement retries with exponential backoff in combination with dead-letter queues for handling failed event delivery to subscribers. This approach allows for the recovery of transient errors without message loss.

- **Addressing Consumer Slowdowns:**

  Throttle event flows in scenarios where slow consumers jeopardize the broker's capacity, ensuring even distribution across consumer instances.

- **Integrating Dead-Letter Channels:**

  Engage dead-letter queues as alternate channels for undelivered events, allowing post-mortem analysis and corrective actions:

  ```
  apiVersion: eventing.knative.dev/v1
  kind: Channel
  metadata:
    name: dlq-channel
  ---
  apiVersion: eventing.knative.dev/v1
  ```

```
kind: Subscription
metadata:
  name: dlq-subscription
spec:
  channel:
    kind: Channel
    name: dlq-channel
  subscriber:
    ref:
      apiVersion: serving.knative.dev/v1
      kind: Service
      name: dlq-service
```

Undelivered messages are rerouted via dlq-channel and processed by dlq-service, ensuring no event is silently dropped.

Advanced Broker and Trigger Patterns

Integrating advanced features can elevate event-driven applications, offering resilience and scalability:

- **Event Replay and Archive:**

  Facilitate replayability by archiving routed events, allowing reconstructions for audit purposes or debugging historical incident data.

- **Global Event Dissemination:**

  Expand brokers across multiple Kubernetes clusters, employing a federated eventing model for distributing workloads in international operations.

- **Customized Event Meshes:**

  Design event meshes using interconnected broker networks, allowing for versatile and redundant routing paths that bolster reliability and minimize latency.

Programming Models for Knative Brokers and Triggers

Developers can create custom brokers or extend existing implementations to suit specialized objectives:

- **Custom Broker Provider Example:**

  Leverage Go language for extending broker functionalities with bespoke event transport workflows:

118

```
package main

import (
    "github.com/cloudevents/sdk-go/v2"
    "knative.dev/eventing/pkg/apis/eventing/v1"
)

func main() {
    broker := v1.Broker{}

    client, err := cloudevents.NewClientHTTP()
    if err != nil {
        panic("Unable to create client: " + err.Error())
    }

    err = client.StartReceiver(context.Background(), func(ctx context.
        Context, event cloudevents.Event) {
        // Custom logic for processing ingested events
    })
}
```

In this template, developers can introduce additional middleware, hybrid transports, or distinctive processing routes aligned with scalable broker constructions.

Best Practices for Optimal Broker and Trigger Utilization

- **Load Testing:**

  Prior to deployment, perform stress testing on brokers and triggers to evaluate their throughput and latency thresholds, ensuring configurations meet expected scale requirements.

- **Version Control Configuration:**

  Maintain version history of broker and trigger configurations using GitOps practices, providing a controlled CI/CD pipeline and rollback mechanisms when deploying updates.

- **Documentation and Governance:**

  Document the architectural compositions of event pipelines, inclusive of broker properties, trigger conditions, and consumer expectations, serving as a central knowledge repository for team collaboration.

In summary, configuring event brokers and triggers in Knative Eventing entails a detailed focus on routing, filtering, and delivering events across various subscribers, where meticulous management of broker resources and trigger conditions delivers a highly responsive and adaptable event-driven architecture. Developers can build leveraging Knative's robust capabilities, dynamically adjusting to application demands, fostering innovative solutions to complex distributed systems challenges in cloud-native environments.

4.6 Building Event-Driven Applications

Building event-driven applications represents a paradigm shift in software development, enabling systems to respond in real-time to diverse stimuli or changes in state. With event-driven architecture (EDA), developers can create applications that are inherently more scalable, flexible, and responsive. In the context of Knative Eventing, event-driven applications are architected to be cloud-native, leveraging Kubernetes for orchestration, and Knative for event management. This section explores comprehensive strategies, patterns, and practical examples to construct sophisticated event-driven applications using Knative Eventing.

1. **Decoupling and Modularity:**

In an event-driven application, components are designed to operate independently, communicating primarily through events. This decoupling ensures changes in one part of the system minimally affect others, thus maintaining modularity, improving maintainability, and enhancing scalability.

2. **Asynchronous Interactions:**

Unlike traditional synchronous request-response systems, event-driven applications leverage asynchronous interactions. Event producers dispatch events, allowing consumers to act on them at their own pace, thereby decoupling process flow and improving system responsiveness.

3. **Eventual Consistency:**

Such architectures prioritize eventual consistency over immediate consistency. Components proceed with available information, achieving consistency over time which aligns well with distributed systems, helping manage network latency and partitioning.

Design Patterns in Event-Driven Architecture

Deploying event-driven applications often necessitates the use of specific design patterns that dictate how events move through the system:

1. Event Notification Pattern:

This common pattern involves events containing only identifiers of changed objects. Subscribers must retrieve the state directly, fostering lightweight event payloads:

```
Event { Type: 'ProductUpdated', Data: { ProductId: '12345' } }
```

2. Event-Carried State Transfer:

Unlike notification, this pattern embeds state changes directly in events, reducing the need for subsequent queries:

```
Event { Type: 'ProductUpdated', Data: { ProductId: '12345', Price: 100.0, Stock: 20
    } }
```

3. Complex Event Processing (CEP):

Leverages rules or algorithms to detect combinations or sequences within events. Such patterns are ideal for applications needing real-time analytics or actionable insights from multiple streams.

Building with Knative Eventing

1. Event Source Configuration:

Initiate event sources to capture signals from external systems. For example, configuring a GitHub source for CI/CD pipelines:

```yaml
apiVersion: sources.knative.dev/v1alpha1
kind: GitHubSource
metadata:
  name: github-source
spec:
  eventTypes:
  - push
  ownerAndRepository: myuser/myrepo
  accessToken:
    secretKeyRef:
      name: github-secret
      key: accessToken
  sink:
    ref:
      apiVersion: serving.knative.dev/v1
      kind: Service
```

```
name: ci-event-handler
```

This setup ensures GitHub events, such as pushes, are correctly fed into application workflows.

2. Handling Events with Knative Services:

Once events are routed appropriately through brokers and triggers, Knative services act on them. Services are containerized applications that scale under load:

```
apiVersion: serving.knative.dev/v1
kind: Service
metadata:
  name: event-processor
spec:
  template:
    spec:
      containers:
        - image: docker.io/myuser/event-processor:latest
          env:
            - name: TARGET
              value: "Process Event"
```

The provided service scales in response to traffic, offering resilience and observability integration.

Advanced Event Processing Techniques

1. Serverless Event Handling:

Abstractions in Knative enable truly serverless event processing, where functions can auto-scale from zero based on demand, optimizing cost-efficiency and operational simplicity.

2. Event Stream Aggregation:

Applications often require aggregation of events from multiple sources. Using Knative channels, developers can define event pipelines that concurrently collect and dispatch conglomerated event streams.

```
apiVersion: messaging.knative.dev/v1
kind: Channel
metadata:
  name: event-aggregate
spec:
  delivery:
    backoffPolicy: linear
    backoffDelay: "10s"
```

122

3. Event Enrichment and Transformation:

Incorporate enrichment services that append metadata, transform data formats, or calculate derived insights, reformulating events traversing the system.

Testing and Ensuring Reliability of Event-Driven Applications

1. Chaos Engineering:

Employ principles of chaos engineering to inject deliberate failures or latency into event flows, observing system responses under stress to improve resilience.

2. Unit and Integration Testing:

Ensure robust testing methodologies incorporating mock event producers and consumers. Testing ensures both the accuracy of event processing logic and seamless integration between components.

Common Challenges and Mitigations in Event-Driven Applications

1. Managing Event Duplication:

Heavy event streams risk duplication, leading to potential state inaccuracies. Employ idempotency in event processing to ensure operations can be repeated without adverse effects. Unique identifiers and deduplication heuristics are critical tactics.

2. Latency and Throughput Balancing:

Architectures must balance between achieving low latency and high throughput. Tune broker configurations, adjust concurrency settings in Knative services, and optimize network paths to address such bottlenecks.

3. Guaranteed Event Delivery:

While employing Knative's built-in 'once' delivery guarantees, reinforce with appropriate retry policies. Leverage dead-letter channels to handle unprocessed events, retriggering them subsequently without data loss.

Deploying Event-Driven Applications at Scale

Deployments involving significant event traffic necessitate

cluster-wide optimizations:

1. Horizontal Scaling:

Leverage Kubernetes' horizontal pod autoscale to dynamically adjust resources in response to event load, ensuring resource efficiency and application uptime.

2. Distributed Data Storage:

High-volume events often necessitate scalable, distributed data frameworks, seamlessly interfacing event flows with databases like Cassandra or message systems like Kafka.

3. Architecture Visualization and Monitoring:

Implement robust observability frameworks using tools like Jaeger for distributed tracing, Prometheus for metrics collection, and Grafana for visualizing flight paths and application performance, which are vital to maintaining health at scale.

Programming Example: Event-Driven Application Using Knative

Consider an application with microservices that processes and analyzes sensor data in real-time:

```python
from flask import Flask, request, jsonify
import json

app = Flask(__name__)

@app.route('/events', methods=['POST'])
def process_event():
    event_data = request.get_json()
    if event_data:
        sensor_id = event_data.get('sensor_id')
        reading = event_data.get('reading')
        print(f"Processing reading from Sensor ID: {sensor_id}, Data: {reading}")
        return jsonify({"status": "success"}), 200
    else:
        return jsonify({"status": "no data"}), 400

if __name__ == '__main__':
    app.run(host='0.0.0.0', port=8080)
```

In this Python Flask-based microservice, incoming event data from sensors is processed, demonstrating the application-centric view of how events are managed in real-time systems.

In summary, building event-driven applications using Knative Eventing within Kubernetes facilitates modern, responsive applications capable of handling varying loads and complex workflows. The successful deployment of such systems depends on careful consideration and implementation of design patterns, error-handling strategies, and scaling methods to address challenges associated with asynchronous processing, high throughput, and resilience in cloud-native environments. Developers can then leverage the flexibility and modularity of these applications to meet diverse operational requirements effectively.

4.7 Integrating External Services and Event Sources

Integrating external services and event sources is essential for constructing comprehensive event-driven architectures. It connects disparate systems and integrates data from various origins into a cohesive, responsive application environment. Knative Eventing provides the infrastructure to seamlessly ingest, process, and react to events from myriad external services, thereby enriching the operational capabilities of cloud-native systems. This section delves into methodologies for integrating external services and event sources, emphasizing best practices, technical configurations, and illustrative examples.

- **External Services Overview:** External services in cloud-native applications can include APIs provided by third-party platforms, data streams from IoT devices, cloud storage systems, databases, and more. These services offer functionalities that augment core application logic, providing additional data, executing specific computations, or enabling connectivity across ecosystems.

- **Event Source Dynamics:** An event source reflects occurrences or state changes in the external services that produce events for upstream processing. The efficiency and functionalities of an event-driven application often hinge upon its capability to tap into relevant external sources tailored to the application's domain logic.

- **RESTful API Integration:** Leveraging HTTP-based RESTful APIs is perhaps the most common approach to interfacing with external services. Knative Eventing allows you to capture events triggered by RESTful interactions effectively, channeling them into cloud-native pipelines:

```
apiVersion: sources.knative.dev/v1beta1
kind: ApiServerSource
metadata:
  name: rest-api-source
spec:
  serviceAccountName: apiserviceaccount
  mode: Resource
  resources:
    - apiVersion: v1
      kind: VirtualMachine
  sink:
    ref:
      apiVersion: serving.knative.dev/v1
      kind: Service
      name: event-consumer
```

This YAML manifests a webhook that listens to interactions with a REST API, converting them into events consumed by the event-consumer service.

- **Webhook Security Considerations:** Securing webhook integrations is paramount when dealing with external interfaces. HMAC signatures, mutual TLS, and OAuth tokens are commonly used to ensure secure transport layers, validating payload authenticity, and protecting against unauthorized access.

Cloud platforms provide native event sources that streamline integration between hosted services and Knative Eventing:

- **Google Cloud Pub/Sub Source:** Integrate Google Cloud Pub-/Sub as an event source to manage events across distributed applications:

```
apiVersion: sources.knative.dev/v1beta1
kind: CloudPubSubSource
metadata:
  name: pubsub-events
spec:
  project: my-gcp-project
```

```
topic: important-topic
sink:
  ref:
    apiVersion: serving.knative.dev/v1
    kind: Service
    name: events-analyzer
```

This configuration streams messages from a topic on Google Pub/Sub into a Knative service, harmonizing multi-cloud architectures.

- **Event-Driven AWS with SQS and SNS:** Leverage AWS services like SQS (Simple Queue Service) and SNS (Simple Notification Service) via custom sources to bring Amazon cloud events into the Knative ecosystem:

  - Develop a custom AWS event adapter to handle authentication and subscription to targeted topics or queues.

  - Utilize AWS SDKs that interface with Knative Eventing to encapsulate event construction and dispatch logic.

- **Edge Device Event Sourcing:** IoT and edge devices enrich event-driven systems by providing real-time data streams from the field, enabling adaptive responses to environmental changes:

  - Create an MQTT source to handle lightweight IoT protocols, connecting edge data to cloud-native workflows.

  - Utilize gateway solutions that bridge proprietary IoT protocols with RESTful or WebSocket transports comprehensible to Knative Eventing.

- **Security in IoT Integration:** Protect sensitive data originating from IoT devices by employing robust encryption protocols, authentication layers, and regular device firmware updates to thwart security threats effectively.

- **Apache Kafka for Event Ingestion:** Apache Kafka serves as a prime candidate for high-throughput event ingestion. Its integration with Knative Eventing supports complex event workflows:

```
apiVersion: sources.knative.dev/v1beta1
kind: KafkaSource
```

```
metadata:
  name: kafka-input
spec:
  consumerGroup: knative-stream-group
  bootstrapServers:
  - kafka-broker1:9092
  topics:
  - sensor-data-stream
  sink:
    ref:
      apiVersion: serving.knative.dev/v1
      kind: Service
      name: stream-processor
```

Kafka sources enable consumption of messages from sensor-data-stream, dispatching them to the stream-processor service.

- **Adopting Stream Processing Patterns:** Implement real-time processing algorithms embodied in services like Apache Flink or Apache Storm to execute complex transformation or aggregation tasks upon event streams captured within the event-driven paradigm.

- **Resilience and Failover:** Design event sources with retry logic, ensuring transient outages in external services do not impact downstream processes permanently. Utilize exponential backoff strategies and circuit breaker patterns for fault-resilient integrations.

- **Performance Tuning:** Optimizing thread pools, connection lifetimes, and payload sizes is crucial for maintaining optimal throughput between event sources and Knative services, especially under load.

- **Event Schema Management:** Define clear event schemas shared externally, promoting data consistency and compatibility. Employ versioning systems for schemas to manage backward-compatible changes efficiently, enriching service interoperability.

Consider a service processing event payloads received from an external API, encoded in JSON format:

```
const express = require('express');
```

```
const app = express();

app.use(express.json());

app.post('/incoming-events', (req, res) => {
    const event = req.body;

    // Validate payload schema
    if (event && event.type && event.data) {
        console.log(`Received event of type: ${event.type} with data: ${JSON.stringify(
            event.data)}`);
        // Implement processing logic here
        res.status(200).send({status: 'Event Processed'});
    } else {
        res.status(400).send({error: 'Invalid event format'});
    }
});

const PORT = process.env.PORT || 8080;
app.listen(PORT, () => {
    console.log(`Server running on port ${PORT}`);
});
```

In this Node.js service, events from an external API are validated and processed, demonstrating a typical integration use case.

- **Navigating Network Latency:** Reduce latency by employing efficient serialization protocols (e.g., Protocol Buffers or Apache Avro) and utilizing network optimizations (e.g., HTTP/2, gRPC).

- **Operational Monitoring:** Implement logging, metrics exportation, and tracing within integration flowpaths. Utilize tools like Grafana, Prometheus, and Jaeger to provide comprehensive visibility into event-driven workflows.

- **Managing Concurrent Events:** Balance concurrency levels across resources to minimize contention, employing tools like Kubernetes' Horizontal Pod Autoscaler for dynamical load adaptations.

Integrating external services and event sources into Knative Eventing extends application connectivity across versatile environments, promoting a dynamic and responsive event-driven ecosystem. By embracing structured approaches, robust security layers, and resilient configurations, developers can harness the full potential of external integrations, broadening the horizon for cloud-native innovations. The principles and practices elaborated herein serve as comprehensive guidelines for constructing well-integrated and scalable event-driven applications amid an ever-evolving service landscape.

Chapter 5

Autoscaling with Knative: Efficient Resource Management

This chapter focuses on the autoscaling capabilities of Knative, explaining how it optimizes resource utilization for applications. It covers the key concepts and metrics the Knative Autoscaler uses to adjust scaling behavior and provides guidance on configuring autoscaling parameters for desired performance. The chapter delves into request-based and concurrency-based scaling to ensure applications handle varying loads efficiently. It also discusses setting scaling limits, managing resource allocation, and handling traffic spikes, ensuring application stability. Additionally, techniques for monitoring autoscaling performance and troubleshooting potential scaling issues are addressed.

5.1 Understanding Autoscaling in Knative

Autoscaling, a fundamental aspect of cloud-native architecture, plays a crucial role in optimizing resource usage, reducing costs, and ensuring the seamless performance of applications. Knative, as an extension of Kubernetes, provides an efficient framework for autoscaling, tailored specifically for serverless environments. This section explores the architecture, design philosophy, and operational mechanisms that govern autoscaling in Knative, providing a detailed understanding of how it manages application workloads dynamically and efficiently.

Given the stateless and ephemeral nature of serverless applications, Knative is designed to react swiftly to changes in demand, scaling applications up and down based on real-time metrics. The design philosophy behind Knative's autoscaling focuses on responsiveness, efficiency, and cost-effectiveness, ensuring that applications have sufficient resources during peaks, while minimizing resource usage during lower demand periods.

Knative's autoscaling mechanism revolves around continuous monitoring of specific metrics such as concurrency and request rates. It leverages these metrics to make informed decisions about scaling the workloads. Unlike traditional static scaling methods where resource allocation is pre-configured, Knative employs a dynamic approach that adjusts the number of instances running your application based on the present load metrics.

The core components facilitating autoscaling in Knative include the Knative Serving component and the Knative Pod Autoscaler (KPA). These components work in tandem to manage the lifecycle and scaling of application instances efficiently. The Knative Serving component is responsible for routing traffic and managing revisions, which lays the foundation for autoscaling decisions driven by traffic patterns. The KPA, on the other hand, ensures that the desired state of the application's replicas matches the actual state, based on strategic metrics.

Within the Knative autoscaling framework, a key concept is the distinguishing of hot and cold path optimizations. The hot path refers to scenarios where the system must scale rapidly either upward or downward to accommodate sudden changes in incoming requests, minimizing latency and ensuring an unbroken user experience. Conversely, the cold path deals with gradual scaling adjustments when changes in demand are less severe or forecast over extended periods.

Consider an environment where an application must handle high volumes of incoming HTTP requests during business hours, with significantly less activity during off-hours. Knative accommodates such scenarios by automatically spinning up multiple instances during peak periods and scaling down as demand decreases. This dynamic adjustment prevents both resource wastage and performance bottlenecks.

To grasp the functionality of Knative's autoscaling, one can delve into the technical specifics by reviewing a sample YAML configuration for a Knative service:

```yaml
apiVersion: serving.knative.dev/v1
kind: Service
metadata:
  name: example-service
spec:
  template:
    metadata:
      annotations:
        autoscaling.knative.dev/minScale: "1"
        autoscaling.knative.dev/maxScale: "10"
        autoscaling.knative.dev/targetUtilizationPercentage: "70"
    spec:
      containers:
      - image: gcr.io/example/image
```

In this example, a Knative service example-service is configured with specific autoscaling parameters. The annotations within the service configuration specify the minimum and maximum number of replicas for the service, ensuring it scales between 1 and 10 instances. With a targetUtilizationPercentage set to 70%, the serverless application aims for optimal resource usage, seeking to maintain utilization around this threshold. Such configurations allow for precise control over resource allocation in response to varying loads.

The operational aspect of autoscaling in Knative is heavily reliant on its interaction with Kubernetes Horizontal Pod Autoscaler (HPA) and Custom Metrics API. Knative's KPA translates the high-level autoscaling requirements into metrics that the HPA can comprehend and act upon, leveraging Kubernetes' innate scalability. The capacity to define custom metrics further enhances Knative's ability to tailor autoscaling behavior to specific application needs.

A deeper examination reveals that Knative's scaling decisions are also guided by the concept of "activation" and "deactivation" of pods. Upon receiving a request, Knative assesses the necessity to activate additional pods. If the load exceeds the capacity of existing replicas, it initiates additional pods aligning with the defined scaling policies. Conversely, during periods of inactivity or low demand, pods are gradually deactivated or scaled down to conserve resources. This mechanism of scaling pods up and down avoids over-provisioning or under-provisioning, striking a balance between performance and cost-efficiency.

Another critical aspect of Knative's autoscaling is its support for different scaling metrics, specifically concurrency-based and request-based autoscaling. While concurrency-based autoscaling scales the application based on simultaneous active requests, request-based scaling adjusts resources based on incoming request rates. This bifurcated approach allows developers to select the metric that best aligns with their application's scaling needs.

Consider another crucial component of Knative autoscaling: the autoscaling classes. Users can specify the autoscaling behavior by setting the autoscaling.knative.dev/class annotation, where options such as kpa.autoscaling.knative.dev (Knative Pod Autoscaler) or hpa.autoscaling.knative.dev (Horizontal Pod Autoscaler) can be chosen based on specific use cases. The KPA class is optimal for concurrency-based scaling, while HPA suits CPU-based metrics more closely.

While Knative itself is inherently robust, in practical scenarios, the reliability and efficiency of the autoscaling mechanism are often subjected to environmental constraints such as cluster capacity and network bandwidth. These factors can influence the response time and scaling limits imposed by the infrastructure, necessitating advance planning to ensure scalable solutions are not hampered by hardware limitations.

Additionally, a noteworthy benefit of Knative autoscaling is its native compatibility with cloud environments, allowing seamless integration with platforms like Google Cloud, AWS, and Azure. This compatibility simplifies the deployment of serverless applications, leveraging the autoscaling capabilities inherent to these cloud platforms.

To enhance understanding, consider a scenario where autoscaling is tested by a simulated traffic increase using a simple application:

```
# Stress Testing the Application
hey -z 30s -c 50 http://example-service.default.example.com
```

This command uses a tool like hey to send a multitude of concurrent requests to the specified Knative service (example-service) for 30 seconds. Observing resource allocation changes in real-time could provide clear insights into how Knative adjusts instances, demonstrating its autoscaling responsiveness.

The evolution of Knative autoscaling continues to incorporate advanced AI and ML techniques, where predictive analytics drive more accurate forecasting of demand, guiding scaling decisions. The integration of machine learning models allows for proactive scaling, rather than reactive, enhancing the predictability and reliability of autoscaling outcomes.

For effective utilization of Knative's autoscaling, a thorough understanding of configuration parameters, metrics, and backend integration pathways is vital. This involves frequent performance analysis, adjustments to threshold values, and careful observation of metric patterns during diverse operational states.

Knative's autoscaling stands as a testament to the intricate interplay between software design and operational efficiency, focusing unequivocally on dynamic adaptation to application demands. It encapsulates the principles of elasticity and resource economy, ensuring that applications not only scale to meet performance expectations but also operate sustainably within budgetary constraints. Only through detailed configuration, combined with continuous monitoring and iterative optimization, can the full power of Knative autoscaling be harnessed.

5.2   Knative Autoscaler Concepts

The Knative Autoscaler is a pivotal component in the automated resource management ecosystem within Knative, specifically addressing the challenge of dynamically adjusting the number of active instances of an application in response to fluctuating demand. This section delves into the core concepts underlying the Knative Autoscaler, presenting an in-depth analysis of the scaling factors, decision-making criteria, and advanced features that govern its behavior.

Central to the Knative Autoscaler's functionality is the management of demand-driven scaling, where key metrics determine how and when resources are allocated or released. At the heart of the autoscaling process is an understanding of concurrency and request rates, which serve as the primary indicators for autoscaling decisions. These metrics provide insights into the application's workload, informing the autoscaler when to scale up or down.

Concurrency is defined as the number of simultaneous requests that an application instance can handle. By setting a target concurrency threshold, developers can instruct the Knative Autoscaler to maintain an optimal number of active pods to meet real-time demand. For instance, if the target concurrency is set to 100, the autoscaler ensures that the available instances are sufficient to handle 100 concurrent requests without degradation in performance.

Consider the following illustrative code snippet configuring concurrency-based autoscaling:

```
apiVersion: serving.knative.dev/v1
kind: Service
metadata:
  name: concurrency-example-service
spec:
  template:
    metadata:
      annotations:
        autoscaling.knative.dev/target: "100"
        autoscaling.knative.dev/class: "kpa.autoscaling.knative.dev"
    spec:
      containers:
      - image: gcr.io/example/concurrency-image
```

The configuration specifies that the autoscaler will adjust the number of active pods to ensure the target concurrency of 100 is sustained. By integrating concurrency-based metrics, the autoscaler evaluates the aggregate demand across all instances, scaling the application dynamically to accommodate incoming workloads efficiently.

Request-based metrics offer an alternative scaling approach, focusing on the rate at which requests arrive at the application rather than the number concurrently handled. This approach suits applications with well-defined request handling patterns, where sudden spikes in request arrivals necessitate quick scaling actions to preserve throughput and quality of service.

Furthermore, the Knative Autoscaler supports **custom metrics**, providing users with the flexibility to define application-specific criteria for scaling decisions. Custom metrics broaden the scope of autoscaling beyond generic concurrency or request rate metrics, accommodating varied workload characteristics.

To deploy custom metrics, developers can integrate with the Kubernetes Custom Metrics API, thereby extending the autoscaler's capabilities to incorporate domain-specific performance indicators. Utilizing custom metrics requires precise configuration and alignment with unique application demands, demanding a deep understanding of the application's operational parameters and variability.

Another crucial concept within the Knative Autoscaler is **scale-to-zero** capability. Scale-to-zero enables applications to reduce their instance count to zero during idle periods, conserving resources and reducing operational costs. When demand resurges, Knative quickly reactivates instances, ensuring minimal latency in responding to new requests. The autoscaler, therefore, makes a binary decision when scaling down – whether to keep a minimal number of instances active or scale down to zero, maintaining readiness for incoming traffic.

Activation latency is a consideration in scale-to-zero scenarios, requiring the autoscaler to balance resource savings against the delay in serving new requests. Developers can configure thresholds to optimize this trade-off, tailoring the autoscaling strategy to meet latency requirements without incurring undue costs.

A sophisticated facet of the Knative Autoscaler is its ability to perform predictive scaling, leveraging past traffic patterns and trends to forecast future demands. This predictive capability allows the autoscaler to pre-emptively adjust resources ahead of anticipated demand spikes or troughs, improving performance efficiency. Predictive scaling relies on extensive telemetry data collection and analysis, requiring integration with monitoring tools and data pipelines to supply accurate forecasts.

Consider the following YAML configuration which enables scaling capabilities with predictive insights:

```
apiVersion: serving.knative.dev/v1
kind: Service
metadata:
  name: predictive-scaling-service
spec:
  template:
    metadata:
      annotations:
        autoscaling.knative.dev/targetUtilizationPercentage: "75"
        autoscaling.knative.dev/predictiveScaling: "enabled"
      spec:
        containers:
        - image: gcr.io/example/predictive-image
```

In this configuration, the service sets a target utilization percentage of 75 for predictive scaling, enabling the predictive algorithm to control the scaling decisions proactively based on historical and real-time data.

The Knative Autoscaler extends its capabilities through its **lifecycle hooks** for startup and pre-stop events, which allow the autoscaler to execute specific operations during these lifecycle stages. Lifecycle hooks give developers added control over state management and cleanup tasks during scaling transitions, ensuring graceful scaling events without service interruption.

A critical aspect of utilizing the Knative Autoscaler is correctly **tuning scaling parameters** such as target utilization percentages, scaling thresholds, and stabilization windows. These parameters directly influence the responsiveness and stability of the autoscaler. For example, a low target utilization might lead to rapid scaling, potentially causing resource oscillations, whereas a high value could slow scaling responses, impacting service levels during peak demand.

Effective parameter tuning is achieved through iterative experimentation, leveraging tooling for real-time metrics visualization, and employing performance testing frameworks that simulate realistic workloads. These tests validate scaling behaviors under controlled conditions, offering insights into parameter adjustments needed to optimize functionality.

In addition, Knative's autoscaling architecture incorporates **safety measures** to prevent erratic scaling behaviors that could destabilize services. These measures include rate limits on scaling actions to avoid excessive scaling operations that add churn to the system, and configuring cool-down periods to allow state consistency before the next scaling adjustment.

To further illustrate the autoscaler's intricacies, we can present a simple experiment that monitors and logs the scaling process over time during various load conditions. Consider a Python script that simulates traffic and uses the Kubernetes API to observe the scale events:

```
import time
from kubernetes import client, config

def simulate_traffic(service_url, duration=60, concurrency=10):
    # Simulate traffic to the Knative service
    # Pseudo-code for generating requests to the service
    pass

def monitor_scaling(namespace, service_name):
    config.load_kube_config()
    v1 = client.CoreV1Api()

    while True:
        pods = v1.list_namespaced_pod(namespace)
        active_pods = [p for p in pods.items if service_name in p.metadata.name and
            p.status.phase == "Running"]
        print(f"Active pods: {len(active_pods)}")
        time.sleep(30)

if __name__ == "__main__":
    service_url = "http://predictive-scaling-service.default.example.com"
    simulate_traffic(service_url, duration=300, concurrency=20)
    monitor_scaling("default", "predictive-scaling-service")
```

This script sets up traffic simulations against a Knative service while concurrently monitoring the number of active pods, logging scaling events in synchronization with changing demand profiles. By employing such tools, developers gain empirical insights that enrich their understanding of the autoscaler's behavior in real-world applications.

The Knative Autoscaler embodies a sophisticated convergence of responsive architecture, operational agility, and resource efficiency. It fosters an environment where application scalability aligns agile engineering practices with cost-conscious architecture, ensuring an inherently adaptable serverless deployment framework. As developers master these core concepts, they unlock the potential to craft highly scalable, resilient, and economically efficient applications that stand robust in the face of evolving demand profiles and operational challenges.

5.3 Configuring Autoscaling Parameters

Configuring autoscaling parameters within the Knative framework is a pivotal task that directly influences an application's scalability, performance efficiency, and resource utilization strategy. This section provides a comprehensive analysis of the essential autoscaling parameters, illustrating their importance, configuration techniques, and impact on the dynamic scalability of serverless applications.

Autoscaling in Knative is primarily governed by annotations applied to service configurations. These annotations define the autoscaling behavior, dictate the scaling limits, and establish the metrics upon which scaling decisions are based. Understanding and correctly setting these parameters is critical to optimizing the utilization of cloud resources while maintaining desired service levels.

- **Concurrency Target** (CT) is an important parameter that designates the optimal number of requests an application instance can handle concurrently. The value assigned to the concurrency target directly affects the scaling behavior of the autoscaler. A lower concurrency target results in more instances being activated to distribute the load evenly, minimizing latency during peak loads. Conversely, a higher target reduces the number of instantiated replicas needed for the same request throughput, potentially conserving resources but risking higher latency due to increased load on each instance.

```
apiVersion: serving.knative.dev/v1
kind: Service
metadata:
  name: custom-concurrency-service
spec:
  template:
    metadata:
      annotations:
        autoscaling.knative.dev/target: "75" % Concurrency Target
      spec:
        containers:
        - image: gcr.io/example/concurrency-image
```

In the configuration above, the concurrency target is set at 75, which configures each instance to manage approximately 75 simultaneous requests, guiding the autoscaler to dynamically adjust the number of instances to meet this threshold.

- **MinScale and MaxScale** represent the minimum and maximum number of instances, respectively, that can be scaled by the service. These parameters serve as safety bounds, preventing overly aggressive scaling or under-provisioning. MinScale ensures a baseline level of instance availability, providing a buffer against sudden demand surges, while MaxScale limits resource allocation to prevent excessive scaling that could otherwise deplete available infrastructure resources or incur undue costs.

```
apiVersion: serving.knative.dev/v1
kind: Service
metadata:
  name: bounded-scale-service
spec:
  template:
    metadata:
      annotations:
        autoscaling.knative.dev/minScale: "2"
        autoscaling.knative.dev/maxScale: "10"
    spec:
      containers:
      - image: gcr.io/example/bounded-scale-image
```

Here, the bounded scale service is configured with a minimum scale of 2 and a maximum scale of 10, ensuring that the service will always have at least two instances available but will not exceed ten, irrespective of demand.

- **TargetUtilizationPercentage** is a crucial parameter that guides the autoscaler in maintaining an ideal balance between resource utilization and service performance. It indicates the percentage of the current capacity that should be utilized before triggering a scale-up event. For applications where maintaining specific performance metrics is crucial, tuning the target utilization helps adjust the sensitivity of the autoscaler to varying loads, offering flexibility in response time or cost effectiveness.

```
apiVersion: serving.knative.dev/v1
kind: Service
```

```
metadata:
  name: utilization-tuned-service
spec:
  template:
    metadata:
      annotations:
        autoscaling.knative.dev/targetUtilizationPercentage: "85"
    spec:
      containers:
      - image: gcr.io/example/utilization-image
```

In the configuration above, a target utilization percentage of 85% has been set, indicating that the service should leverage up to 85% of its scaling capacity before additional scaling actions are initiated.

- **ScaleToZero and ActivationThreshold** serve vital roles in managing idle resources efficiently. The scale-to-zero feature allows automatically reducing pod count to zero when no requests are being processed, drastically cutting costs during idle periods. The activation threshold parameter defines the minimum traffic level at which scaling should begin, optimizing the reconfirmation delay following a zero-scale phase.

```
apiVersion: serving.knative.dev/v1
kind: Service
metadata:
  name: zero-scale-service
spec:
  template:
    metadata:
      annotations:
        autoscaling.knative.dev/scale-to-zero: "true"
        autoscaling.knative.dev/activationThreshold: "5"
    spec:
      containers:
      - image: gcr.io/example/zero-scale-image
```

In this scenario, the 'zero-scale-service' is configured to scale down to zero during extended idle periods, with an activation threshold set to 5. This ensures scaling does not initiate until there is a definitive surge in request traffic.

- **Stabilization Window** is another key parameter, setting a time duration to average metrics before making scaling decisions. A well-tuned stabilization window helps dampen erratic scaling actions due to transient load changes, ensuring more consistent and predictable resource allocation.

```
apiVersion: serving.knative.dev/v1
kind: Service
metadata:
  name: stable-scaling-service
spec:
  template:
    metadata:
      annotations:
        autoscaling.knative.dev/stabilizationWindow: "60s"
    spec:
      containers:
      - image: gcr.io/example/stable-scaling-image
```

Utilizing a stabilization window of 60 seconds as shown in the configuration above, the autoscaler averages the metrics over this period to determine scaling actions, filtering out short-lived fluctuations that do not warrant immediate scaling adjustments.

- **Custom Metrics Integration** is made possible through annotations and enables applications with unique scaling requirements to scale based on specific business-related metrics. Such metrics may include response times, application-specific load factors, or other tailored metrics, involving integration with monitoring and metric collection tools like Prometheus and Grafana.

Configuring custom metric scaling requires understanding how to expose metric endpoints and configuring Kubernetes to perform metric retrieval. An illustrative example for a custom metric is provided:

```
apiVersion: autoscaling.knative.dev/v1alpha1
kind: Metric
metadata:
  name: custom-response-time-metric
spec:
  type:
    name: "pods"
    selector:
      app: response-time-app
    metric:
      name: response_time_ms
      target:
        type: "Value"
        value: "200ms"
```

In this example, a custom metric configuration instructs the autoscaler to consider response time as a metric, setting a target threshold of 200 milliseconds for optimal scaling decisions. Effectively configuring and utilizing custom metrics requires a complete ecosystem of metric instrumentation and ingestion workflows, including considerations for data resolution and collection frequency.

- **Predictive and Reactive Scaling** harnesses a combination of real-time metric evaluation and historical data analysis to implement a comprehensive scaling strategy. This dual approach leverages predictive models, often based on machine learning, to anticipate load changes and preemptively adjust instance counts, resulting in smoother performance transitions and reduced latency during demand shifts.

Ultimately, configuring autoscaling parameters within Knative is an exercise in trade-offs, balancing resource consumption with application responsiveness, and aligning autoscaling behavior with business objectives. Mastery of these parameters involves iterative experimentation, continuous monitoring, and ongoing adjustment of configurations. By leveraging available tooling and maintaining an acute awareness of workload patterns and application demands, organizations can refine autoscaling strategies to achieve robust, scalable, and cost-effective serverless applications within the Knative landscape.

5.4 Concurrency and Request-Based Autoscaling

Concurrency and request-based autoscaling stand as cornerstones of the dynamic scaling capabilities within Knative, framing the strategies by which applications responsively adjust resource allocations in response to changing demands. This section provides a detailed exposition of these autoscaling methodologies, exploring their architectural underpinnings, implementation nuances, and impact on application performance and resource efficiency.

Concurrency-based autoscaling in Knative revolves around monitoring and managing the simultaneous execution of multiple requests within a service, subsequently optimizing the allocation of instances required to efficiently process these requests. The concept is principally applied in scenarios where application throughput and latency are directly tied to the number of concurrent executions that active instances can support.

The core metric in concurrency-based autoscaling is the concurrency target, which specifies the ideal number of concurrent requests each service instance should handle. By configuring this target, the Knative Autoscaler dynamically adjusts the number of instances deployed to meet this concurrency level without compromising application performance. The flexibility to modify the concurrency target ensures that scaling behavior aligns with both performance specifications and cost constraints.

```
apiVersion: serving.knative.dev/v1
kind: Service
metadata:
  name: concurrency-optimized-service
spec:
  template:
    metadata:
      annotations:
        autoscaling.knative.dev/target: "50"
        autoscaling.knative.dev/minScale: "3"
        autoscaling.knative.dev/maxScale: "20"
    spec:
      containers:
      - image: gcr.io/example/concurrency-optimized-image
```

In the configuration above, the service is optimized for concurrency-based scaling with a target of 50 concurrent requests per instance. Parameters including minScale and maxScale delineate the allowable scaling boundaries, ensuring efficient utilization of infrastructure resources while maintaining robust performance characteristics.

Concurrency-based autoscaling is inherently beneficial for applications that feature variable but predictable loads, enabling fine-tuned control over resource allocation in environments where latency reduction is paramount. This model complements microservices architectures where individual services perform distinct functions, each potentially requiring specific concurrency thresholds.

In contrast, request-based autoscaling operates by monitoring the arrival rate of requests, subsequently dictating the capacity of application instances required to handle incoming demands without bottlenecks. This is particularly suited to applications with sporadic or un-predictable workloads, where balancing request processing capacity with incoming request rates is crucial to sustained service provision.

The configuration of request-based autoscaling engages the request rate target, setting the expected request processing rate for each instance. It enables the autoscaler to match the influx of new requests with the available processing capacity, scaling resources as needed to preserve response times and minimize queuing delays.

```
apiVersion: serving.knative.dev/v1
kind: Service
metadata:
  name: request-rate-service
spec:
  template:
    metadata:
      annotations:
        autoscaling.knative.dev/metric: "rps" % Requests per Second
        autoscaling.knative.dev/target: "200" % Target RPS per instance
    spec:
      containers:
      - image: gcr.io/example/request-rate-image
```

This request-rate-service handles fluctuations in incoming request rates by utilizing a requests-per-second metric as its scaling determinant. By setting a target of 200 RPS, the service aims to sustain this throughput, dynamically allocating instances to meet demand effectively.

By integrating both concurrency and request-based autoscaling measures, Knative provides a flexible and comprehensive framework that supports a diverse range of workload characteristics and application types. Both methodologies utilize a rigorous data-driven approach, analyzing current load conditions and historical usage patterns to inform scaling decisions in real time.

An important consideration in both concurrency and request-based autoscaling strategies is the evaluation period and stabilization window, which govern the time frames over which metrics are aggregated and evaluated before scaling actions are triggered. A shorter evaluation period fosters a more responsive scaling environment, albeit potentially at the cost of increased scaling fluctuations. Conversely, longer evaluation periods yield more stable scaling responses but may incur delays in reacting to sudden demand spikes.

Real-world application scenarios often necessitate the hybridization of

146

concurrency and request-based autoscaling. Applications that experience seasonal traffic patterns, such as e-commerce platforms during shopping events or media streaming services during major broadcast events, can leverage these autoscaling strategies to ensure optimal operation under various load conditions.

Consider an extended use case where both types of autoscaling are dynamically adjusted based on external factors such as promotional events or marketing campaigns. A Kubernetes operator could be configured to adjust concurrency and request rate targets in anticipation of expected load increases, aligning scaling behavior with business objectives.

```
apiVersion: serving.knative.dev/v1
kind: Service
metadata:
  name: hybrid-autoscaling-service
spec:
  template:
    metadata:
      annotations:
        autoscaling.knative.dev/class: "kpa.autoscaling.knative.dev"
        autoscaling.knative.dev/metric: "concurrency,rps"
        autoscaling.knative.dev/target: "100,300"
        autoscaling.knative.dev/stabilizationWindow: "90s"
    spec:
      containers:
      - image: gcr.io/example/hybrid-image
```

In this configuration, the hybrid-autoscaling-service employs both concurrency and request-based metrics to drive scaling actions, indicating a target concurrency of 100 and a request rate of 300 RPS. This dual approach allows for precise management of diverse load conditions, maintaining robustness against unexpected demand shifts.

Advanced implementations of autoscaling can incorporate predictive analytics and machine learning to enhance decision-making accuracy. By analyzing extensive telemetry data and incorporating predictive models, these advanced methodologies anticipate future demands, delivering proactive scaling adjustments which smooth out performance variability and optimize resource planning.

Moreover, effective implementation of these approaches necessitates comprehensive monitoring and logging infrastructure to track autoscaling behavior, capture metrics, and visualize trends. Tools such as Prometheus, Grafana, and Elasticsearch can provide

147

invaluable insights into autoscaler performance and efficacy, enabling operators to refine autoscaling configurations and improve outcomes continually.

Performance testing and scenario-based simulations are essential cornerstones in validating concurrency and request-based autoscaling strategies. These simulated environments replicate authentic workloads, enabling developers to evaluate scaling effectiveness under controlled stress conditions. Such tests inform parameter tuning efforts and facilitate ongoing improvements to autoscaler configurations.

Ultimately, mastering concurrency and request-based autoscaling requires a balanced synthesis of data-driven insights and adaptive control, ensuring that application services remain responsive, resilient, and resource-efficient. As Knative matures, its autoscaling capabilities continue to evolve, enabling scalable serverless applications that seamlessly align with modern agile development practices and the dynamic needs of distributed cloud environments.

5.5 Scaling Limits and Controls

Scaling limits and controls within the Knative framework are essential for balancing application performance with infrastructure constraints and resource budgets. Setting these parameters strategically allows organizations to manage compute resource allocations effectively, minimize potential over-provisioning costs, and ensure dependable service performance. This section provides a comprehensive discussion of the diverse scaling limits and control mechanisms available in Knative, their configuration, practical implications, and the strategies that leverage these attributes to optimize autoscaling behaviors for serverless applications.

- **Maximum and Minimum Scale Constraints** are foundational parameters shaping the scope of resource allocation and application scalability. **MaxScale** restricts the upper bound for the number of replica pods that can be provisioned, effectively preventing resource wastage and avoiding excessive scaling operations that could overwhelm cluster capacity or inflate costs unnecessarily.

Setting a maximum scale constraint requires an assessment of the application's peak demand characteristics, evaluating the compute and memory load needed to maintain desired Quality of Service (QoS) metrics even during spikes. Consider the following configuration example:

```
apiVersion: serving.knative.dev/v1
kind: Service
metadata:
  name: max-scale-controlled-service
spec:
  template:
    metadata:
      annotations:
        autoscaling.knative.dev/maxScale: "15"
    spec:
      containers:
      - image: gcr.io/example/max-scale-image
```

In this configuration, 'maxScale' is assigned a value of 15, indicating that the service should not scale beyond fifteen pods irrespective of traffic load. The parameter provides a safeguard against potential resource depletion during extreme demand scenarios.

- **Minimum Scale Constraints**, specified by **MinScale**, ensure a base level of service availability, guaranteeing that a certain number of instances are always provisioned and ready to handle incoming requests. This constraint enhances resilience against sudden traffic increases and maintains the service's reactive capability even during lulls in demand.

```
apiVersion: serving.knative.dev/v1
kind: Service
metadata:
  name: min-scale-controlled-service
spec:
  template:
    metadata:
      annotations:
        autoscaling.knative.dev/minScale: "2"
    spec:
      containers:
      - image: gcr.io/example/min-scale-image
```

The example above sets a 'minScale' value of 2, implying that at least two replicas must persist under all conditions. This configuration is particularly relevant for applications demanding high availability and those serving critical or time-sensitive missions.

- **Concurrency Limits** define boundaries on the concurrent request processing capacity of service instances, which, in turn, dictate how autoscaling decisions are enacted based on real-time load assessments. These limits facilitate load distribution across available instances, mitigating risks of request overload and ensuring even strain under increasing demand conditions.

```
apiVersion: serving.knative.dev/v1
kind: Service
metadata:
  name: concurrency-control-service
spec:
  template:
    metadata:
      annotations:
        autoscaling.knative.dev/target: "80"
    spec:
      containers:
      - image: gcr.io/example/concurrency-control-image
```

By setting a concurrency target to 80, as shown in this configuration, each instance is tuned to handle up to eighty concurrent requests, steering autoscaler interventions to bolster resource allocations accordingly.

- **Resource Limits and Requests** place caps on CPU and memory availability for each pod, thereby instilling resource control on a per-instance basis. Kubernetes implements these limitations to streamline resource provisioning, thereby avoiding contention issues that could degrade application performance or reliability.

```
apiVersion: serving.knative.dev/v1
kind: Service
metadata:
  name: resource-limited-service
spec:
  template:
    metadata:
    spec:
      containers:
      - image: gcr.io/example/resource-limited-image
        resources:
          limits:
            cpu: "1"
            memory: "512Mi"
          requests:
```

```
cpu: "500m"
memory: "256Mi"
```

This service configuration designates specific CPU and memory resources for each instance, setting a cap of 1 CPU and 512 MiB of memory with reserved requests of 500 milli-CPU and 256 MiB. These constraints prevent arbitrary resource consumption, ensuring systems operate within architectural capacity.

The usage of **Scaling Policy Controls** involves fine-tuning scaling granularity, establishing rules that guide the autoscaler in its execution of scaling operations, and incorporating stabilization windows that alleviate transient state oscillations.

The 'stabilizationWindow' parameter dictates how long the autoscaler should delay scaling actions post-threshold breach to allow for data variation smoothing:

```
apiVersion: serving.knative.dev/v1
kind: Service
metadata:
  name: stable-policy-service
spec:
  template:
    metadata:
      annotations:
        autoscaling.knative.dev/stabilizationWindow: "30s"
      spec:
        containers:
        - image: gcr.io/example/stable-policy-image
```

A window of 30 seconds establishes a regulatory cadence for scaling operations, instructed to adjust instance counts only after assessing the steadiness of the utilization metrics—a practice effective against noisy metric environments.

- **Rate Limits** can establish a ceiling on the growth rate of service instance numbers, meaningful for controlling aggressive scaling up/down operations in volatile environments. Rate limits foster predictability in instance provisioning, aligning with budgetary and infrastructure capacity considerations.

Consider also implementing more advanced control mechanisms, such as **Dynamic Limits** which modulate constraints based on present traffic characteristics or forecasted trends, thus providing adaptability favorably poised for seasonally variant loads or promotions.

- **Real-time Monitoring and Alerting** serve pivotal roles, offering insights into scaling efficacy and identifying thresholds that could benefit from recalibration. Technologies like Prometheus and Grafana facilitate continuous observation of operational metrics, enabling alerts for when scaling behavior diverges from strategic norms or when resource limits are imminently reached.

An example of deploying a basic alert in Prometheus for monitoring CPU saturation might appear as follows:

```
groups:
- name: instance_alerts
  rules:
  - alert: HighCpuUsage
    expr: container_cpu_usage_seconds_total{image="resource-limited-image",
        namespace="default"} > 0.9
    for: 5m
    labels:
      severity: warning
    annotations:
      summary: "High CPU use on instance {{$labels.instance}}"
      description: "{{$labels.instance}} is using over 90\% CPU for more than 5
        minutes."
```

Throughout this advanced setup, the interplay between these scaling limitations and control paradigms necessitates a detailed comprehension of application-specific requirements, environmental constraints, and architectural drivers to ultimately attenuate unnecessary expenditures and cultivate efficient autoscaling mechanisms.

Crucially, the configuration of scaling limits and controls hinges upon continuous iterative improvements and empirical refinement. Engaging in ongoing performance assessments, stakeholder input review, and planned stress-testing cycles across representative load conditions enhances confidence in scaling configurations, emboldening organizations' capacity to adapt swiftly to ever-changing market and user dynamics.

5.6   Handling Traffic Spikes and Load

Effective management of traffic spikes and load fluctuations is crucial in ensuring the stability and responsiveness of applications, especially in serverless environments powered by Knative. The autoscaling capabilities of Knative are designed to dynamically adapt to changing demands, thereby ensuring service reliability and performance even under varying load conditions. This section delves into strategies for managing traffic spikes, exploring architectural mechanisms, configuration best practices, and advanced techniques that facilitate comprehensive scale management.

Traffic spikes represent sudden and often unpredictable surges in demand, which, if not addressed swiftly, can potentially overwhelm application resources, resulting in degraded performance or service outages. These spikes can be episodic, such as during promotional events, viral media content releases, or breaking news, requiring applications to absorb increased traffic seamlessly and maintain user satisfaction.

Reactive Autoscaling forms the backbone of managing sudden traffic spikes in Knative. The autoscaler reacts to real-time metrics by provisioning additional resources to accommodate increased load. The fundamental metrics employed for reactive autoscaling include request rates, concurrency levels, and latency indicators. By leveraging these metrics, Knative scalably allocates the necessary computing power to handle spike-induced loads temporally.

For instance, a Knative service may be configured to adjust dynamically based on incoming requests per second (RPS):

```
apiVersion: serving.knative.dev/v1
kind: Service
metadata:
  name: spike-tolerant-service
spec:
  template:
    metadata:
      annotations:
        autoscaling.knative.dev/metric: "rps"
        autoscaling.knative.dev/target: "200"
    spec:
      containers:
      - image: gcr.io/example/spike-tolerant-image
```

In this configuration, the service is optimized to scale responsively to request rates, ensuring that an abrupt surge in traffic is met with proportional instantiation of additional pods to sustain the desired throughput.

Concurrency Scale control is another strategy for reacting to traffic spikes where the concurrency target is finely tuned to limit the number of requests processed concurrently, thereby enabling proactive scaling when this concurrency threshold is crossed. This ensures efficient resource allocation during high-load periods while maintaining low-latency operations.

```
apiVersion: serving.knative.dev/v1
kind: Service
metadata:
  name: concurrency-sensitive-service
spec:
  template:
    metadata:
      annotations:
        autoscaling.knative.dev/target: "75"
    spec:
      containers:
      - image: gcr.io/example/concurrency-sensitive-image
```

Within this configuration, a concurrency target of 75 ensures that each instance efficiently manages up to 75 simultaneous requests, demanding timely scaling actions when these levels are exceeded.

Employing a Dynamic Scaling Policy can enhance strategic spike management by incorporating run-time adjustments based on business logic and operational insights. This involves utilizing context-aware parameters that modify scaling attributes, e.g., anticipating increased demand during anticipated large-scale events or responding to temporary surges in consumer activity with rapid provisioning.

Rate Limiting is a strategic control point in handling excessive traffic spikes, placing a cap on request influx and thus protecting backend systems from overload. Implementing APIs or service controllers to enforce rate limits ensures equitable service delivery and prevents individual components from becoming performance bottlenecks.

In Knative, rate limiting can be applied through service proxy configurations using tools such as Istio or nginx. Employing middleware strategies for request throttling stabilizes load dispersion and mitigates variances caused by unexpected rushes. Here's an example using nginx configuration directives:

154

```
http {
    limit_req_zone $binary_remote_addr zone=mylimit:10m rate=100r/s;

    server {
        location /service-endpoint {
            limit_req zone=mylimit;
            proxy_pass http://backend-service;
        }
    }
}
```

This configuration demonstrates the use of nginx to limit each source address to 100 requests per second, acting as a tactical mechanism to prevent backend strain when servicing traffic spikes.

Load Balancing across distributed instances further ensures that no single node becomes a bottleneck under heightened demand conditions. Knative orchestrates intelligent load distribution via Kubernetes' native balancing mechanics, juxtaposed with external traffic management systems where cross-regional workloads necessitate globally distributed solutions.

Exploiting Traffic Mirroring and Shadowing offers a robust means of addressing latent issues by replicating production traffic into parallel testing environments. By gauging service performance under mirrored conditions, developers can preemptively identify potential choke points and adjust resource policy accordingly before traffic spikes impact production environments.

In multi-tenancy deployments, understanding request prioritization ensures certain critical loads retain precedence over less vital ones during capacity crunches. This differentiation, based on importance or specific user profiles, ensures that quality services persistently deliver essential outcomes.

Caching Strategies further mitigate spike impact by enabling rapid data retrieval absent the need for repeated backend processing. Comprehensive utilization of distributed caching solutions—such as Redis or Memcached—across service layers capitalizes on reduced infrastructure load pressure, freeing computational resources for processing non-cacheable requests.

During periods of high activity, Elastic Scaling leverages cloud-native durability for resourcing flexibility, epitomizing an on-demand resource elasticity ethos. Taking advantage of cloud infrastructure that supports autoscaling, like Google Cloud's Kubernetes Engine, AWS Elastic Kubernetes Service, or Azure Kubernetes Service, extends autoscaling provisions beyond communal limits.

Scenario Planning and Simulation Testing afford critical insights into application behavior under theoretical spike load situations, demanding scheduled testing cycles that validate the durability of scaling configurations and predict application performance metrics. Solutions such as Apache JMeter or k6 employ scriptable load execution, showcasing profitable avenues for tuning thresholds and response mechanisms.

For continuous refinement, Monitoring and Alerting Integration enables the capture of operational metrics, reflecting autoscaling efficacy and providing critical data for on-the-fly adjustments. Platforms like Prometheus, alongside visualization frameworks like Grafana, deliver dynamic metrics observations, offering direct feedback loops to refine scaling strategies.

By specifically targeting alert conditions pertinent to spikes and stress, such as sudden latency increases or prolonged CPU saturation, a comprehensive alerting strategy signals intervention requirement thresholds, effectively anchoring stability management protocols and orchestrating intelligent escalations where necessary.

Proactivity and strategic preparedness underpin effective traffic spike management in Knative, embracing an assortment of predictive and reactive scaling tactics which enhance application agility amidst fluctuating demands. As infrastructure and application domains evolve, adopting technological advancements and instituting operational excellence will ensure applications ubiquitously and gracefully manage diverse load challenges, securing robust, scalable, and economically viable deployments.

5.7 Monitoring and Troubleshooting Scaling

Monitoring and troubleshooting scaling behaviors in Knative is an essential component of maintaining efficient and reliable serverless operations. This section examines the robust set of tools and methodologies available for observing, analyzing, and resolving scaling-related issues, providing insights into best practices for ensuring that scaling actions align with both system demands and performance expectations.

Monitoring Scaling Activities encompasses tracking the real-time status and historical metrics of application instances, which are critical for understanding scaling dynamics. Effective monitoring involves integrating with observability platforms that can ingest and analyze data related to request rates, concurrency, CPU and memory usage, instance counts, and latency. These platforms often utilize a combination of dashboards, alerts, and logs to provide a comprehensive view of scaling behaviors.

Prometheus and **Grafana** are widely adopted solutions within the Kubernetes ecosystem, offering extensive capabilities for capturing and visualizing metrics from Knative services. Prometheus collects metrics at regular intervals via endpoints exposed by instrumented applications and Kubernetes itself, while Grafana enables users to create dynamic, interactive dashboards to interpret these metrics.

An exemplary Prometheus configuration might include the following scrape configuration for collecting Knative metrics:

```
scrape_configs:
  - job_name: 'knative_serving'
    kubernetes_sd_configs:
      - role: endpoint
    relabel_configs:
      - source_labels: [__meta_kubernetes_namespace,
          __meta_kubernetes_pod_name]
        action: keep
        regex: 'knative-serving;(activator|autoscaler)-.*'
    metric_relabel_configs:
      - source_labels: [__name__]
        regex: 'knative_serving_(request_count|autoscaler_pod_count).*'
        action: keep
```

This Prometheus configuration captures metrics related to the Knative

Serving component, specifically targeting request counts and the number of autoscaler-managed pods. By restricting data collection to relevant metrics, storage and query efficiency are enhanced, delivering focused insights into scaling events.

Grafana dashboards then visualize this metrical data, furnishing operational teams with real-time and historical perspectives of how applications scale in response to demand. A typical Grafana dashboard might feature panels displaying request latency over time, concurrency levels, pod counts, and resource consumption patterns, furnishing stakeholders with key performance indicators and trends.

Here is a simple Grafana query example that visualizes average concurrency for a given time frame:

```
avg_over_time(knative_serving_average_concurrency_count[5m])
```

This PromQL query calculates the average concurrency count for Knative Serving workloads over a rolling five-minute window, facilitating identification of workload variations and anomalies.

To complement metric collection, **Logging** offers critical diagnostic information, capturing event-level intelligence that assists in identifying root causes of scaling issues. Kubernetes and Knative generate logs related to autoscaler actions, pod lifecycle events, and resource allocations. Centralized logging solutions like the **ELK Stack** (Elasticsearch, Logstash, Kibana) aggregate and index these logs, enabling complex queries and in-depth analyses.

Alerts and Notifications play pivotal roles in proactive scaling management. By configuring alerts based on key metrics—such as high request latency, excessive error rates, or anomalous pod scaling activities—teams can promptly respond to adverse scaling behaviors. Throttling or degraded performance alerts can trigger investigation protocols, guiding operators towards preventive or corrective measures.

For example, a Prometheus alert rule targeting latency might be structured as follows:

```
groups:
- name: scaling_alerts
  rules:
  - alert: HighRequestLatency
    expr: histogram_quantile(0.95, rate(
```

```
        knative_serving_request_duration_seconds_bucket[5m])) > 2
for: 10m
labels:
  severity: high
annotations:
  summary: "High request latency detected"
  description: "The 95th percentile request latency is above 2 seconds for over 10
    minutes."
```

This rule activates a high-severity alert when the 95th percentile of request latency exceeds two seconds for a duration longer than ten minutes, encompassing both transient and sustained performance degradations.

Troubleshooting Scaling Challenges involves resolving issues that prevent effective scaling, such as configuration errors, resource bottlenecks, and application-specific constraints. This process often requires a methodical approach, employing a combination of monitoring insights, log analysis, and iterative testing to isolate and address underlying factors.

During troubleshooting, consider the following common scaling issues and solutions:

- **Resource Allocation Conflicts**: Scaling may be impeded if resources exceed configured cluster limits or if allocations are inadequately specified. Ensuring that resource requests and limits are aligned with application needs and cluster capabilities can resolve these conflicts. Review and adjust Kubernetes Resource-Quotas and LimitRanges to relax constraints as necessary.

```
apiVersion: v1
kind: ResourceQuota
metadata:
  name: compute-resources
spec:
  hard:
    requests.cpu: "10"
    requests.memory: "32Gi"
```

- **Incorrect Autoscaler Configuration**: Misconfigured scaling parameters may lead to undesired behaviors such as insufficient scaling or excessive instance creation. Verifying the accuracy of annotations governing autoscaling logic can align actions with intent.

159

- **Excessive Scaling Latency**: Investigate the stabilization windows and cooldown periods if pods do not scale promptly during demand spikes. These temporal settings may cause delays in scaling response time. Reducing stabilization windows can increase responsiveness but risk scaling oscillations.

- **Failed Pod Scheduling**: If the autoscaler triggers new pods but they fail to enter the Running state, inspect cluster capacity, node taints, and affinity rules that may be obstructing efficient scheduling. Address node failures or adjust PodAntiAffinity rules to enhance flexibility.

- **External Dependencies**: Intermittent endpoint failures or external service latencies may manifest as perceived scaling inefficiencies. Introduce resilient retry mechanisms, circuit breaker patterns, or enhanced caching to buffer applications against external variability.

Finally, **Load Testing** simulates scaling conditions, providing valuable performance data and insights into thresholds and failure modes. Tools such as **Apache JMeter**, **k6**, and **Locust** offer customizable scenarios that anticipate peak loads and stress-test applications to identify weaknesses prior to production incidents.

Consider a k6 load test script for simulating request load:

```
import http from 'k6/http';
import { check } from 'k6';

export default function () {
  let res = http.get('http://spike-tolerant-service.default.example.com');
  check(res, {
    'status is 200': (r) => r.status === 200,
    'response time < 500ms': (r) => r.timings.duration < 500,
  });
}
```

Running this script in distributed mode replicates peak conditions, ensuring the service scales effectively, maintaining performance metrics within predefined boundaries. Load testing, coupled with rigorous monitoring and alerting frameworks, lays the foundation for reliable, scalable, and responsive Knative application environments.

In essence, scaling monitoring and troubleshooting require unified visibility across metrics, timely detection of scaling lags or irregularities,

and proactive examination of scaling conditions. By fully implementing these strategies, operators can maintain robust, efficiently scaling
applications capable of adapting gracefully to intricate and evolving
serverless demands.

Chapter 6

Knative Integrations and Ecosystem

This chapter examines the expansive Knative ecosystem and its seamless integration with cloud and open-source platforms. It explores how Knative enhances development workflows by integrating with CI/CD tools such as Jenkins, GitLab CI/CD, and Tekton. The integration with Istio and other service meshes is discussed for advanced networking management. Strategies for connecting Knative Eventing to various cloud services for comprehensive event handling are presented. The chapter highlights Knative's role in improving DevOps practices and introduces community-driven tools and extensions that enhance its capabilities. Real-world case studies demonstrate effective Knative integrations in solving complex challenges across industries.

6.1 Exploring the Knative Ecosystem

The Knative ecosystem presents a comprehensive suite of tools designed to abstract the complexities associated with developing, deploying, and managing modern cloud-native applications atop Kubernetes.

163

At its core, Knative is built on a foundation that enhances Kubernetes by introducing higher-level application lifecycle management primitives streamlined for developer productivity and operational efficiency.

Knative divides its functionality into two primary domains: Serving and Eventing. Each is a discrete component, yet they are inherently interconnected to provide a seamless operational experience.

Knative Serving:

Knative Serving focuses on deploying and managing serverless workloads. It allows developers to build modern, container-based applications and ensures those applications can automatically scale based on real-time demand. The key aspects of Knative Serving include:

- *Services:* A Service in Knative encapsulates the containerized workloads, allowing them to evolve over time while maintaining stable access URLs for clients.

- *Routes:* Routes provide networking components with the ability to target a specific configuration of a service, thus enabling smooth traffic splitting and progressive rollout strategies.

- *Configurations:* Configurations maintain the desired state for software delivery when a new revision is created. Changes in configuration can automatically lead to new revision creation.

- *Revisions:* Each change in a configuration results in a revision, representing an immutable snapshot of code and configuration.

The following example illustrates a declarative YAML configuration for a simple Knative service. The configuration manages the deployment of a Docker container to the Kubernetes cluster:

```yaml
apiVersion: serving.knative.dev/v1
kind: Service
metadata:
  name: helloworld-go
spec:
  template:
    spec:
      containers:
        - image: gcr.io/knative-samples/helloworld-go
          env:
            - name: TARGET
              value: "World"
```

164

Upon applying this configuration to a Kubernetes cluster, Knative establishes the necessary infrastructure to schedule, serve, and scale the Docker-based application.

Knative Eventing:

Event-driven architectures are central to modern cloud applications, and Knative Eventing facilitates building these kinds of services by providing essential constructs for producing and consuming events.

- *Brokers and Triggers:* Brokers act as a central hub that receives events, while Triggers define event filters and subscriber relationships.

- *Channels and Subscriptions:* Channels represent event routing path collections. Subscriptions enable services to subscribe to specific channels for event consumption.

- *Source Adapters:* Knative provides out-of-the-box source adapters that can be integrated with various external systems to bring events into your environment.

A critical feature of Knative Eventing is its pluggability, allowing integration of different messaging backends such as Apache Kafka or NATS, to suit diverse operational requirements. Here is an example of setting up an event broker:

```
apiVersion: eventing.knative.dev/v1
kind: Broker
metadata:
  name: default
```

Following the broker creation, triggers are defined to link events with appropriate handlers:

```
apiVersion: eventing.knative.dev/v1
kind: Trigger
metadata:
  name: my-trigger
spec:
  broker: default
  filter:
    attributes:
      type: my-event-type
  subscriber:
    ref:
```

```
apiVersion: serving.knative.dev/v1
kind: Service
name: event-display
```

Here, the broker routes tagged specified events to the appropriate Knative services for processing.

Integrations with Cloud Platforms:

Knative's design integrates seamlessly with a variety of cloud providers and open-source platforms. Kubernetes, GKE (Google Kubernetes Engine), EKS (AWS Elastic Kubernetes Service), and AKS (Azure Kubernetes Service) provide managed Kubernetes offerings that inherently support Knative deployment. These integrations allow teams to leverage serverless technology while maintaining the ability to utilize cloud-native tools and services.

For example, GKE offers built-in support for deploying Knative directly, streamlining the provisioning and management of serverless applications across Google's cloud infrastructure.

```
gcloud container clusters create knative-demo \
  --addons=HttpLoadBalancing,CloudRun,ConfigConnector \
  --machine-type n1-standard-2 \
  --enable-stackdriver-kubernetes \
  --zone us-central1-b
```

After setting up the cluster, Knative components can be installed via Helm or directly using the kubectl CLI tools.

Multiplatform Interoperability:

One of Knative's notable features is its interoperability with multiple execution platforms. This is particularly valuable for applications built using hybrid or multi-cloud strategies. Knative treats all resources, regardless of their underlying cloud provider, as first-class citizens.

The open nature of the Kubernetes API and Knative's abstractions allows developers to encapsulate the complexity of details into a simple, cohesive API that can run uniformly across any compliant Kubernetes platform.

Extending Functionality:

Knative's ecosystem is extensible, allowing for custom extensions and additive features. Developers can create custom sources, event brokers, or choose among a growing community of integrations and plugins. As the ecosystem evolves, new options continue to enrich the adaptability and flexibility that Knative offers.

The versatility of Knative is enhanced by its community-driven approach, fostering a home for various auxiliary tools, such as Tekton for CI/CD, which seamlessly align with the Knative model, ensuring concurrent incorporation into DevOps workflows.

Overall, Knative serves as a formidable framework for abstracting the underlying complexities of Kubernetes operations, facilitating the deployment, management, and scaling of containerized services, making it an indispensable component of the cloud-native application stack.

6.2 Integration with CI/CD Tools

The integration of Knative with Continuous Integration and Continuous Deployment (CI/CD) tools such as Jenkins, GitLab CI/CD, and Tekton enhances development workflows by automating application build, testing, and deployment processes. Knative's capabilities align with the principles of DevOps, embracing agility, scalability, and efficiency. This section delves into how Knative can be effectively integrated with popular CI/CD tools, providing insights into achieving a streamlined, automated pipeline.

Jenkins Integration

Jenkins is a widely-used open-source automation server. Its adaptability is leveraged by integrating with Knative to deploy serverless applications automatically. By using Jenkins pipelines, users can orchestrate complex workflows that deploy applications with minimal manual intervention.

Jenkins can interact with a Kubernetes cluster through the Kubernetes plugin, providing an interface to manage resources, including Knative services. Here is a basic Jenkins pipeline example that builds a Docker image based on source code and deploys it to a Knative service:

```
pipeline {
```

167

```
agent any
stages {
    stage('Checkout') {
        steps {
            checkout scm
        }
    }
    stage('Build Docker Image') {
        steps {
            script {
                docker.build("my-knative-app:${env.BUILD_ID}")
            }
        }
    }
    stage('Deploy to Knative') {
        steps {
            script {
                sh 'kubectl apply -f k8s/knative-service.yaml'
            }
        }
    }
}
}
```

In this pipeline, source code is checked out from version control, a Docker image is built from it, and then the image is deployed as a Knative service using 'kubectl'.

GitLab CI/CD Integration

GitLab CI/CD provides an integrated approach to software delivery, facilitating automation through pipeline definitions within the repository using '.gitlab-ci.yml'. Knative leverages this integration for continuous deployment, allowing developers to push updates automatically from source code repositories to Knative-enabled Kubernetes clusters.

Consider the following '.gitlab-ci.yml' file that defines a basic workflow for deploying a Knative application:

```
image: docker:latest

stages:
  - build
  - deploy

variables:
  IMAGE_TAG: $CI_REGISTRY_IMAGE:$CI_COMMIT_REF_SLUG

build:
  stage: build
  script:
    - docker build -t $IMAGE_TAG .
    - docker push $IMAGE_TAG
```

```
deploy:
  stage: deploy
  script:
    - kubectl apply -f knative/service.yaml
```

By using GitLab's built-in capabilities to manage container registries, the process seamlessly builds and deploys containerized applications, capturing the efficiencies of end-to-end pipeline management.

Tekton Pipelines

Tekton represents a modern Kubernetes-native CI/CD solution that fits naturally with the Knative ecosystem. Developed as part of the Continuous Delivery Foundation (CDF), Tekton Pipelines offers a standardized way to build CI/CD systems, benefiting from container orchestration practices provided by Kubernetes itself.

A Tekton pipeline is composed of tasks that define discrete steps in the process. For example, a task may clone a repository, build an application, and deploy it. The task is a first-class resource within the Kubernetes API, and can be version-controlled and utilized in different contexts. Below is an exemplary Tekton task specification that performs a simple build and deployment workflow:

```
apiVersion: tekton.dev/v1beta1
kind: Task
metadata:
  name: build-and-deploy
spec:
  steps:
    - name: clone-repo
      image: alpine/git
      script: |
        git clone https://github.com/example/myrepo.git /workspace
    - name: build-image
      image: gcr.io/cloud-builders/docker
      script: |
        docker build -t gcr.io/my-project/my-image /workspace
        docker push gcr.io/my-project/my-image
    - name: deploy-knative
      image: bitnami/kubectl
      script: |
        kubectl apply -f /workspace/knative/service.yaml
```

Within this setup, the 'clone-repo' step handles repository cloning, 'build-image' step builds and pushes the Docker image, and 'deploy-knative' applies the Knative service configuration to the cluster.

Streamlining the Continuous Deployment Process

Incorporating CI/CD with Knative simplifies and accelerates development cycles, creating a responsive and agile delivery pipeline that can rapidly respond to changing demands and circumstances. By automating repetitive tasks traditionally managed manually, developers can focus on higher-level logic and optimizations.

CI/CD pipelines ensure systematic integration and testing, reducing risk and time-to-market for new features. Consistency across environments is achieved via infrastructure-as-code principles, allowing software developers and engineers to deploy consistent versions of applications irrespective of the environment, whether in development, testing, or production.

Each of the CI/CD tools above augments Knative's inherent capabilities, enabling scalable and robust deployments while maintaining the flexibility necessary for modern software engineering practices. Integrating these tools into your Knative development lifecycle provides:

- Reduced manual errors through automation.

- Enhanced collaboration within teams leveraging repositories and shared pipelines.

- Early and integrated testing processes, allowing for quicker identification of issues.

- Revisable artifacts, such as Docker images and configuration files, that are easily version-controlled and auditable.

The holistic art of combining CI/CD with Knative goes beyond mere deployments—it touches upon broader organizational objectives by promoting a sustainable, reliable, and predictable delivery pipeline. As the nature of applications continues to evolve towards microservices and serverless models, integrating powerful CI/CD tools provides both the framework and operational leverage necessary for success in an increasingly competitive technological landscape. Through methodological experimentation and customized configurations, development environments become truly organic, adapting in real-time to enhance deliverable quality and robustness.

Knative's compatibility with varying CI/CD solutions also points towards its versatility, granting diverse organizational infrastructures the power to deploy best practices aligned with internal policies and goals.

As the ecosystem expands, these tools—Jenkins, GitLab, and Tekton—are continuously updated with plugins and modules enhancing compatibility, facilitating an ongoing evolution that equips developers to adjust seamlessly to emerging technological paradigms.

6.3 Knative with Istio and Service Mesh

The integration of Knative with Istio and additional service mesh technologies provides a robust platform for orchestrating advanced networking and traffic management needs in cloud-native environments. This capability leverages the infrastructure advantages of Kubernetes, merging them with the unified traffic control and resilient service-to-service communication offered by service meshes. Here, we examine the interplay between Knative and Istio, illustrating its applications for managing network policies, security, observability, and more.

Understanding Service Mesh and Istio

A service mesh abstracts and manages complex, microservice service-to-service interactions within cloud environments. At its essence, it provides network-layer functionality such as load balancing, traffic management, security enforcement, and observability without altering application code. Service meshes typically employ a data plane, comprised of proxies for managing service traffic, and a control plane, managing configuration.

Istio is a leading open-source service mesh that seamlessly integrates with Kubernetes. It provides tools to successfully connect, secure, control, and observe services. Istio's architecture includes Envoy as the sidecar proxy underpinning its robust traffic management capabilities; it also supports increased observability via telemetry collection and heightened security through mutual TLS.

Integrating Knative with Istio

Knative requires a service mesh to effectively route requests and apply networking features transparently, initially designed with Istio as its primary integration. Istio enhances Knative's serving functionalities by enabling fine-grained traffic control through its routing rules, facilitating efficient load balancing, and managing network ACLs.

Start by ensuring Istio is correctly deployed within your Kubernetes cluster. Here is a simplified guide to deploying Istio:

```
istioctl install --set profile=default
```

This command installs Istio using the default configuration profile, which includes core features and extensions. Once Istio is operational, you can proceed to integrate Knative.

Deploying Knative with Istio

Deploying Knative together with Istio involves configuring Knative components to use Istio's capabilities for advanced networking. Below is an approach to deploy Knative in a Kubernetes environment with Istio as the service mesh:

```
kubectl apply -f https://github.com/knative/serving/releases/download/v0.25.0/
    serving-core.yaml

kubectl apply -f https://github.com/knative/net-istio/releases/download/v0.25.0/
    release.yaml
```

In these commands, we apply Knative components and specify the use of Istio for networking by applying the net-istio manifest.

Traffic Management and Routing

With Istio, nuanced routing and traffic management capabilities become available to Knative applications. These functionalities are vital for operations like intelligent request routing, canary deployments, and blue-green deployments. Istio provides several custom resource definitions, such as VirtualService and DestinationRule, which enable declarative traffic control policies.

Consider an example manifest demonstrating a canary deployment:

```
apiVersion: networking.istio.io/v1alpha3
kind: VirtualService
metadata:
  name: knative-service-canary
spec:
  hosts:
    - my-knative-app.default.svc.cluster.local
```

```
http:
 - route:
   - destination:
       host: my-knative-app.default.svc.cluster.local
       subset: v1
     weight: 80
   - destination:
       host: my-knative-app.default.svc.cluster.local
       subset: v2
     weight: 20
```

In this scenario, traffic is split with an 80/20 ratio between version 1 and a freshly deployed version 2 of the application. This flexibility affords developers sufficient control over their deployment processes, enabling careful monitoring and a gradual rollout of new features.

Security Enhancements

Istio offers a suite of security features that strengthen the holistic security posture of applications running on Knative. Vital capabilities include mutual Transport Layer Security (mTLS), service identity and policy management, and detailed authentication. By enforcing mTLS, all in-cluster traffic between microservices remains encrypted, protecting it from eavesdropping and tampering.

Consider enabling mTLS for a Knative service within an Istio environment using the following PeerAuthentication resource:

```
apiVersion: security.istio.io/v1beta1
kind: PeerAuthentication
metadata:
  name: default
spec:
  mtls:
    mode: STRICT
```

Strict mode mandates secure connections between services. These security capabilities are vital as developers transition monolithic applications to microservices, guaranteeing inter-service communication remains secure.

Observability Capabilities

Observability in microservices is critical for understanding system behavior and performance. Istio enriches Knative's observability by integrating features such as distributed tracing, metrics collection, and logging. Built-in adapters for tools like Prometheus, Jaeger, and Grafana deliver insightful and real-time data, facilitating quicker mitigation of potential issues and efficient performance tuning.

For deploying observability add-ons:

```
kubectl apply -f https://github.com/istio/istio/releases/download/1.9.7/istio-kiali.yaml
kubectl apply -f https://github.com/istio/istio/releases/download/1.9.7/istio-
    prometheus.yaml
kubectl apply -f https://github.com/istio/istio/releases/download/1.9.7/istio-grafana.
    yaml
```

These commands install Kiali for service mesh visualization, Prometheus for metrics, and Grafana for dashboards, ensuring a comprehensive observability stack is available for monitoring Knative applications.

Service Mesh Alternatives to Istio

While Istio is a widely regarded option for a service mesh, several alternatives exist, each with unique attributes that developers can use alongside Knative. These include Linkerd, Consul Connect, and Kuma. Evaluating these alternatives involves examining factors like ease of use, latency overhead, feature sets, and community support.

For instance, Linkerd provides lightweight functionality and simple Kubernetes-based deployment, whereas Consul Connect excels in multi-platform and multi-cloud service mesh strategies. These varied feature sets help development teams align specific mesh functionality with organizational needs.

Advancements and Future Directions

Service mesh development remains a dynamic field within cloud-native infrastructure. Recent trends include the evolution toward zero-touch service meshes, reducing the necessity for complex operations expertise. As Knative and Istio progress, their convergence could lead to broader abstractions that offer easier adoption and management.   Emerging standards and advancements in mesh federation may unify disparate meshes, promoting interoperability and collaborative scaling across multiple environments.

The Knative-Istio integration empowers developers to architect applications rooted in performance consistency, security, and innovation. By leveraging Knative's serverless paradigm with Istio's sophisticated networking, deployment becomes precision-oriented and adaptive. Such enhancements are invaluable for organizations seeking operational excellence and enhanced resilience in cloud-native applications.

Knative's integration with Istio and other service meshes defines a pivotal moment in the evolution of modern software architecture, bridging the gap between disparate services while promising a unified, comprehensive application experience. Through further exploration, enhancement, and adoption, integrated offerings continue to refine and redefine the realms of cloud computing possibilities.

6.4 Connecting Event Sources to Cloud Services

Knative Eventing is a sophisticated system designed to manage the flow of event data from diverse sources and route it effectively to services that process these events. By integrating with cloud services like AWS, Google Cloud, and Azure, Knative Eventing enables seamless event handling across different service ecosystems, streamlining the workflow automation processes crucial for modern, event-driven architectures.

Fundamentals of Knative Eventing

At its core, Knative Eventing facilitates building event-driven applications by defining constructs for declaring and managing event flow. The primary components involved are:

- *Event Sources:* These are incoming data streams and triggers from external components that Knative Eventing manages.

- *Brokers:* Event distribution hubs that manage event reception and provide one or more targets for the events.

- *Triggers:* Facilitate filtering of events based on custom criteria—routing events to specific services or sinks.

- *Subscriptions and Channels:* Enable decoupled, asynchronous event processing, directing events from sources to consumers.

These constructs allow users to build loosely-coupled, reliable event-driven applications that can scale seamlessly across diverse environments.

AWS Event Source Integration

For integrating AWS event sources such as S3 bucket events or DynamoDB Streams into Knative, AWS introduces AWS EventBridge, serving as a conduit for event ingress classification and routing. One can configure AWS EventBridge to associate with SNS (Simple Notification Service) topics or Lambda functions, creating an event forwarding strategy.

The steps for bridging AWS Event Sources with Knative include setting up connectivity from AWS resources to an EventBridge and then defining AWS source adapters in Knative:

```
apiVersion: sources.knative.dev/v1alpha1
kind: AWSS3Source
metadata:
  name: sample-s3-source
spec:
  bucket: "myS3Bucket"
  eventTypes:
  - "s3:ObjectCreated:*"
  serviceAccountName: aws-eventing-sa
  sink:
    ref:
      apiVersion: serving.knative.dev/v1
      kind: Service
      name: event-consumer
```

This example creates a Knative source for AWS S3 to respond to object creation events, deploying them to a Knative service for processing.

Google Cloud Event Source Integration

Google Cloud supports Knative Eventing integration primarily through Google Cloud Pub/Sub, providing asynchronous messaging between independent services. Pub/Sub's reliability and message delivery guarantees ensure that events from Google Cloud services such as Cloud Storage or Google Cloud Functions maintain both timeliness and accuracy.

To wire Google Cloud Pub/Sub with Knative, define a PullSubscription:

```
apiVersion: pubsub.cloud.run/v1
kind: PullSubscription
metadata:
```

```
  name: my-gcp-subscription
spec:
  topic: "projects/my-project/topics/my-topic"
  sink:
    ref:
      apiVersion: serving.knative.dev/v1
      kind: Service
      name: event-handler
```

This PullSubscription resource configures automatic subscription to a Pub/Sub topic, piping payload data to a handler service in your Kubernetes environment.

Azure Event Source Integration

Azure facilitates event-driven architectures using Event Grid, a highly scalable event routing service. It offers native integration with various Azure services like Azure Functions, Azure Storage, and third-party sources, acting as a publisher and subscriber endpoint.

To integrate Azure Event Grid with Knative, one can define Event Source configurations:

```
apiVersion: sources.knative.dev/v1alpha1
kind: AzureEventSource
metadata:
  name: sample-azure-source
spec:
  eventSource: "/subscriptions/MySub/resourceGroups/MyResourceGroup/providers/
      Microsoft.EventGrid/eventSubscriptions/MySubscription"
  sink:
    ref:
      apiVersion: serving.knative.dev/v1
      kind: Service
      name: azure-event-consumer
```

Linking an Azure Event Source such as Azure Storage Blob service thus becomes seamless, allowing events to be systematically ingested into a Kubernetes Processing Service.

Cross-Cloud Strategy and Considerations

Operating seamlessly across diverse cloud environments offers unmatched agility but also necessitates careful consideration of proprietary and security constraints, not least regulatory compliance and data residency concerns. By employing cloud-native descriptions, Knative abstracts the underlying differences between cloud providers, giving developers a unified configurable platform for interacting with

CI/CD plumbing, application microservices, and discrete cloud capabilities.

Event-driven approaches yield several benefits: agile and responsive applications, reactive programming templates, and natural fault tolerance realized via event reply techniques and temporal decoupling barriers. Leveraging cloud-based services like AWS Lambda, Google Cloud Pub/Sub, and Azure Functions, alongside Knative Eventing, also offers the opportunity to reduce manual orchestration effort by automating flows and triggering fine-grained dependencies.

To achieve efficient cross-cloud deployments, consideration must be given to:

- *Network Latency:* Optimize critical path placements, minimizing the latency resulting from multi-hop message transit across clouds.

- *Cost Monitoring:* Quell unexpected deviations in resource usage which could incur variable cost impacts.

- *Security Management:* Adopt uniform policies to govern access controls, maintain consistent security postures, and promote auditing fidelity where sensitive client data transit event flows.

- *Compliance Obligations:* Ascertain that all data governance policies comply with necessary jurisdictional and regulatory frameworks.

Deploying an End-to-End Multi-Cloud Example

To exemplify, consider an application where events generated in AWS are to be processed by Google Cloud services with Azure acting as a data storage endpoint. Knative Eventing serves as the connective glue binding these cloud providers together:

1. *AWS S3 to Google Cloud Pub/Sub:* Events generated by AWS can be retried and pushed to an EventBridge which interacts with a dedicated Google Cloud Pub/Sub Topic.

2. *Google Cloud Processing:* Deployed Knative Service hooks into the Pub/Sub subscription, processing event data by running appropriate workloads.

3. *Azure Storage Actions:* Event processing prompts other actions within the Knative service aligned with Azure Blob Storage uploads or updates, forwarding resultant output back to Azure.

Each cloud layer—AWS, Google Cloud, and Azure—works within its strength but coalesces into a harmonized event workflow ensuring robust real-time response to cloud events. By managing separate Knative deployments across domains, a distributed yet cohesive development model results, driving better compliance risk strategies, exploiting cloud resources better, and refining operation metrics visualization using built-in observability tools present on each platform.

Knative enables the deployment of scalable, reliable event-driven systems, connecting robustly with major cloud providers. This technology stack helps developers create synchronous or asynchronous processing paths that span various cloud ecosystems efficiently—a testament to its significance in shaping the next chapter of cloud computing evolution.

6.5 Utilizing Knative with DevOps Practices

Integrating Knative into DevOps practices significantly enhances the development, deployment, and operational processes within cloud-native environments. Knative supports increased automation, collaboration, and efficiency, aligning naturally with the underlying principles of DevOps. This section explores how Knative's capabilities can be leveraged to streamline continuous integration, continuous deployment, monitoring, and automated operations.

Acceleration of Continuous Integration and Continuous Deployment

The CI/CD pipelines form the backbone of modern software deployment, ensuring that application code transitions smoothly from development to production. Knative serves as a critical component in configuring serverless deployments, managing containerized applications that inherently support rapid delivery and scalability. By leveraging Knative, DevOps practices can evolve towards more dynamic, on-demand application deployment models.

Knative supports automated rollouts and rollbacks in response to testing and real-time monitoring, reducing operational overheads significantly. For instance, employing Knative Serving, services can be rapidly deployed, with traffic updated via configurations responsive directly to source control commits.

Consider the following Kubernetes configuration involving Knative deployments that auto-trigger based on updated build artifacts:

```
apiVersion: build.knative.dev/v1alpha1
kind: Build
metadata:
  name: my-service-build
spec:
  source:
    git:
      url: https://github.com/example/my-app.git
      revision: master
  steps:
    - name: build-and-push
      image: gcr.io/kaniko-project/executor:latest
      args:
        - --dockerfile=/workspace/Dockerfile
        - --destination=gcr.io/my-project/my-image
```

For persistent environments, this architecture ensures that any code push triggers a build pipeline, with the endpoints updating following successful tests.

Infrastructure as Code Management

Infrastructure-as-code (IaC) is a critical component of modern software development, enabling precise and reliable control over environments. Knative facilitates this approach, ensuring infrastructure remains versionable, testable, and replicable. Knative itself can be employed to deploy services in a Kubernetes environment precisely as defined in IaC scripts, enabling teams to configure numerous instances of applications reproducibly across differing staging and production environments.

Consider using Helm charts or Kubernetes custom resource definitions (CRDs) alongside Knative to manage compute resources effectively. Below is an example where Helm templates manage Knative service configurations:

```
apiVersion: serving.knative.dev/v1
kind: Service
metadata:
```

```
  name: {{ .Values.service.name }}
spec:
  template:
    spec:
      containers:
        - image: "{{ .Values.image.repository }}/{{ .Values.image.name }}:{{ .Values.
            image.tag }}"
          resources:
            limits:
              memory: "{{ .Values.resources.limits.memory }}"
              cpu: "{{ .Values.resources.limits.cpu }}"
```

Helm provides a higher-level templating engine, facilitating dynamic configurations across environments, thereby fitting snugly within IaC paradigms.

Enhanced Collaboration through DevOps Culture

A fundamental tenet of DevOps culture is fostering enhanced collaboration between developers and operations teams. Knative's unified API approach aligns with this principle, equipping teams to utilize shared tooling and definitions to depict service lifecycles accurately. Teams experience reduced friction when proposing changes, as Knative abstracts service management by adopting the well-known Kubernetes resource model.

Developers and operators gain more precise control over applications, collaborating over service definitions that determine runtime characteristics, such as scalability and networking behavior. Knative also provides observability metrics through integrations with tools like Prometheus and Grafana allowing stakeholders from different teams to gain consistent insights into application performance.

Automated Monitoring and Observability

Monitoring and observability serve as pillars for sustaining high operational standards in any deployment setting. Knative's event-driven architecture enhances typical monitoring setups with improved automatic metrics generation and log capture. An ecosystem built around tools like Prometheus for metrics collection, Grafana for visualization, and Fluentd for logging, becomes seamlessly integrated within Knative environments.

The following example shows deploying a ServiceMonitor resource for observing Knative services with Prometheus:

181

```
apiVersion: monitoring.coreos.com/v1
kind: ServiceMonitor
metadata:
  name: knative-service-monitor
spec:
  selector:
    matchLabels:
      knative-dev/service: your-service-name
  endpoints:
  - port: http
    interval: 30s
    path: /metrics
```

This Prometheus ServiceMonitor resource ensures that essential metrics around Knative services are collected and made available for operational oversight in data-rich visualizations with tools like Grafana.

Operational Efficiency via Automation

Automation within Knative environments extends beyond mere deployment scripts to encompass an ecosystem that supports seamless, automated event handling and infrastructure scaling. The convergence of Knative with CI/CD tools allows for lower mean times to discovery (MTTD) and mean times to resolution (MTTR), contributing directly to improved software quality and user experience.

For example, based on incoming cyclical demand, Knative automatically scales instances up or down, aligning resource acquisition in direct proportion to load, thus achieving operational cost efficiencies.

By leveraging Knative Eventing, teams can react to real-time system events proactively, building architectures resilient to high-throughput consumer demands without extensive manual intervention:

```
apiVersion: eventing.knative.dev/v1
kind: Broker
metadata:
  name: default
---
apiVersion: eventing.knative.dev/v1
kind: Trigger
metadata:
  name: high-load-trigger
spec:
  broker: default
  filter:
    attributes:
      type: high-load
  subscriber:
    ref:
      apiVersion: serving.knative.dev/v1
```

```
kind: Service
name: scale-handler
```

Here, events tagged as 'high-load' solicit scaling responses, enabling service resilience without exhaustive resource pre-allocation.

Expanding DevOps Horizons with Knative

The fusion of Knative with DevOps marks the dynamic expansion in software innovation—an evolution where microservices and serverless components interact fluidly within a coherent DevOps framework. Emphasizing collaboration, integration, and efficiency, Knative empowers teams to derive maximum value from hybrid cloud deployments, driving reduced time-to-market and superior service reliability.

Knative's embrace of Kubernetes' declarative syntax, expanded event-driven processing capabilities, and native CI/CD integration paves new avenues within DevOps culture. Organizational agility increases as teams shift focus towards site reliability engineering, emphasizing application performance and availability, enabled by truly integrated development operations regimes.

The ever-expanding Knative ecosystem, supported by community-driven tools and contributions, heralds a future where DevOps practices adapt swiftly to ongoing technological developments, fostering heightened innovation and more symmetry between development, operational efficiency, and client satisfaction.

6.6   Community Tools and Extensions

The vibrant and dynamic ecosystem around Knative encompasses a multitude of community-driven tools and extensions that significantly augment its capabilities. These community contributions further streamline the development, deployment, and management of serverless applications in Kubernetes environments. This section delves into these tools and extensions, highlighting their functionality and the benefits they offer to developers and DevOps teams.

Knative Client (kn)

The Knative client (kn) is an essential CLI tool that simplifies interaction with Knative components, providing a user-friendly command-line interface for managing Knative Serving and Eventing resources on Kubernetes. The kn client allows developers and operators to perform common tasks such as deploying services, managing traffic, and subscribing to event streams with minimal effort.

Installing the kn client can be done using a package manager like Homebrew:

```
brew install kn
```

Having installed the kn client, developers can quickly deploy a new Knative service from a container image:

```
kn service create hello-world --image gcr.io/knative-samples/helloworld-go
```

This command efficiently handles creating the underlying Kubernetes resources necessary for the service, simplifying what would otherwise demand a more intricate YAML configuration.

Kail: Kubernetes Tail for Debugging Logs

Kail is another noteworthy utility that fits seamlessly within a Knative-managed Kubernetes environment. It provides a streamlined approach to tailing logs from multiple resources consistently and simultaneously. This logging utility helps developers diagnose issues directly within their Kubernetes cluster, particularly useful given Knative's serverless and often ephemeral nature, where diagnostics require real-time visibility.

To install Kail, proceed with:

```
go get github.com/boz/kail
```

Kail empowers developers to capture logs for Knative services with labels, thereby improving debugging timelines and resolutions:

```
kail -l serving.knative.dev/service=hello-world
```

Kail's robust capability to identify these labels simplifies monitoring tasks across dynamically managed services, thereby reducing the complexity associated with diverse logging formats.

Kourier: Lightweight Traffic Management

Kourier serves as an alternative lightweight ingress controller for Knative, offering efficient integration and reduced resource overhead compared with heavier solutions like Istio, primarily oriented for setups requiring simpler traffic management without extensive service mesh features.

Deploy Kourier for minimalistic ingress management in Knative environments:

```
kubectl apply -f https://github.com/knative/net-kourier/releases/download/v0.25.0/
    kourier.yaml
```

Kourier leverages Envoy as the data plane, and its architecture aims to support environments where Istio's advanced capabilities (such as mutual TLS or complex routing rules) might be unnecessary. This facilitates efficient Knative utilization in resource-constrained environments.

GitOps with Knative: Utilizing Argo CD

Argo CD, a declarative, GitOps continuous delivery tool, supports Knative application management by governing deployments wholly from a Git repository. Emphasizing the GitOps principle—where Git is the source of truth for applications' desired state—Argo CD complements Knative by ensuring deployment configurations are tightly coupled with version control.

The transition to GitOps can be orchestrated with Argo CD by first deploying it into your Kubernetes cluster:

```
kubectl create namespace argocd
kubectl apply -n argocd -f https://raw.githubusercontent.com/argoproj/argo-cd/stable/
    manifests/install.yaml
```

By defining applications as code and managing them directly from a Git repository, Argo CD provides visibility, traceable deployments, and automated rollbacks for Knative-enabled workflows.

Knative Kafka Source: Event Streaming Integration

Kafka integration expands Knative's reach into real-time, high-throughput event streaming environments, in which Apache Kafka acts as both an ingress and egress channel, connecting event producers and consumers. By adopting the Kafka Channel implementation, Knative Eventing can ingest Kafka streams while processing messages in a nature characteristic of cloud-native applications—scalable, resilient, and asynchronous.

To set up Kafka with Knative Eventing, begin by deploying the Knative Kafka controller:

```
kubectl apply -f https://github.com/knative/eventing-contrib/releases/download/v0
    .25.0/kafka-source.yaml
```

Following this, define Kafka sources to tie Kafka topics to specific Knative services:

```
apiVersion: sources.knative.dev/v1alpha1
kind: KafkaSource
metadata:
  name: my-kafka-source
spec:
  consumers: 1
  bootstrapServers: my-cluster-kafka-bootstrap.kafka:9092
  topics: my-topic
  sink:
    ref:
      apiVersion: serving.knative.dev/v1
      kind: Service
      name: kafka-event-display
```

This definition ensures a fluent transition for Kafka events to decoupled processing services, preserving event order and delivery semantics including at-least-once guarantees where required.

Tekton: Pipelines for Continuous Delivery

Part of the rich ecosystem surrounding Knative includes Tekton Pipelines, a Kubernetes-native framework for CI/CD systems enabling continuous integration and delivery directly on Kubernetes. Tekton facilitates granular, atomic deployment steps organized into pipelines, with each step supported by its dedicated container for optimal resource allocation and isolation.

Below you see a fragment of Tekton Pipeline for building and deploying a Knative service:

```
apiVersion: tekton.dev/v1beta1
kind: Pipeline
metadata:
  name: knative-build-deploy
spec:
  tasks:
    - name: build-app
      taskRef:
```

```
    name: kaniko # Assuming predefined build task
workspaces:
  - name: source
params:
  - name: pathToDockerFile
    value: /workspace/source/Dockerfile
- name: deploy-to-knative
  taskRef:
    name: knctl # Assuming predefined deploy task
  runAfter:
    - build-app
```

Inclusion of Tekton Pipelines in DevOps practices enables efficient resource management and builds a bridge between development and operations through fine-grained automation processes.

Extending Knative's Functionality with Community Efforts

The vibrant nature of Knative's community continues to spur extensions and integrations, such as Knative HPA autoscaler configurations, Knative Sugar for simplified CRD handling, and Knative Quickstarts providing easy setup scripts for bare metal and cloud deployments. Each addition fuels broadened support for the evolving microservices ecosystem, forging pathways for enhanced multi-cloud, hybrid-cloud approaches.

These community-driven contributions help Knative encompass new paradigms and practices, reflecting the innovative spirit of the intertwined Kubernetes and Knative communities. This expansionary vision ensures that novel methodologies are seamlessly incorporated, paving the way for broader dissemination and adoption of compelling Knative-based solutions across a variably cloud-distributed enterprise landscape.

Community tools and extensions reinforce Knative's core strengths while paving new paths of resilience, extensibility, and innovation with every iteration. This vibrant ecosystem continues to equip developers, architects, and operators with unmatched resources for sculpting modern, efficient, cloud-native applications tailored around specific scalability and domain requirements.

6.7 Case Studies of Effective Knative Integrations

Knative, leveraging the underlying capabilities of Kubernetes, provides a comprehensive framework for serverless applications and event-driven architectures. This section presents several detailed case studies depicting how various organizations have effectively integrated Knative into their infrastructure, showcasing its versatility and performance in solving complex challenges.

Case Study 1: Streamlining Continuous Deployment at a Fintech Startup

A fintech startup, specializing in providing micro-lending solutions, needed a robust platform to manage its application scaling demands, driven by fluctuating request loads during peak business hours. Traditional deployment strategies were impacting their operational efficiency, necessitating a shift towards serverless architectures.

Integration Strategy:

Knative became the core backend service framework comprising both Serving and Eventing components. Here's how:

- Deployed Knative Serving for dynamically scaling microservices that controlled core transactional APIs. The auto-scaling based on active connections led to significant cost reductions during non-peak hours.

- Integrated Knative Eventing to handle inter-service events. This event-driven model ensured reliable asynchronous processing of loan application requests, thereby boosting app responsiveness.

- Implemented CI/CD pipelines using Tekton, synchronized with Git repositories, ensuring automated deployment and rollback when changes to service APIs occurred.

Implementation:

The core application was broken into several Knative services. Here's a snippet defining a crucial transaction service in Knative:

```
apiVersion: serving.knative.dev/v1
kind: Service
metadata:
  name: transaction-service
spec:
  template:
    spec:
      containers:
        - image: gcr.io/fintech-project/transaction-app:latest
          resources:
            limits:
              cpu: 1000m
              memory: 512Mi
```

Outcomes:

The startup observed a 25% reduction in cloud infrastructure expenditure along with improved request handling performance. Knative's adaptive scaling significantly minimizes over-provisioning while maintaining low latency and high availability.

Case Study 2: Event Streaming in an E-commerce Platform

An e-commerce giant faced challenges preserving the integrity and consistency of inventory data across its multi-node seller platform, especially during sale events. Real-time data processing with scalable architectures was critical.

Integration Strategy:

To address these issues, the organization deployed Knative integrated with Apache Kafka for real-time stream processing as follows:

- Knative Eventing installed on top of Kubernetes provided an interface to Capricorn Kafka, orchestrating asynchronous event processing mitigating data desync challenges across services.

- Created Knative Channels and KafkaSource to transmit data streams when inventory status changes occurred, ensuring immediate availability updates were processed across the entire platform.

Implementation:

Below is an example setup of Knative KafkaSource and Channel configurations:

189

```
apiVersion: messaging.knative.dev/v1
kind: KafkaChannel
metadata:
  name: inventory-updates
spec:
  numPartitions: 3
  replicationFactor: 1

apiVersion: sources.knative.dev/v1beta1
kind: KafkaSource
metadata:
  name: inventory-source
spec:
  consumerGroup: inventoryGroup
  bootstrapServers:
  - my-kafka-bootstrap:9092
  topics: inventory-updates
  sink:
    ref:
      apiVersion: serving.knative.dev/v1
      kind: Service
      name: inventory-processing
```

Outcomes:

The incorporation of Knative Eventing with Apache Kafka drastically reduced data synchronization lag times from several seconds to milliseconds, ensuring the platform maintained a high standard of real-time inventory accuracy during major promotional events.

Case Study 3: On-Demand Media Processing for a Streaming Service

A media streaming service provider needed to efficiently process and transcode video files uploaded by content creators. The existing pipeline struggled under peak loads resulting in delays and increased processing costs.

Integration Strategy:

The solution deployed involved orchestrating tasks using Knative Serving for elastic scalability and Knative Eventing for robust event handling capacities:

- Employed Knative Serving to deploy transcoding services dynamically, scaling instances based on incoming load.

- Integrated Knative Eventing to decouple video upload events from processing workflows, distributing tasks using brokers and triggers effectively handling large-scale concurrent uploads.

Implementation:

Workflow implementations included Knative services running transcoding operations deployed in response to Knative Triggers receiving new video data:

```
apiVersion: eventing.knative.dev/v1
kind: Trigger
metadata:
  name: video-transcoding-trigger
spec:
  filter:
    attributes:
      type: video.upload
  subscriber:
    ref:
      apiVersion: serving.knative.dev/v1
      kind: Service
      name: transcoder
```

Notifications on upload completion initiated event flows to transcode processes. Output from these services was systematically logged for future analytics and quality assessments.

Outcomes:

After implementation, the provider experienced a 40% increase in throughput efficiency with turnaround times for video processing workloads decreasing by 30%. The serverless approach using Knative led to an optimized media processing workflow aligned with variable demand metrics.

Case Study 4: Data Processing in Scientific Research

A scientific research institution faced challenges in processing data from large-scale experiments. Existing pipelines were fragmented, causing data processing bottlenecks and impeding rapid iteration over datasets.

Integration Strategy:

The institution leveraged Knative to unify and expedite their data analysis frameworks:

- Configured Knative Serving to automate provisioning of data processing services, focusing resources during intensive computational workloads.

- Implemented Knative Eventing for integrating batch processing workflows, allowing distributed processing tasks to be queued and completed efficiently.

Implementation:

Services were organized to handle discrete aspects of the analytics workload orchestrated by event patterns linked to disparate data sources:

```
apiVersion: serving.knative.dev/v1
kind: Service
metadata:
  name: data-analyzer
spec:
  template:
    spec:
      containers:
        - image: gcr.io/research-project/data-analyzer:latest
          args:
            - --dataset
            - "$(dataset.url)"
```

Data ingestion events were mapped through Knative Eventing sources connected to triggers managing intermediate result handoffs between data processing states.

Outcomes:

The enhancement in data processing pipelines using Knative facilitated a 50% improvement in data throughput and analysis speed. The research institution could iterate experimental setups faster, enhancing their research efficacy.

Conclusion of Case Study Insights

These case studies reveal Knative's ability to seamlessly integrate within various organizational infrastructures, supporting distinct industry-specific demands. Whether addressing real-time event handling, cost-efficient scaling, or advanced automation in CI/CD workflows, Knative's strengths bridge the gap between raw computational needs and practical, deployable solutions. Organizations implementing Knative report substantial gains in operational efficiency, cost savings, and system responsiveness, translating these into tangible business outcomes, showcasing

Knative's compelling promise in modern cloud-native ecosystems.

Chapter 7

Developing with Knative and Continuous Deployment

This chapter addresses the process of developing serverless applications with Knative, focusing on best practices and tool utilization. It provides guidance on setting up effective development environments, both locally and in cloud settings, and delves into leveraging the Knative CLI and related tools for efficient application management and deployment. The chapter outlines steps to implement continuous deployment pipelines using Knative, ensuring automation and seamless integration with source control systems like Git. Testing and debugging strategies specific to Knative applications are explored, as well as methods for managing rollbacks and updates within a continuous deployment framework to maintain application quality and reliability.

7.1 Building Serverless Applications with Knative

The concept of serverless computing represents a paradigm shift that abstracts the complexities of infrastructure management by allowing developers to focus solely on application logic. Knative, an open-source platform based on Kubernetes, significantly extends the Kubernetes capabilities to facilitate the creation, deployment, and management of serverless applications. This section delineates the essential components and practices for building robust serverless applications using Knative, emphasizing efficiency, scalability, and maintainability.

Knative introduces two core components that are fundamental to its serverless architecture: Knative Serving and Knative Eventing. These components provide a flexible and powerful framework to manage stateless services and event-driven architectures, respectively.

Knative Serving is designed to run and scale applications on-demand. It serves four essential abstractions: Service, Route, Configuration, and Revision. The interaction between these constructs enables efficient request handling and version management.

A **Service** in Knative encapsulates the application's lifecycle. It binds together a Route and Configuration to maintain the endpoint management and deployment configurations.

```
apiVersion: serving.knative.dev/v1
kind: Service
metadata:
  name: helloworld-go
spec:
  template:
    spec:
      containers:
        - image: gcr.io/knative-samples/helloworld-go
          env:
            - name: TARGET
              value: "Go Sample v1"
```

In this example, the service 'helloworld-go' refers to a specific container image and environmental variable. This declarative approach facilitates seamless deployments.

A **Route** maintains the URL path responsibility. It dynamically allocates traffic to different Revisions of a service. Routes simplify traffic splitting and canary deployments, safeguarding application stability during updates.

Configurations in Knative hold the deployed code and relevant configurations, forming a base template for creating Revisions. These Revisions are immutable snapshots capturing the application's deployment state. Knative uses these Revisions to provide historical versions, enabling efficient rollbacks or comparisons.

Knative Eventing facilitates event-driven architectures by establishing a robust mechanism for event producers and consumers. Core objects include Sources, Brokers, and Triggers, which orchestrate event flow.

Consider the following simple Knative Service deployment:

```
apiVersion: sources.knative.dev/v1alpha1
kind: ApiServerSource
metadata:
  name: testevents
spec:
  serviceAccountName: events-sa
  mode: Resource
  resources:
    - apiVersion: v1
      kind: Event
  sink:
    ref:
      apiVersion: serving.knative.dev/v1
      kind: Service
      name: event-display
```

In this example, 'ApiServerSource' listens for Kubernetes events and sends these to the 'event-display' Knative Service. Such integrations demonstrate Knative's versatility in handling varied event sources.

When designing serverless applications with Knative, it is essential to leverage its autoscaling capabilities. Knative automatically scales workloads based on demand, scaling down to zero during inactivity to minimize costs. This scalability is paramount to achieving operational efficiency in cloud environments.

```
apiVersion: serving.knative.dev/v1
kind: Service
metadata:
  name: autoscaler
spec:
  template:
    metadata:
      annotations:
```

```
      autoscaling.knative.dev/maxScale: "10"
  spec:
    containers:
      - image: example/autoscaler
```

In the example above, the Knative service is configured with autoscaling properties, capping the service to a maximum of 10 pods, thus ensuring resource constraints are respected while meeting demand.

Security in serverless functions is critical. Implementing strict authentication and authorization protocols, such as OAuth2, enhances security postures. Knative enables the seamless integration of such protocols through extensions and is compatible with various identity providers.

Performance optimization also plays a pivotal role. Developers should aim to create lightweight functions, ensuring that application logic remains concise and efficient. Leveraging caching, optimizing network requests, and minimizing cold start latencies contribute to enhanced performance metrics.

Observability and monitoring are indispensable in maintaining reliable serverless applications. Knative seamlessly integrates with observability tools such as Prometheus and Grafana, providing insights into application behaviours, latency issues, and potential bottlenecks.

Finally, developers should adhere to best practices, such as using Continuous Integration and Continuous Deployment (CI/CD) pipelines to streamline application updates and testing. With Knative, these pipelines can be further enhanced by leveraging tools like Tekton.

Building serverless applications with Knative inherently ties into a broader ecosystem. The synergy between Knative components and Kubernetes ensures a robust, scalable foundation for modern cloud-native application development. Through meticulous planning and implementation, developers can harness Knative to deploy serverless applications that not only meet but exceed performance, scalability, and security expectations.

7.2 Setting Up Development Environments

A conducive development environment is paramount for enhancing productivity, ensuring consistency, and facilitating the seamless integration of applications, particularly when working with sophisticated frameworks like Knative. This section explores methodologies for setting up robust development environments for Knative applications, encompassing both local and cloud-based configurations.

The creation of an effective development environment for Knative demands an understanding of its underlying architecture and dependencies. Knative runs atop Kubernetes, thereby necessitating a functional Kubernetes cluster as a prerequisite. Developers have multiple options to deploy Kubernetes for Knative development, including Minikube, Kind (Kubernetes IN Docker), and cloud-based Kubernetes services such as Google Kubernetes Engine (GKE), Amazon Elastic Kubernetes Service (EKS), and Azure Kubernetes Service (AKS).

- Local Development Environment

For developers opting for a local setup, Minikube and Kind are popular choices due to their ease of installation and resource efficiency. Minikube facilitates the deployment of a Kubernetes cluster on a local machine, allowing developers to emulate production environments closely.

```
curl -Lo minikube https://storage.googleapis.com/minikube/releases/latest/minikube-
    linux-amd64 \
  && chmod +x minikube
sudo install minikube /usr/local/bin/
minikube start --memory=4096 --cpus=3 --kubernetes-version=v1.20.0
```

This series of commands installs Minikube and starts a Kubernetes cluster with specified resources. It is advisable to allocate sufficient memory and CPU to emulate a functional production-like environment needed for Knative services.

Following the Kubernetes setup, developers must install Knative. The installation involves deploying two primary components: Knative Serving and Knative Eventing.

```
kubectl apply --filename https://github.com/knative/serving/releases/download/v0
    .19.0/serving-crds.yaml
kubectl apply --filename https://github.com/knative/serving/releases/download/v0
    .19.0/serving-core.yaml

kubectl apply --filename https://github.com/knative/eventing/releases/download/v0
    .19.0/eventing-crds.yaml
kubectl apply --filename https://github.com/knative/eventing/releases/download/v0
    .19.0/eventing-core.yaml
```

The above commands will install Knative Serving and Eventing into the Kubernetes cluster, respectively.

Moreover, establishing effective development environments necessitates configuring essential tools such as Docker and kubectl. Docker aids in containerizing the application, while kubectl is indispensable for managing and interacting with the Kubernetes deployment.

- Integrating IDEs and Developer Tools

An IDE (Integrated Development Environment) or code editor like Visual Studio Code or IntelliJ IDEA significantly enhances productivity by providing features such as syntax highlighting, autocompletion, and integrated terminal access. Visual Studio Code is particularly favorable due to its wide range of extensions tailored for cloud-native development, including Kubernetes and Knative plugins.

```
Extensions:
- Kubernetes Extension
- Docker Extension
- Knative Extension
```

By installing these extensions, developers can manage Kubernetes resources, handle Docker images, and monitor Knative services directly within the IDE, promoting an efficient workflow.

- Cloud-Based Development Environments

For teams preferring cloud solutions, managed Kubernetes services offer a reliable alternative. These cloud services abstract the complexity of cluster setup and maintenance, allowing developers to focus on application logic and architecture.

Cloud-based development environments facilitate large-scale collaborative development and ensure everyone on the team has congruent configurations, minimizing discrepancies between development, staging, and production environments.

- Google Kubernetes Engine (GKE):

GKE provides a robust and scalable Kubernetes service with native integration of Knative. It simplifies the deployment process with built-in load balancing, scalability settings, and monitoring tools.

```
gcloud container clusters create knative-cluster --zone us-central1-a --cluster-version
       1.20.0 --machine-type e2-standard-4 --num-nodes 3
```

This command initiates a GKE cluster with a specified Kubernetes version and machine type, optimized for a Knative deployment.

- Security Configurations

Security is an integral aspect of setting up development environments. Developers should implement stringent access controls, ideally using IAM (Identity and Access Management) roles for authentication and authorization in cloud-based settings. This ensures that only authorized personnel have access to critical infrastructure and resources.

Implementing network policies within Kubernetes clusters further restricts unauthorized access. Policies should dictate ingress and egress rules, defining which services can communicate with each other.

In a local setting, securing Docker images using verified sources and scanning images for vulnerabilities are recommended practices. Tools like Anchore and Clair can integrate with Docker to provide automated security assessments.

- Continuous Integration/Continuous Deployment (CI/CD)

Incorporating CI/CD pipelines in the development environment is vital for automation and efficiency. Tools like Jenkins, Jenkins X, or GitLab CI/CD can streamline the process by building, testing, and deploying Knative applications continuously.

A prototypical Jenkins pipeline file for a Knative service might look like:

```
pipeline {
  agent any
  stages {
    stage('Build') {
      steps {
        script {
          sh 'docker build -t myknativeapp .'
        }
      }
    }
    stage('Test') {
      steps {
        sh 'docker run --rm myknativeapp tests'
      }
    }
    stage('Deploy') {
      steps {
        script {
          sh 'kubectl apply -f myknativeapp.yaml'
        }
      }
    }
  }
}
```

This script automates the build-test-deploy cycle, ensuring that any codebase changes are promptly validated and released.

- Conclusion

Establishing a meticulous development environment for Knative applications requires methodical planning and execution, integrating optimal tools and configurations. Both local and cloud-based setups have their merits, often contingent on team preferences, resource availability, and specific project requirements.

With the right tools and practices in place, developers can harness Knative's powerful features to create scalable, efficient, and resilient serverless applications without the overhead of infrastructure management. Consistent and robust configurations across environments further ensure the smooth progression from development to deployment, enabling developers to focus on innovation and application logic.

7.3 Utilizing Knative CLI and Tools

Effectively leveraging the Knative CLI (Command-Line Interface) and associated tools is vital for managing, deploying, and monitoring serverless applications within the Knative ecosystem. This section provides an in-depth exploration of the Knative CLI's capabilities and its integration with various developer tools to streamline operational workflows.

Knative CLI, known as kn, simplifies interaction with Knative resources, abstracting intricate Kubernetes configurations and providing user-friendly commands for application management. This serves as an indispensable asset for developers and operators aiming to enhance productivity within a serverless architecture.

7.3.1 Installing Knative CLI

Before utilizing the Knative CLI, it must be installed correctly in the working environment. The installation process varies slightly depending on the operating system but is generally straightforward.

```
# For Linux
curl -LO https://github.com/knative/client/releases/download/v0.19.0/kn-linux-amd64
chmod +x kn-linux-amd64
sudo mv kn-linux-amd64 /usr/local/bin/kn
```

The command sequence above downloads and installs the Knative CLI on a Linux system. For Windows and macOS, analogous steps can be followed to install using the appropriate binaries or package managers.

7.3.2 Fundamental Commands and Operations

With the Knative CLI installed, basic operations for managing Knative Service resources become simple and intuitive. Commands typically follow the pattern kn <resource> <action>, significantly reducing the cognitive load associated with more verbose Kubernetes command syntax.

- **Creating Services:**

The creation of a Knative service involves specifying the container image and environmental parameters vital for execution:

```
kn service create helloworld-go --image=gcr.io/knative-samples/
helloworld-go --env TARGET="Knative"
```

This command results in the deployment of helloworld-go, with the image pulled from the specified container registry and the TARGET environment initialized.

- **Updating Services:**

  Updates entail modifying service parameters, such as the container image, without impacting ongoing operations:

```
kn service update helloworld-go --env TARGET="Updated Knative"
```

  Here, helloworld-go is updated to use a new environment variable value, promoting dynamism and flexibility in development workflows.

- **Deleting Services:**

  Deletion of services reclaims resources, maintaining a tidy operational environment:

```
kn service delete helloworld-go
```

  Efficient resource management through clean deletion is crucial for long-term sustainability and scalability within clusters.

7.3.3   Advanced Knative CLI Features

Beyond basic service management, the Knative CLI accommodates advanced functionalities, such as traffic splitting and event management. These capabilities underpin more nuanced deployments and operational efficiencies.

- **Traffic Splitting and Version Control:**

  Traffic splitting enables simultaneous routing to multiple service revisions, assisting in progressive deployments and A/B testing.

```
kn service update helloworld-go --traffic v1=50,v2=50
```

This command splits inbound traffic equitably between two distinct revisions (v1 and v2), facilitating empirical evaluations and minimizing deployment risk.

- **Eventing Management:**

  Knative Eventing operates on the premise of event producers and consumers, allowing integration with myriad services and systems.

  ```
  kn trigger create new-trigger --broker default --filter type=dev.knative.
  kafka.event --sink ksvc:event-display
  ```

Through trigger creation, specific events are channeled to designated services, streamlining event-driven architecture.

7.3.4 Tooling and Integration

Integration of the Knative CLI with development tools and environments extends its functionality and enriches the user experience. Tools such as Visual Studio Code and Jenkins offer plugins and integrations to enhance Knative operation management directly from their interfaces.

Visual Studio Code:

By installing the Knative plugin for Visual Studio Code, developers can visualize services, manage deployments, and track revisions efficiently. The plugin experiences seamless integration with existing Kubernetes tooling, providing a comprehensive development environment.

```
Knative Plugin Capabilities:
- List all services
- Monitor traffic routes
- View service details and logs
```

Jenkins and CI/CD Pipelines:

Jenkins enables automated workflows through its plugins specifically designed for Kubernetes and Knative. By automating tasks such as testing, building, and deployment, developers secure a robust, scalable CI/CD pipeline.

```
pipeline {
```

```
agent any
stages {
  stage('Deploy') {
    steps {
      script {
        sh 'kn service update myservice --image new-image:latest'
      }
    }
  }
}
}
```

This automated deployment script empowers teams to focus on code enhancements by reducing deployment complexity and manual intervention.

7.3.5 Monitoring and Observability

Effective observability is crucial for maintaining high-performance serverless applications, with tools supporting log aggregation, tracing, and metrics.

Integration with Prometheus and Grafana:

Prometheus and Grafana, prominent monitoring solutions, can seamlessly integrate with Knative to offer real-time insights and visually interactive dashboards, aligning performance metrics with business objectives.

Configuration of Prometheus involves scraping metrics from Knative components, which can then be aggregated and presented within Grafana's dashboard.

```
scrape_configs:
  - job_name: 'knative'
    kubernetes_sd_configs:
    - role: pod
    relabel_configs:
    - source_labels: [__meta_kubernetes_namespace]
      action: keep
      regex: 'knative-serving|knative-eventing'
```

This monitoring setup shepherds proactive identification and rectification of performance bottlenecks, ensuring sustained operational efficacy.

7.3.6 Leveraging Community and Resources

Active engagement in the Knative community can significantly aid in maximizing the potential of the Knative CLI and related tools. The community provides copious resources, including detailed documentations, forums, and open-source repositories, which furnish developers with timely updates and best practices.

7.3.7 Conclusion

The Knative CLI and its suite of extended tools form an integral component of an efficient serverless application lifecycle management. By utilizing the CLI's powerful capabilities alongside critical technological integrations for development, deployment, and monitoring, developers are adeptly positioned to overcome challenges inherent in modern cloud-native computing.

As these tools evolve, staying abreast of new developments is critical to sustaining competitiveness and leveraging the full extent of Knative's potential. With well-defined practices and clear objectives, teams can effectively manage serverless environments, focusing on innovation and application logic rather than infrastructural complexities.

7.4 Implementing Continuous Deployment Pipelines

Continuous Deployment (CD) is a sophisticated and automated approach that facilitates the rapid and reliable delivery of software updates by leveraging CI/CD pipelines. This section delves into the methodologies and best practices for implementing continuous deployment pipelines in the context of Knative applications, elucidating on tools, techniques, and the seamless integration of Knative with existing deployment frameworks.

Continuous Deployment builds upon Continuous Integration (CI) by automating the release of code into production environments, contingent on passing a series of predefined tests and quality checks. Unlike

Continuous Delivery, where manual approval acts as a checkpoint before deployment, Continuous Deployment continuously deploys code changes to production once they meet quality standards.

Core Components of a Continuous Deployment Pipeline

The architecture of a robust CD pipeline typically comprises several critical stages: Source Control Integration, Build Automation, Testing, Deployment, and Monitoring. Each stage plays an integral role in ensuring the pipeline's seamless functionality and effectiveness.

- **Source Control Integration:**

  Source Control Systems (SCS) like Git help manage codebases, track changes, and facilitate collaboration. Repositories are organized to maintain version histories, branch strategies, and merge requests, providing well-documented frameworks necessary for consistent CD pipelines.

  Integration with repositories is often automated using webhooks or polling mechanisms, which trigger pipeline execution upon code changes.

- **Build Automation:**

  Build automation encapsulates compiling code, resolving dependencies, creating Docker images, and tagging versions. Tools like Docker use Dockerfiles to build container images that ensure consistent environments across development and production.

```
FROM gcr.io/distroless/base
COPY my_application /app
CMD ["/app/my_application"]
```

  The Dockerfile provides instructions for containerizing applications, forming the backbone of build automation.

- **Testing:**

  Testing is indispensable in validating code integrity and functionality. Unit tests, integration tests, and end-to-end tests are automated using frameworks such as JUnit, Selenium, or TestNG, depending on the application's nature and scope.

```
import org.junit.jupiter.api.Test;
import static org.junit.jupiter.api.Assertions.*;

public class MyApplicationTests {
    @Test
    void basicFunctionalityTest() {
        assertEquals(2, 1 + 1);
    }
}
```

Automated testing ensures confidence in the quality and reliability of the code being deployed.

- **Deployment:**

  Deployment automates the process of releasing applications to target environments. With Knative, the deployment phase involves updating services and managing traffic across service revisions, leveraging the Knative CLI for efficient resource management.

  ```
  kn service update myapp --image=myregistry/myapp:latest
  ```

  This command promotes seamless service updates, marking specific application states ready for production.

- **Monitoring and Logging:**

  Implementing monitoring tools like Prometheus and Grafana aids in visualizing application performance and operational metrics, essential in verifying the success of deployments and diagnosing issues post-deployment.

  Logging frameworks, such as Elasticsearch, along with Kibana dashboards, offer real-time insights into application health and behavior.

CI/CD Tools

Multiple tools and platforms provide end-to-end support for CI/CD pipelines. Jenkins, GitLab CI/CD, and Tekton are prominent choices in the industry, each offering distinct capabilities and integrations tailored to different developmental needs.

Jenkins:

209

Jenkins, a versatile and widely-adopted automation server, manages CD pipelines through its extensible plugin architecture. By integrating Jenkins with Knative, developers can automate complex workflows, set triggers, and manage deployments efficiently.

```
pipeline {
  agent any
  stages {
    stage('Build') {
      steps {
        script {
          sh 'docker build -t myapp .'
        }
      }
    }
    stage('Test') {
      steps {
        script {
          sh 'docker run myapp:test'
        }
      }
    }
    stage('Deploy') {
      steps {
        script {
          sh 'kn service update myapp --image myregistry/myapp:latest'
        }
      }
    }
  }
}
```

The Jenkins pipeline script provides a declarative approach to define and control these processes, promoting repeatability and reproducibility within deployment systems.

GitLab CI/CD:

GitLab CI/CD integrates deeply with GitLab repositories, offering a seamless experience from source control to deployment. With powerful features like Auto DevOps and Merge Request Pipelines, GitLab facilitates efficient CD processes while maintaining high security standards.

```
stages:
  - build
  - test
  - deploy

build:
  stage: build
  script:
```

```
    - docker build -t myapp .

test:
  stage: test
  script:
    - docker run --rm myapp:test

deploy:
  stage: deploy
  script:
    - kn service update myapp --image registry.gitlab.com/mygroup/myapp:latest
```

Tekton:

Tekton is a cloud-native CI/CD pipeline designed for Kubernetes environments. By encoding tasks and workflows as Kubernetes-native resources, Tekton integrates seamlessly with Knative and other Kubernetes-based applications, facilitating diverse deployment scenarios.

```
apiVersion: tekton.dev/v1beta1
kind: Task
metadata:
  name: build-and-deploy
spec:
  steps:
    - name: docker-build
      image: gcr.io/cloud-builders/docker
      script: |
        docker build -t gcr.io/$PROJECT_ID/myapp .
    - name: knative-deploy
      image: gcr.io/cloud-builders/kubectl
      script: |
        kn service apply myapp --image gcr.io/$PROJECT_ID/myapp
```

By using Tekton tasks, developers construct modular and reusable components across projects, ensuring consistency and reducing the manual overhead.

Best Practices for Continuous Deployment

Implementing CD pipelines entails adopting best practices that align processes, improve security, and ensure operational excellence.

- **Infrastructure as Code (IaC):**

  Treat infrastructure setup and configurations as code using tools like Terraform and Ansible. IaC lends version control, repeatabil-

211

ity, and automation to pipeline execution, facilitating rapid provisioning and consistent environments.

- **Security Integrations:**

  Embed security checks and vulnerability scanning within builds. Utilize tools like Snyk for Docker image scans and SonarQube for static code analysis to ensure adherence to security standards and protect deployment environments.

- **Rollback Strategies:**

  Predefine rollback procedures and integrate them into deployment plans. Rollbacks serve as a safeguard to promptly revert to a stable state in the case of errors or failures during deployments.

- **Canary Releases and Blue-Green Deployments:**

  Deploy updates using canary releases or blue-green deployment techniques to evaluate production changes incrementally or in parallel environments, reducing risk and improving user experience.

- **Continuous Feedback Loops:**

  Establish feedback mechanisms using monitoring and logging tools to provide insights and early detections of anomalies. Continuous feedback loops enable proactive troubleshooting and iterative improvements.

Conclusion

Constructing continuous deployment pipelines for Knative applications involves strategic planning, leveraging diverse tools, and aligning industry best practices. By automating workflows and ensuring seamless integration across development environments, CD pipelines afford efficiency, scalability, and reliability, essential for thriving in modern software delivery landscapes.

Through optimizing each stage of the pipeline—from build automation to deployment and monitoring—development teams become adept at delivering high-quality applications expediently, focusing on innovation rather than infrastructural burdens. In the evolving domain of

212

cloud-native technologies, mastering CD pipelines is imperative for sustaining competitive advantage and meeting the dynamic needs of users and businesses alike.

7.5 Integrating with Source Control Systems

Integrating Knative applications with Source Control Systems (SCS) is foundational for maintaining code integrity, facilitating collaboration, and automating deployment pipelines. Source Control Systems, such as Git, serve as repositories that manage changes to codebases, emulating a robust framework for version control and project management. This section expounds on the methodologies and best practices for leveraging source control within the Knative ecosystem, offering insights on automated workflows, branch management, and collaboration strategies.

Overview of Source Control Systems

Source Control Systems are integral to software development, enabling teams to collaborate efficiently by tracking changes, managing branches, and maintaining historical versions of projects. Such systems promote distributed development, where contributions from different developers or teams coexist seamlessly. Git is the de facto standard in the industry, characterized by its distributed nature and extensive integration capabilities with CI/CD platforms and development tools.

Implementing Git for Knative Applications

Git repositories house application source code and facilitate continuous integration, ensuring that codebases remain consistent and up-to-date. Integrating Knative applications with Git unlocks numerous advantages, including traceable changes, simplified code reviews, and the ability to implement sophisticated CI/CD pipelines.

```
# Initialize a new Git repository
git init

# Add remote origin
git remote add origin https://github.com/user/knative-app.git
```

```
# Track files and commit
git add .
git commit -m "Initial commit"
git push -u origin master
```

These preliminary commands illustrate setting up a Git repository for a Knative application, establishing the foundation for collaborative development and versioned code management.

Branching Strategies and Collaboration

Effective branching strategies are paramount in managing concurrent development efforts, testing, and deployments. Popular strategies include:

- **Feature Branching:** Dedicated branches for individual features isolate development efforts, facilitating parallel progression and reducing integration complexities.

- **Git Flow:** A model where branches represent various development states — namely, master for stable releases and develop for integrating changes before release. This model supports structured release cycles and is conducive to large teams.

- **Trunk-Based Development:** A minimalist approach that involves frequent integration into a central branch, encouraging rapid iterations and simplification of merge conflicts.

Implementing these strategies within Knative projects necessitates consideration of team dynamics, project scale, and release cadences. Branching supports modularity and cohesion across development efforts, permitting targeted code reviews and testing.

```
# Create and switch to a new feature branch
git checkout -b feature/new-routing

# Commit changes to feature branch
git commit -a -m "Add new routing feature"

# Push feature branch to remote
git push origin feature/new-routing
```

By leveraging these branching techniques, teams can orchestrate more structured and manageable workflows, accommodating multifaceted development needs.

Pull Requests and Code Reviews

The code review process is vital for maintaining code quality, enhancing team collaboration, and ensuring adherence to coding standards. Pull requests act as a medium for code reviews, amalgamating feedback loops into the integration process. Establishing a robust pull request process ensures all changes are reviewed, commented, and approved before merging into primary branches.

```
Pull Request Workflow:
1. Developer completes feature or bugfix.
2. Changes are pushed to a dedicated branch.
3. A pull request is opened, targeting the primary branch.
4. Peer reviews are conducted, with feedback provided.
5. Reviewer approves, and changes are merged after resolution.
```

This systematic approach ingrains quality assurance into the development cycle, minimizing bugs and fostering knowledge sharing among team members.

Automation with CI/CD Workflows

Automating interaction with source control systems through CI/CD pipelines is the linchpin of contemporary software delivery practices. By integrating Knative applications with systems like GitHub Actions, GitLab CI/CD, or Jenkins, the process benefits from reduced human intervention, streamlined deployments, and consistent development standards.

GitHub Actions:

GitHub Actions provide native integration with repositories, facilitating automated workflows in response to repository events, such as commits and pull requests. For Knative applications, actions can be configured to build, test, and deploy containerized services upon code modifications.

```
name: Knative CI

on:
  push:
    branches:
      - master

jobs:
  build-and-deploy:
    runs-on: ubuntu-latest
    steps:
```

```
- name: Checkout code
  uses: actions/checkout@v2
- name: Set up Docker Buildx
  uses: docker/setup-buildx-action@v1
- name: Log in to Docker Hub
  uses: docker/login-action@v1
  with:
    username: ${{ secrets.DOCKER_USERNAME }}
    password: ${{ secrets.DOCKER_PASSWORD }}
- name: Build and Push Docker Image
  run: |
    docker build -t myapp:latest .
    docker push myapp:latest
- name: Deploy to Knative
  run: |
    kn service update myapp --image mydockerhub/myapp:latest
```

This workflow automates the build and deployment cycle, ensuring that every change is systematically validated and deployed to Knative environments.

Integration with Security Practices

Ensuring security within the source control environment is crucial, particularly in public repositories where code is visible to wide audiences. Strategies include leveraging encryption for sensitive data, generating and storing secrets securely, and conducting security scans as part of CI/CD workflows.

Code Scanning:

GitHub and GitLab offer automated code scanning tools capable of identifying vulnerabilities and non-compliant code patterns, contributing to a secure development lifecycle.

Security Checklist:
- Enable two-factor authentication for repository access.
- Use secret management tools for sensitive environment variables.
- Employ code scanning tools to identify vulnerabilities.

Utilizing GitOps with Knative

GitOps, an operational model that uses Git as the single source of truth for deploying infrastructure and applications, synchronizes the state of Knative services with declared configurations stored in repositories. Frameworks such as ArgoCD and Flux simplify GitOps implementations by continuously monitoring repositories and synchronizing changes with deployed environments.

216

GitOps marries code and infrastructure management, fostering comprehensive traceability, auditability, and repeatable deployments — especially useful in complex cloud-native architectures reliant on configuration management and automated reconciliations.

Conclusion

Integrating source control systems with Knative applications encompasses a holistic approach to code management, collaboration, and automation. Emphasizing version control, branching strategies, automated workflows, and security, this integration represents a continuous commitment to quality and operational excellence.

As teams navigate the intricacies of modern software development, an adept source control partnership becomes vital, ensuring efficiency and innovation. By leveraging rigorous systems and practices, developers can extend the potential of Knative and maintain competitive superiority in progressively dynamic tech landscapes.

7.6 Testing and Debugging Knative Applications

Testing and debugging are critical components in the lifecycle of Knative applications, ensuring functionality, reliability, and performance across diverse environments. This section delves into nuanced strategies and best practices for effectively testing and debugging Knative applications, providing detailed instructions, illustrative scenarios, and coding examples that emphasize precision and resilience.

Comprehensive Testing Strategies

Testing Knative applications entails multiple facets, including unit testing, integration testing, end-to-end testing, and performance testing. Each type of testing serves a distinct purpose, collectively ensuring that applications meet quality standards and are resilient to varied scenarios.

Unit Testing

Unit testing focuses on verifying the functionality of individual components or functions, providing a granular view of potential defects within the codebase. Tools such as JUnit for Java, pytest for Python, and Mocha for JavaScript offer frameworks for constructing and executing unit tests.

```
import org.junit.jupiter.api.Test;
import static org.junit.jupiter.api.Assertions.*;

class KnativeFunctionTests {

    @Test
    void additionTest() {
        assertEquals(4, KnativeFunction.add(2, 2));
    }
}
```

The test above verifies a simple add function, serving as a basic template for unit tests. These tests are automated and included in continuous integration workflows to detect issues at the earliest stages.

Integration Testing

Integration testing evaluates how different components of the application work together within a unified environment. This is critical for applications with complex data flows, dependencies, or those involving external services. Tools like Testcontainers enable creating ephemeral test environments with containerized services.

```
import org.junit.jupiter.api.Test;
import org.testcontainers.containers.GenericContainer;
import static org.junit.jupiter.api.Assertions.*;

public class MyIntegrationTest {

    @Test
    public void integrationTest() {
        try (GenericContainer redis = new GenericContainer("redis:5.0.3-alpine").
            withExposedPorts(6379)) {
            redis.start();

            String response = myService.callService(redis.getContainerIpAddress(), redis
                .getFirstMappedPort());
            assertEquals("SUCCESS", response);
        }
    }
```

```
}
```

This example demonstrates how to use Testcontainers to bring up a Redis service as part of the testing process.

End-to-End Testing

End-to-end (E2E) testing simulates user journeys and interactions, ensuring that applications behave as expected from start to finish. E2E tests often involve automating browser interactions using tools such as Selenium or Puppeteer.

```
const puppeteer = require('puppeteer');

(async () => {
    const browser = await puppeteer.launch();
    const page = await browser.newPage();
    await page.goto('http://myknativeapp.local');

    const title = await page.title();
    console.assert(title === 'Expected Title', 'Page title does not match');

    await browser.close();
})();
```

Performance Testing

Performance testing ensures that applications perform well under load, identifying bottlenecks and verifying resource utilization scalability. Tools such as Apache JMeter or Gatling are often employed for automated performance testing.

```
jmeter -n -t load_test_plan.jmx -l results.jtl
```

Creating a comprehensive suite of performance tests is crucial for optimizing application performance metrics, particularly in cloud-native environments where resource efficiency can significantly influence operational costs.

Debugging Knative Applications

The debugging process involves systematically detecting, diagnosing, and resolving defects within Knative applications. Debugging becomes intricate in distributed systems, necessitating specialized tools and approaches to effectively address issues.

Logging and Monitoring

Logs are indispensable for debugging, providing insights into application behavior, operational states, and error conditions. Centralized logging platforms, such as Elasticsearch and Kibana, store structured logs, enabling detailed analysis and visualization.

```
apiVersion: serving.knative.dev/v1
kind: Service
metadata:
  name: my-knative-service
spec:
  template:
    spec:
      containers:
        - image: mydockerhub/my-knative-app
          env:
            - name: LOG_LEVEL
              value: "DEBUG"
```

Incorporating log level configurations within applications maximizes insight during debugging. Traditional log files complement real-time monitoring tools like Prometheus and Grafana by recording metrics, which highlight performance issues.

Distributed Tracing

Distributed tracing tracks requests across microservice architectures, elucidating the path and duration of transaction flows. Useful tools such as Jaeger or OpenTelemetry integrate with Knative, enabling end-to-end tracking and detailed performance visualization.

```
service:
  name: knative-tracer

exporters:
  jaeger:
    endpoint: "http://jaeger-collector:14268/api/traces"
```

```
service_name: "my-knative-service"
```

The configuration above sets up tracing information to be sent to a Jaeger instance, contributing to a comprehensive tracing ecosystem.

Debugging with IDEs

Integrated Development Environments (IDEs) provide tooling and extensions tailored for debugging Knative applications. Visual Studio Code, IntelliJ IDEA, and Eclipse support remote debugging, breakpoint management, and code evaluation, facilitating intricate code analysis and troubleshooting.

Examples include leveraging Visual Studio Code extensions with stepping, variable inspection, and console outputs for real-time insights.

Tailoring Tests and Debugging for Knative-Specific Contexts

Testing and debugging Knative applications involve particular nuances due to the nature of serverless environments:

- Cold Starts: Identify and mitigate delays associated with the initialization of applications under idle conditions.

- Event Sources: Validate all configurations related to Knative Eventing, ensuring event sources and brokers are configured to trigger functions properly.

- Autoscaling: Test the scaling behavior of services under load to ascertain correctness and effectiveness of resource allocation.

- Traffic Management: Test Canary releases and A/B testing configurations to ensure reliable traffic splits and transitions between versions.

Given these contexts, detailed test plans should be framed that encompass both the idiosyncrasies of Knative and the broader application landscape.

Conclusion

Effectively testing and debugging Knative applications calls for a comprehensive approach spanning multiple layers of application architecture. By adopting rigorous testing protocols and leveraging modern debugging tools, developers can ensure that applications are not only stable and efficient but also quick to adapt to changes.

The specialized nature of serverless functions and the distributed nature of cloud-native applications necessitate a deep understanding and adept deployment of tools, structures, and methods articulated in this section. Mastery of these practices ensures that Knative applications remain robust and reliable, even as they scale and evolve to meet ever-increasing user demands.

7.7 Managing Rollbacks and Updates

Managing rollbacks and updates is a crucial aspect of application lifecycle management, particularly in environments where continuous delivery and integration methodologies are employed. In the context of Knative, the serverless nature of applications adds a layer of complexity, requiring a keen understanding of its underlying architecture to execute robust rollbacks and updates. This section articulates the strategies, best practices, and tools for managing these operations efficiently within the Knative framework.

Understanding Knative's Architecture

Knative runs on Kubernetes, offering a suite of features that are crucial for smooth application rollbacks and updates. Two fundamental components of Knative aiding these processes are Knative Serving and Knative Eventing.

- **Knative Serving:** This component is responsible for deploying and managing the lifecycle of serverless services. It includes the creation of Revisions, which are immutable snapshots of your code and configuration. Revisions are pivotal in rollbacks since they track historical states of an application, allowing a return to a previous state when needed.

- **Knative Eventing:** While its primary function is to handle event-driven workloads, understanding the event sources and triggers is essential during updates, ensuring that the new version of an application handles events correctly.

Strategies for Updates and Rollbacks

Updates and rollbacks require different strategies depending on the complexity and requirements of the application. The following methods are widely adopted in Knative environments:

Canary Releases

A canary release is a deployment strategy allowing incremental updates where a new version is slowly introduced to a subset of users. This approach minimizes risk, as issues only affect a small user percentage initially.

```
# Update Service with New Revision
kn service update myapp --image=mycontainer/myapp:new-version --traffic new-
    revision=5,old-revision=95
```

In this command example, Knative directs 5% of the traffic to the new revision (new-revision) while maintaining the remaining 95% for the existing version (old-revision).

Blue-Green Deployments

This strategy involves maintaining two environments: one currently serving all production traffic (blue) and another running the new application version (green). The green environment fully replaces the blue after testing and verification.

```
# Create Green Version with No Traffic
kn service create myapp-green --image=mycontainer/myapp:green-version --traffic 0

# Test Green Version
kn service describe myapp-green
```

223

```
# Shift 100% Traffic to Green
kn service update myapp --traffic blue=0,green=100
```

After successful testing of myapp-green, traffic switches entirely from the blue version to the green, minimizing downtime and disruptions.

Rolling Updates

A rolling update gradually replaces the parts of a running application with new components, distributing updates incrementally to minimize potential disruption.

```
# Modify Knative Service with Incremental Rollout
for i in {1..10}; do
  kn service update myapp --image=mycontainer/myapp:v$((i)) --traffic "v$(i)"=$((10*
      i))
done
```

Each iteration adjusts the percentage of traffic handled by the new versions, providing fine-grained control over the update process.

Rollback Mechanisms

Given the modern emphasis on fast-paced deployments, rollbacks are as critical as updates to maintain service reliability and performance. Here's how Knative facilitates the rollback procedure:

Revision Management

In Knative, each service update creates a new revision. Rollback involves promoting an earlier, stable revision to replace the current one.

```
# Retrieve and List Revisions
kn revision list -s myapp

# Rollback to Previous Stable Revision
kn service update myapp --revision-name previous-stable-rev
```

This command sequence provides an efficient mechanism for rolling back while ensuring minimal disruption.

Automated Rollback Policies

Implementing automated rollback policies reduces human error and time-to-recovery during critical failures:

- **Traffic Monitoring:** Continuous monitoring detects anomalies such as increased error rates or latency. This monitoring can trigger alerts and initiate automated rollbacks if thresholds are breached.

- **Health Checks and SLOs:** Establish Service Level Objectives (SLOs) and define health checks for critical endpoints. Automated rollbacks should trigger when the application fails to meet predefined SLOs after an update.

Tooling and Best Practices

Proper tooling accelerates and simplifies update management, ensuring rollbacks are swift when needed.

GitOps

GitOps leverages Git as a source of truth for declaratively managing infrastructure and application configurations. Rollbacks in GitOps are straightforward: reverting to prior commits and observing continuous reconciliation with running configurations.

```
# Revert to Previous Commit
git revert <commit_hash>

# Push Changes to Remote Repository
git push origin main
```

Tools such as Flux or ArgoCD for GitOps automate deployment after repository changes, ensuring synchronicity between codebase and runtime state.

Continuous Integration and Continuous Deployment (CI/CD)

Integrating CI/CD pipelines with rollback capabilities enhances resilience:

- **Smoke Tests and Canary Tests:** Deploy smoke tests post-deployment to validate that applications run correctly. Canary tests extend this by verifying a small user segment using automated checks before wider rollout.

- **Rollback Automation in Jenkins/GitLab:** Scripts within Jenkins or GitLab pipelines automatically rollback upon detecting failures during deployment.

```
stage('Deploy') {
    steps {
        sh 'kn service update myapp --image=mycontainer/myapp:new-version'
    }
}
post {
    failure {
        echo 'Deployment failed, initiating rollback!'
        sh 'kn service update myapp --revision-name=previous-stable-rev'
    }
}
```

Final Considerations

Efficient management of rollbacks and updates underpins successful Knative application operations, ensuring smooth transitions and high service availability. A clear strategy, combined with automated tooling and vigilant monitoring, forms a robust system capable of responding to dynamic operational needs.

Developers should regularly review their rollback and update practices, incorporating ongoing learnings and technological advancements. Mastery of these processes strengthens the capacity to innovate rapidly and effectively adapt to user needs while preserving operational stability in evolving serverless environments. Through continuous refinement, rollbacks and updates enhance the reliability and responsiveness of serverless applications, supporting both development agility and user satisfaction.

Chapter 8

Monitoring and Observability in Knative

This chapter focuses on the principles of monitoring and observability, emphasizing their critical roles in managing Knative applications. It details the setup of monitoring tools such as Prometheus and Grafana to track application performance and health. The use of tracing and logging is explored to gain actionable insights into application behavior. Techniques for visualizing metrics are discussed to facilitate performance optimization. The chapter also covers configuring alerts and incident management to proactively address issues. Integration with third-party monitoring solutions is examined to enhance observability, and case studies illustrate the effective use of monitoring tools in maintaining robust Knative deployments.

8.1 Concepts of Monitoring and Observability

In software systems, particularly within cloud-native environments, monitoring and observability are indispensable concepts. Both are vital in ensuring that applications function optimally, maintaining their reliability, and facilitating prompt responses to any issues that may arise. Despite their interconnectedness, monitoring and observability possess distinct attributes which merit a clear differentiation.

Monitoring is primarily concerned with collecting data related to the system's performance and health. It involves the systematic observation of system metrics to detect deviations from normal operation patterns, thereby identifying potential issues. Monitoring answers the question, "Is everything working as expected?" It focuses on the representation of superficial system health indicators through metrics like CPU usage, memory consumption, error rates, and request counts. These are aggregated into timeseries dashboards, often visualized through tools like Grafana, leveraging data collected via systems such as Prometheus.

Observability, on the other hand, delves deeper into the inner workings of systems. It implies a qualitative understanding of the internal states of a system based on external outputs. Observability seeks to answer, "Why is something not functioning correctly?" by recompiling data from logs, metrics, and traces to provide a comprehensive picture of system behavior. While monitoring gauges system output at a high level, observability enables the inference of internal states, granting a more profound level of insight.

For an application deployed within Knative, a cloud-native computing project, disaggregating these two dimensions is essential for ensuring resilient and high-performing service delivery.

```
# Example command to install Prometheus for basic monitoring
kubectl apply -f https://github.com/prometheus-operator/prometheus-operator/blob/
    main/bundle.yaml
```

The above command initiates the deployment of Prometheus, a system integral to basic monitoring architectures. After installation, tracking various application metrics becomes seamless, offering an initial foray into understanding Knative application performance.

Knative is conducive to high-level monitoring due to its event-driven, auto-scaling characteristics. By defining services declaratively using Kubernetes API resources, developers can harness the scalability features native to Kubernetes environments. Thus, when these services are monitored with both telemetric data and observability tools, developers acquire meaningful insights into system performance and behavior patterns over time.

In a typical Knative environment, monitoring focuses on the quantifiable aspects of workflows through predefined telemetry and health metrics. Here, essential metrics can include:

- Request Latency: Measures the time taken to process a request from start to finish. High latency values could indicate a congested network or under-provisioned computational resources.

- Error Rates: A critical metric that captures the count or rate of requests resulting in error responses, indicating potential issues in code execution or integration points.

- Resource Usage: Observes CPU and memory allocations, providing insights into the system's efficiency and scaling behavior.

Once metrics are established, visualization tools such as Grafana can construct dashboards for these data points, lending immediate visibility into the system's status.

```
{
  "dashboard": {
    "panels": [
      {
        "type": "graph",
        "title": "Request Latency",
        "targets": [
          {
            "expr": "rate(http_request_duration_seconds_bucket[5m])"
          }
        ]
      },
      {
        "type": "stat",
        "title": "CPU Usage",
        "targets": [
          {
```

```
        "expr": "sum by(namespace, pod) (rate(
            container_cpu_usage_seconds_total{container!=\"\",namespace
            !=\"\",pod!=\"\"}[5m])"
      }
    ]
  }
 ]
}
}
}
```

The JSON above illustrates a basic Grafana dashboard panel setup, which visualizes real-time data that could reveal patterns relevant to system performance issues.

In juxtaposition, observability tools capture deeper insights into the application's functional inner states. By leveraging logging and tracing capabilities within Knative, developers can diagnose systemic issues that may not manifest through high-level monitoring metrics alone.

Logging captures a timestamped record of events, enabling the inspection of system actions as they occur. Fluent Bit or Fluentd are typical choices for forwarding logs to dedicated log management systems. Examining these logs through tools such as Elasticsearch and visualized via Kibana allows developers to uncover complex interdependencies by exploring context-rich data.

For tracing, tools such as OpenTelemetry provide standardized support in capturing distributed trace data across Knative's microservices architecture. Traces document the journey of a request through each facet of the infrastructure, providing a detailed map of execution paths and revealing latency bottlenecks or anomalies.

```java
import io.opentelemetry.api.GlobalOpenTelemetry;
import io.opentelemetry.api.trace.Tracer;
import io.opentelemetry.context.Scope;
import io.opentelemetry.api.trace.Span;

public class ExampleTracing {
    private final Tracer tracer = GlobalOpenTelemetry.getTracer("exampleTracer");

    public void exampleMethod() {
        Span span = tracer.spanBuilder("overwriteSpanName").startSpan();
        try (Scope scope = span.makeCurrent()) {
            // Business logic goes here
        } finally {
            span.end();
        }
    }
}
```

Instrumenting a simple Java application with tracing through Open-Telemetry permits an unbroken view of transaction flows, illuminating operation inefficiencies or misconfigurations within the observed application components.

Furthermore, blending monitoring and observability strengthens an enterprise's capability to conduct advanced root cause analysis. While monitoring flags an anomaly requiring attention, observability empowers the infrastructure or SRE teams to zero in on the root cause by examining rich contextual data.

Within cloud-native architectures, this synergy allows for dynamic scaling decisions based on just-in-time demand signal receipts. By employing autoscalers that consider both monitored resources and observable signals, systems can increase or decrease resources more intelligently and in real-time.

As cloud systems grow more complex, adopting a proactive monitoring and observability strategy underpins an efficient DevOps cycle. This empowers developers to transition from mere reactive troubleshooting to crafting a more predictable performance-driven maintenance framework, ultimately leading to an optimized end-user experience.

Effective observability also necessitates cultural adoption within technology teams. Developers must collaboratively decide on appropriate service-level indicators (SLIs) and service-level objectives (SLOs) that delineate essential performance and reliability metrics according to business and end-user expectations.

This collaboration extends across development, operations, and business analysis stakeholders to ensure that observability efforts align with critical business outcomes. By establishing error budgets and recovery plans, teams possess clear guidelines on threshold breaches and agreed-upon recovery strategies.

Through a meticulous union of monitoring and observability within Knative deployments, organizations can maintain a comprehensive understanding of their system architecture, offering enhanced reliability, agility, and informed decision-making processes. Conclusively, this holistic approach is pivotal for sustaining high availability and service quality, especially in environments characterized by volatility and rapid scalability.

8.2 Setting Up Monitoring Tools for Knative

Establishing a robust monitoring setup is imperative in ensuring the availability, performance, and reliability of Knative applications. Given the dynamic and distributed nature of cloud-native environments, leveraging specialized tools such as Prometheus and Grafana is essential. These tools provide the necessary visibility into system metrics and offer powerful querying and visualization capabilities essential for diagnosing and understanding the behavior of Knative services. This section provides a comprehensive guide to setting up and configuring these monitoring tools specifically tailored for Knative applications.

Prometheus is a popular open-source systems monitoring and alerting toolkit widely adopted for collecting and storing metrics as time series data. Its potency lies in its robust multi-dimensional data model, operational simplicity, and rich querying language, PromQL. It integrates seamlessly with Kubernetes, making it a natural fit for monitoring Knative applications that run atop Kubernetes clusters.

To begin setting up Prometheus for Knative, you'll want to deploy Prometheus using the Prometheus Operator, a Kubernetes-specific controller that automates and simplifies the deployment and management of Prometheus instances.

```
# Install Prometheus Operator
kubectl apply -f https://raw.githubusercontent.com/prometheus-operator/prometheus-
    operator/release-0.48/bundle.yaml

# Apply Prometheus Instance
kubectl apply -f https://raw.githubusercontent.com/prometheus-operator/prometheus-
    operator/release-0.48/example/prometheus-prometheus.yaml
```

The above commands deploy the Prometheus Operator and create a Prometheus instance within your Kubernetes cluster. The Prometheus Operator encapsulates the complexity associated with managing Prometheus infrastructure by dynamically configuring Prometheus instances within Kubernetes, monitoring ServiceMonitors and PodMonitors deployed alongside your applications.

In Knative, various metrics pertinent to system behaviors are exposed through metrics endpoints by default. These metrics are critical for assessing service performance, auto-scaling decisions, and identifying potential system bottlenecks. Integrating these metrics with Prometheus involves configuring the monitoring stack to scrape exposed endpoints.

```
apiVersion: monitoring.coreos.com/v1
kind: ServiceMonitor
metadata:
  name: knative-service-monitor
  labels:
    release: prometheus
spec:
  endpoints:
  - port: metrics
  namespaceSelector:
    matchNames:
    - knative-serving
  selector:
    matchLabels:
      serving.knative.dev/revision: ""
```

This ServiceMonitor configuration instructs Prometheus to scrape metrics from endpoints under the 'knative-serving' namespace. Understanding and configuring these components is a crucial step towards end-to-end observability.

Grafana complements Prometheus by offering dynamic and flexible dashboards to visualize the metrics collected by Prometheus. It aids in illustrating trends, comparing metrics, and providing tangible insights into system performance over time.

```
# Install Grafana
kubectl apply -f https://raw.githubusercontent.com/grafana/grafana/master/deploy/
    kubernetes/custom-resources.yaml
```

To connect Grafana to Prometheus, create a data source within Grafana that targets Prometheus' query endpoint. This linkage facilitates the visual representation of telemetry data and allows for constructing various dashboards suited to the particular needs of your Knative environments.

```
{
  "name": "Prometheus",
  "type": "prometheus",
  "url": "http://prometheus-server:9090",
  "access": "proxy",
  "isDefault": true
}
```

With this integration, exploring and customizing dashboards offers unique perspectives into how well Knative services are performing. Grafana supports creating intricate visualizations, including time-series graphs, heatmaps, and alert panels that trigger when predetermined thresholds are exceeded.

A significant advantage of aligning Prometheus and Grafana for Knative monitoring lies in their extensive support for alerting. Alerts are essential for proactive incident management, helping teams address issues before they evolve into service failures. Prometheus evaluates rule expressions and triggers alerts via its Alertmanager component based on predefined thresholds.

```
apiVersion: monitoring.coreos.com/v1
kind: PrometheusRule
metadata:
  name: knative-alerts
  namespace: knative-monitoring
spec:
  groups:
  - name: knative.rules
    rules:
    - alert: HighRequestLatency
      expr: job:request_latency_seconds:mean5m > 0.5
      for: 5m
      labels:
        severity: critical
      annotations:
        summary: "High request latency detected"
        description: "The average request latency over 5 minutes exceeded 500ms."
```

This rule detects abnormally high request latency and generates a critical alert, alerting about potential performance degradation.

Integrating tracing into monitoring ecosystems further enriches the intelligence derived from collected metrics. Observability tools like OpenTelemetry can be configured to emit traces into a common backend such as Jaeger or Zipkin. These trace data points interlink with metrics, not only simplifying root cause analysis through detailed request adventures but highlighting interdependencies between Knative services.

Setting up a complete monitoring suite involves attention to security, resource allocation, and scalability. Configuration best practices include securing endpoints with authentication measures (such as OAuth for Grafana), setting resource limits and requests in Kubernetes manifests to ensure efficient resource use, and scaling monitoring components appropriately to handle anticipated data ingestion volumes.

It's also essential that robustness and resiliency in monitoring architectures are addressed through multi-cluster or highly available deployments, ensuring that monitoring doesn't become a single point of failure within your surveillance strategy.

Alerting and tracing aren't only aimed at engineers but can provide operational insights across the business stack. Developers, site reliability engineers, and product managers can harness insights to optimize not only performance but also feature velocity and service uptime assurance.

Incorporating automated monitoring testing, through tools like chaos engineering and failure simulation, tests the operational limits of your monitoring configurations by validating alerting mechanisms and monitoring thresholds under real pressure scenarios. This positions teams to adopt a mitigation- and learning-focused approach to incrementally improve their Knative deployments' performance.

Through a detailed and well-planned monitoring setup, Knative applications can achieve high observability and maintain their operational integrity, bolstering their ability to scale dynamically as traffic demands flex. This forms a foundation for resilience in modern cloud-native application landscapes, equipping teams with the data-driven insights necessary to facilitate ongoing refinement, optimization, and innovation.

8.3   Tracing and Logging in Knative

In cloud-native environments like Knative, tracing and logging are indispensable for gaining deep insights into application behavior and performance. These two mechanisms form the backbone of application observability, providing developers and operations teams with the tools necessary to comprehend dynamic interactions within distributed systems. This section delves into the intricacies of tracing and logging in Knative, exploring how these tools can be effectively utilized to enhance system understanding and reliability.

Tracing in Knative captures the propagation of requests across various services, offering a transparent view of service calls and enabling precise performance analysis. Tracing helps identify latency issues, service bottlenecks, and dependencies across microservices, thereby facilitating root cause analysis.

Knative natively supports tracing through integration with OpenCensus or OpenTelemetry and tracing backends such as Jaeger or Zipkin. These integrations allow for detailed recordkeeping of transactions and service interactions, effectively tagging and timing them as they traverse the system.

The following is an example of integrating OpenTelemetry tracing within a Knative serverless function written in Go:

```
import (
    "go.opentelemetry.io/contrib/instrumentation/net/http/otelhttp"
    "net/http"
)

func main() {
    tracerProvider := initTracer()
    defer func() { _ = tracerProvider.Shutdown(context.Background()) }()

    http.Handle("/", otelhttp.NewHandler(http.HandlerFunc(handler), "YourOperation
        "))
    log.Fatal(http.ListenAndServe(":8080", nil))
}

func handler(w http.ResponseWriter, req *http.Request) {
    ctx := req.Context()
    span := trace.SpanFromContext(ctx)
    span.AddEvent("handling request")
    w.Write([]byte("Hello, Knative!"))
}

func initTracer() *trace.TracerProvider {
    tp := otel.GetTracerProvider()
    return tp
}
```

This example setup initializes an OpenTelemetry tracer to automatically instrument incoming HTTP requests, providing seamless tracing data for each request processed by the Knative service. By utilizing OpenTelemetry, developers can gain granular insights into request processing times, helping to pinpoint inefficiencies or errors within the call graph.

Tracing data collected from Knative services is typically forwarded to a backend such as Jaeger. Jaeger provides a centralized view of trace data, offering an intuitive interface for examining traces, understanding service latencies, and analyzing request flows.

Moreover, tracing contextualizes the relationship between services by assigning unique trace IDs to transaction flows. This enables correlation of logs and telemetry events tied to the same trace, thus painting a comprehensive picture of system operations.

Logging, in parallel, serves as an equally critical element of Knative observability. Logs offer historical records of application events, errors, and other informational messages pertinent to the system's lifecycle. Efficient logging provides insights that facilitate debugging, historical analysis, and security auditing.

For Knative applications, Fluent Bit and Fluentd often serve as log collectors, aggregating log data from pods and forwarding it to log management systems such as Elasticsearch or Cloud Logging services.

Configuring Fluent Bit to collect logs from a Knative service involves creating a DaemonSet that runs Fluent Bit on each node and configures it to aggregate logs from the application containers.

```
apiVersion: v1
kind: ConfigMap
metadata:
  name: fluent-bit-config
data:
  fluent-bit.conf: |
    [SERVICE]
        Flush 1
        Daemon Off
        Log_Level info

    [INPUT]
        Name tail
        Path /var/log/containers/*${HOSTNAME}*.log
        Tag kube.*
        Refresh_Interval 10

    [OUTPUT]
        Name stdout
        Match *
```

This configuration captures application logs from Knative services, tagging them for downstream processing. Logs can be enriched with metadata such as trace IDs or service names, enhancing their utility in postmortem analysis and real-time monitoring.

Incorporating log aggregation further empowers organizations to apply sophisticated queries, conduct trend analysis, and create alert conditions based on log patterns or frequency. Advanced logging systems support indices, facilitating quick searches that improve incident response times and provide operational intelligence.

Strategies for effective logging in Knative environments include:

- Ensuring that log messages are both human-readable and structured (e.g., JSON format) to facilitate machine processing.

- Defining an appropriate log retention policy that aligns with organizational compliance, cost, and utility considerations.

- Implementing logging levels (e.g., DEBUG, INFO, WARN, ERROR) to control verbosity and noise in the logs.

- Using correlation IDs within log messages to link them back to distributed trace context for improved trace-log correlation.

By combining tracing and logging, developers gain a holistic understanding of application workflows. Anomalies flagged by metrics or performance outliers revealed through tracing can be further scrutinized with logs, uncovering the annotations, error stacks, and contextual data essential for thorough diagnoses.

Additionally, leveraging service mesh technologies like Istio alongside Knative enables automatic injection of tracing headers into service requests. Service meshes also deliver mTLS encrypted communications, load balancing, and policy control, further extending the security and observability of tracing and logging frameworks.

```
apiVersion: install.istio.io/v1alpha1
kind: IstioOperator
spec:
  meshConfig:
    enableTracing: true
    defaultConfig:
      tracing:
        sampling: 100.0
        zipkin:
          address: "zipkin-service:9411"
```

This Istio configuration enhances observability by enabling automatic tracing for all service requests, significantly boosting trace coverage without necessitating direct code instrumentation.

Finally, fostering a collaborative culture around monitoring solutions ensures that both tracing and logging are not isolated practices but integral components of the entire application lifecycle. By continuously refining observability practices and tools within Knative environments, teams enhance their ability to deliver high-quality, reliable, and scalable services in cloud-native architectures. This pursuit of excellence in observability defines resilient applications capable of rapidly adapting to demand fluctuations and swiftly recovering from disruptions.

8.4 Visualizing Metrics and Data

Data visualization in cloud-native systems like Knative plays a pivotal role in transforming raw data into actionable insights. With a myriad of metrics generated by applications, services, and infrastructure, visualizing these metrics effectively aids in optimizing performance, identifying anomalies, and facilitating informed decision-making. This section explores the methodologies, tools, and best practices for visualizing metrics and data in Knative environments, emphasizing their significance in dynamically scaling and managing applications.

Central to the process of visualizing metrics is the toolset employed to aggregate, query, and display data. Prometheus, coupled with Grafana, constitutes a powerful duo for metric collection, storage, and visualization in Knative setups. Prometheus gathers time-series data from various services, while Grafana translates these datasets into graphical representations that facilitate easy interpretation and comprehension.

Grafana's intuitive dashboard interface allows users to construct custom views that enhance data interplay, enabling swift anomaly detection and operational assessments. To start visualizing metrics, Grafana must be connected to the Prometheus data source, as previously outlined.

Once connected, users can create and customize dashboards specific to the needs of their applications. Creating a useful dashboard involves adding diverse panels, each corresponding to different queries or metrics of interest. A common practice involves visualizing key metrics such as HTTP request rates, CPU usage, memory consumption, and error rates.

```
{
  "type": "timeseries",
  "title": "HTTP Request Rate",
  "target": {
    "expr": "rate(http_requests_total[5m])",
    "legendFormat": "{{instance}} request rate"
  }
}
```

This panel utilizes PromQL, Prometheus' native query language, to display HTTP request rates per instance, offering insights into service demand and highlighting potential performance bottlenecks.

A well-designed Grafana dashboard not only visualizes current states but also draws upon historical data to recognize patterns and predict future trends. Fertile visualization practices in Knative entail the integration of annotations and alerts, which contextualize visualizations with temporal markers and threshold crossings respectively.

Annotations act as reference points directly on the graphs, marking when deployments occurred, incidents were reported, or alerts were triggered:

```
{
  "name": "Deployments",
  "datasource": "Prometheus",
  "showLine": true,
  "expr": "changes(knative_deployment_timestamp[5m])",
  "iconColor": "rgba(54, 42, 226, 0.901)"
}
```

This annotation ties deployments with visual graphs, aiding developers in attributing performance changes to recent application updates.

Additionally, alerting rules in Prometheus can be leveraged to trigger notifications when specific conditions are met, such as sustained high CPU usage or abnormal error rates.

```
groups:
- name: example.rules
  rules:
  - alert: HighCpuUsage
    expr: avg(rate(container_cpu_usage_seconds_total{namespace="knative-serving
        "}[1m])) by (pod) > 0.7
    for: 5m
    labels:
      severity: warning
    annotations:
      summary: "High CPU usage detected"
      description: "CPU usage is above 70\% for 5 minutes."
```

Upon triggering, alerts can integrate with notification channels in Grafana, visibly altering dashboard presentations to signal pertinent alerts and guide users towards potential problem areas.

Heatmaps and Status Panels are additional visualization types that contribute substantially to monitoring and analysis purposes. Heatmaps serve well in representing the distribution and variance of a metric over time, facilitating pattern recognition and anomaly identification.

Status Panels quickly convey the health of various application components at a glance, exhibiting status as visual indicators such as color-coded signals for services' operational states:

```
{
  "title": "Service Health",
  "type": "stat",
  "target": {
    "expr": "sum(increase(http_requests_total{status=~\"5..\"}[5m]))",
    "format": "percentage",
    "thresholds": "80,90",
    "gauge": {
      "thresholdLabels": "critical"
    }
  }
}
```

Beyond dashboard panels, scripting automated reports can systematically distill visual insights. Grafana's API supports generating images of dashboards or specific panels programmatically, which can be incorporated into scheduled reports for wider organizational dissemination.

Efficient visualization strategies must also accommodate diverse analytical views, empowering cross-functional teams to leverage dashboards tailored to their role-specific insights. For instance, operations teams may focus on infrastructure metrics, while development teams prioritize application performance data.

Visualization practices in Knative aren't limited to performance metrics alone, extending to service usage and cost analytics, capacity planning, and user experience metrics such as response times and request success rates. By visualizing these different dimensions, organizations foster a data culture rooted in transparency and evidence-based management.

Exploring additional plugins and extensions within the Grafana ecosystem further enriches visualization capabilities. This includes plugins like WorldMap, which contextualize data geographically, or Pie Chart, useful for representing categorical distributions such as request types or response codes.

Interactive and real-time dashboards promote collaboration and operational agility, allowing stakeholders to gather actionable insights during crises, planning sessions, or routine evaluations. The adaptability of Grafana dashboards ensures they serve as a living instrument, reflective of evolving service dynamics and priorities.

Beyond the traditional monitoring realm, visualizations can extend into predictive analytics, using historical data to anticipate future performance scenarios. Machine learning models could be employed to augment visualization efforts, offering forecasts for resource demands versus current capacity, thereby recommending proactive scaling as per anticipated spikes in workloads.

In summary, the visualization of metrics and data in Knative transcends simple monitoring, empowering teams to act on data-driven insights, uncover latent trends, and orchestrate an iterative performance enhancement regimen. As cloud-native technologies and methodologies evolve, so too will visualization paradigms, continually striving to equip decision-makers with the most comprehensive perspectives on their digital ecosystem's health and potential. Through strategic visualizations, organizations stand to transform data into a formidable asset, guiding them toward achieving operational excellence and sustained competitive advantage.

8.5   Alerting and Incident Management

Effective alerting and incident management are critical components in maintaining the reliability, availability, and performance of cloud-native applications, such as those deployed on Knative. These practices ensure that operational disruptions are detected promptly, communicated effectively, and addressed efficiently to minimize downtime and its impact. This section will delve into the systematic approach to setting up alerting mechanisms and incident management protocols in

Knative environments, discussing tools, configurations, and best practices to prepare for various operational scenarios.

Alerting in Knative Environments

Alerting constitutes the mechanism by which system metrics that cross predefined thresholds trigger notifications. These notifications serve as triggers for operational teams to investigate and resolve underlying issues. In Knative, a typical alerting architecture integrates Prometheus for monitoring, with Alertmanager handling alert distribution and management.

Configuring Alerting Rules

Prometheus rules are used to define alerts based on queries executed against monitored data. Alerts are expressed using PromQL, which allows flexible querying to capture specific conditions of interest.

Consider an example where alerts are configured to detect persistent HTTP error rates, a common issue in microservices that could indicate service degradation or failure.

```
groups:
- name: http-alerts
  rules:
  - alert: HighHttp500ErrorRate
    expr: sum(rate(http_requests_total{status_code=~"5.."}[1m])) by (service) / sum(
        rate(http_requests_total[1m])) by (service) > 0.05
    for: 5m
    labels:
      severity: critical
    annotations:
      summary: "High HTTP Error Rate Detected"
      description: "{{ $labels.service }} has HTTP 500 error rate > 5\% over the last 5
        minutes"
```

In this example, the alert rule triggers if the proportion of HTTP 500 errors exceeds 5% for any given service over a five-minute interval. The rule is categorized with a critical severity label, prompting immediate attention from responders.

Managing Alerts with Alertmanager

Alertmanager is responsible for receiving alerts from Prometheus and handling their distribution to the designated notification channels. It's configured to manage deduplication, grouping, and routing of alerts to appropriate recipients, often through integrations with communication tools like Slack, PagerDuty, or email systems.

A sample Alertmanager configuration might look like this:

```
route:
  receiver: "slack-notifications"
  group_by: ['alertname']
  group_wait: 30s
  group_interval: 5m
  repeat_interval: 1h

receivers:
- name: "slack-notifications"
  slack_configs:
  - api_url: "https://hooks.slack.com/services/T00000000/B00000000/
      XXXXXXXXXXXXXXXXXXXXXXXXX"
    channel: "#alerts"
    title: "{{ .AlertName }} - {{ .Status }}"
    text: "{{ .Annotations.description }}"
```

This configuration specifies Slack as a notification channel, setting parameters for grouping alerts and controlling notification frequency to avoid alert fatigue. Alerts are grouped by name, which aids in categorizing incidents for efficient triage and resolution.

Incident Management Protocols

While alerting is about detection, incident management encompasses the processes and practices used to coordinate the resolution of operational disruptions. Effective incident management minimizes the time from detection to resolution and is measured by metrics such as Mean Time to Acknowledgement (MTTA) and Mean Time to Resolution (MTTR).

Roles and Responsibilities

A defined incident management protocol typically assigns roles and responsibilities, such as:

- **Incident Commander**: Oversees the incident response process, ensuring efficient coordination and communication among teams.

- **Responder**: Technical personnel tasked with diagnosing and resolving specific issues.

- **Communicator**: Keeps stakeholders informed about incident status, progress, and impacts.

Incident Lifecycle

The incident lifecycle comprises several stages: detection, response, mitigation, resolution, and review. Each stage requires careful documentation and communication to ensure transparency and continual improvement.

1. **Detection**: Triggered by alerts, detection marks the beginning of the incident lifecycle. It's essential to have clear guidelines on how alerts are verified and assessed for priority.

2. **Response and Mitigation**: Involves deploying resources and efforts to contain the impact of the incident. This stage is crucial for preventing further escalation and includes implementing temporary fixes or workarounds.

3. **Resolution**: Permanently resolves the underlying cause of the incident. This involves updating code, scaling resources, or remediating configuration issues as necessary.

4. **Review**: Conduct a post-incident review (postmortem) to evaluate the incident response process, identify root causes, and apply learnings for future improvement. This is a collaborative process involving all stakeholders, producing an incident report that outlines what happened, how it was resolved, and what changes will be made to prevent recurrence.

Tools for Incident Management

Incident management is bolstered by using collaboration tools and platforms that facilitate coordination and documentation. Integrations between alerting tools and incident management platforms (e.g., Opsgenie, PagerDuty) streamline processes by automating task assignments, managing communication logs, and maintaining an audit trail of actions taken during an incident.

Automating Incident Responses

Advanced systems incorporate automated responses to common incidents, reducing response times and freeing human resources for more complex issues. Automation scripts can handle predefined scenarios, such as rebooting a service or updating a configuration parameter, as exemplified below:

```
#!/bin/bash
SERVICE_NAME=$1
NAMESPACE=$2

kubectl rollout restart deployment/${SERVICE_NAME} -n ${NAMESPACE}
echo "Restart command invoked for service ${SERVICE_NAME} in namespace ${
    NAMESPACE}."
```

Though automation accelerates handling repeated tasks, care must be taken to ensure that scripts are safe, tested, and linked to proper alert conditions to avoid inadvertent escalations.

Continuous Improvement

Incident management processes should be regularly reviewed and refined based on insights gained from past incidents. Implementing feedback loops ensures continuous improvement, paving the way towards a more resilient and robust infrastructure. Incorporating machine learning for anomaly detection and predictive analytics may provide early warnings, enhancing proactivity in incident management.

Organizational Culture

Lastly, the effectiveness of alerting and incident management is highly dependent on organizational culture. Encouraging a culture of accountability, transparency, and learning fosters a proactive stance in addressing operational challenges. Organizations should maintain a blameless postmortem culture to encourage honesty and openness, leading to more substantive learnings and improvement opportunities.

The symbiotic relationship between alerting systems, incident management protocols, and the organizational readiness plays a foundational role in safeguarding Knative applications against potential threats and disruptions. Through meticulous implementation and continuous refinement of these processes, teams are best positioned to uphold the reliability and efficiency of their cloud-native services, ensuring seamless and uninterrupted user experiences.

8.6 Integrating Third-Party Monitoring Solutions

In cloud-native environments such as Knative, leveraging third-party monitoring solutions enhances observability and operational insights, enabling teams to proactively manage and optimize application performance. These solutions often provide advanced analytics, seamless integration capabilities, and robust visualization tools that transcend the basic monitoring functionalities. This section explores the integration of third-party monitoring solutions with Knative, emphasizing the benefits, methodologies, and considerations necessary to implement effective monitoring strategies.

- **Benefits of Third-Party Monitoring Solutions**

  Third-party monitoring solutions offer several advantages over self-hosted setups. Key benefits include:

  - **Scalability**: Many third-party solutions are designed to effortlessly scale with your application infrastructure, accommodating dynamic workloads and fluctuations in data volume.

  - **Advanced Analytics**: Sophisticated analytics and machine learning capabilities enable intelligent alerting, anomaly detection, and predictive insights, often beyond what's feasible in self-managed setups.

  - **Ease of Use**: A streamlined setup process, coupled with intuitive dashboards and reporting tools, simplifies the monitoring experience, minimizing the operational overhead.

  - **Integration Ecosystem**: These platforms often provide rich ecosystems of integrations with various services, tools, and programming languages, enhancing data aggregation and contextual insights.

- **Popular Third-Party Monitoring Solutions**

  Numerous third-party monitoring solutions can integrate seamlessly with Knative. Prominent examples include Datadog, New

Relic, Dynatrace, and AWS CloudWatch. Each platform offers distinct capabilities and features suited to different organizational needs and preferences.

- **Integration Methodology**

Integrating third-party monitoring solutions with Knative environments involves several steps, generally encompassing the setup of monitoring endpoints, configuration of agents, and customization to align with service-specific metrics and alerts.

- **1. Datadog**

Datadog provides extensive observability capabilities, supporting metrics, traces, and logs with unified dashboards and machine learning-powered alerting. It is particularly noted for its ease of integration and support for a wide array of technologies.

Integration Steps:

- **Agent Installation**: Install the Datadog Agent within the Kubernetes cluster. The agent collects traces, logs, and metrics from Knative services.

```
kubectl apply -f "https://raw.githubusercontent.com/DataDog/
datadog-agent/main/Dockerfiles/manifests/datadog-
agent.yaml"
```

- **Configuration**: Specify monitoring requirements in the Datadog UI, such as which Knative services to monitor and which metrics to collect. Service discovery within Datadog automatically detects Knative services, thus simplifying the configuration process.
- **Observing Traces**: Enabling APM (Application Performance Monitoring) generates detailed insights into service calls. Instrument applications with the Datadog APM library for supported programming languages to start capturing trace data.

- **2. New Relic**

New Relic provides a comprehensive set of observability tools, including distributed tracing, metrics, and logs, built on a robust, AI-driven platform that offers deep application insights.

248

Integration Steps:

- **Kubernetes Integration**: Deploy the New Relic Kubernetes integration, which involves creating a Kubernetes secret with your New Relic license key and installing the New Relic Infrastructure Agent.

```
kubectl create secret generic newrelic-license --from-literal=
    licenseKey=YOUR_LICENSE_KEY
```

- **Deploying the Infrastructure Agent**: Use Helm to install the New Relic Infrastructure Agent, which collects data from Kubernetes clusters and automatically integrates with Knative components.

```
helm repo add newrelic https://helm-charts.newrelic.com
helm upgrade --install newrelic-infrastructure \
  --set cluster=my-cluster-name \
  --set licenseKey=$(kubectl get secret newrelic-license -o=
      jsonpath='{.data.licenseKey}' | base64 --decode) \
  stable/newrelic-infrastructure
```

- **Custom Dashboards and Alerts**: New Relic offers customizable dashboards and alerts, supporting in-depth analysis and proactive incident management tailored to Knative deployments.

- **3. Dynatrace**

Dynatrace excels in providing automated monitoring and dynamic baselining, with powerful AI capabilities that uncover root causes and improve real-time decision-making.

Integration Steps:

- **Dynatrace Operator**: Install the Dynatrace Operator to manage the lifecycle of the OneAgent within your Kubernetes environment. The operator auto-discovers applications and injects OneAgent automatically.

```
kubectl apply -f https://github.com/Dynatrace/dynatrace-
    operator/releases/latest/download/kubernetes.yaml
```

- **Enabling Cloud-Native Monitoring**: The OneAgent automatically detects Knative service transactions, providing full-stack visibility and detailed service flows across inter-connected components.

- **Zero Touch Instrumentation**: Dynatrace provides seamless, no-code instrumentation for Kubernetes environments, effectively capturing traces, dependencies, and service metrics without additional configuration requirements.

- **4. AWS CloudWatch**

For those running Knative on AWS, Amazon CloudWatch offers a native and integrated solution for monitoring AWS-hosted resources, providing insights into application infrastructure and performance.

Integration Steps:

- **CloudWatch Container Insights**: Enable Container Insights to collect, ingest, and process metrics and logs generated by Knative applications in AWS EKS.

```
aws eks update-cluster-config --name my-cluster --region us-west-2 --container-insights enable
```

- **Custom Metrics and Alarms**: CloudWatch supports the creation of custom metrics and alarms via its user interface or AWS CLI. Monitor metrics specific to Knative workloads, such as request latency or auto-scaling statistics, and trigger alerts when thresholds are breached.

- **Data Visualization and Reporting**

Third-party solutions offer sophisticated data visualization capabilities that improve the comprehension of complex metrics. This often includes customizable dashboards, prebuilt templates specific to Kubernetes or Knative environments, and rich graphing libraries that facilitate exploratory data analysis.

By integrating multiple data sources (e.g., infrastructure, applications, business metrics), these platforms provide a comprehensive observability experience, supporting unified views that promote cross-functional insights and alignment.

250

- **Best Practices and Considerations**

  When integrating third-party monitoring solutions, consider the following best practices and considerations to ensure a seamless and valuable implementation:

  - **Performance Impact**: Although valuable, monitoring solutions introduce overhead. It's essential to assess the impact that agents and integrations impose on system resources to avoid performance degradation.

  - **Security**: Pay attention to data sovereignty and security compliance standards, particularly the handling of application data within third-party systems. Secure all data transmission and adhere to internal and external compliance policies.

  - **Cost Management**: Be aware of the subscription models and costs associated with third-party monitoring solutions, given that over-collection of metrics may result in unnecessary expenses.

  - **Customization**: Tailor the monitoring setup to fit the unique operational and business needs of your organization. This may involve custom metrics, trace annotation, or log enrichment to derive maximum value.

  - **Training**: Ensure that involved teams are trained and conversant with the setups and dashboards of third-party tools to fully leverage their capabilities.

- **Conclusion**

  Integrating third-party monitoring solutions with Knative can significantly uplift the observability posture of an organization through enhanced scalability, rich analytics, and seamless visualization. The success of such integrations hinges on thoughtful implementation, attentive configuration, and continual adaptation to evolving application landscapes. By selecting suitable tools that align with organizational objectives and investing in their proper administration, teams can ensure their applications remain robust, responsive, and reliable in increasingly complex cloud environments.

8.7 Case Studies of Monitoring in Action

The efficacies of monitoring systems in cloud-native architectures such as Knative are best illustrated through real-world case studies. These insights provide tangible examples of how diverse organizations leverage monitoring and observability tools to achieve operational excellence and optimize service performance. This section presents comprehensive case studies demonstrating the implementation and impact of monitoring tools in Knative deployments, underscoring challenges faced, strategies employed, and successes achieved.

Case Study 1: E-commerce Platform's Resilience through Proactive Monitoring

Background: A major e-commerce company operating on a Kubernetes-based architecture uses Knative for its microservices, handling massive transaction volumes, especially during peak periods like Black Friday. Ensuring consistent user experience with minimal downtime during high traffic surges is a business-critical requirement.

Challenges:

- Managing peak loads with auto-scaling.

- Identifying and resolving performance bottlenecks proactively.

- Minimizing the response time to incidents to prevent lost revenue.

Solution: The e-commerce organization adopted a comprehensive monitoring strategy, integrating Prometheus and Grafana with their Knative infrastructure. Custom Terraform scripts were used to deploy and manage the monitoring stack in a repeatable manner.

```
resource "helm_release" "prometheus" {
  name = "prometheus"
  namespace = "monitoring"
  chart = "prometheus"
  repository = "https://prometheus-community.github.io/helm-charts"
}
```

Implementation Steps:

- **Metrics Collection:** Prometheus scrapes metric endpoints from Knative services, collecting data on HTTP request latencies, error rates, and resource utilization.

- **Auto-scaling with Metrics:** Custom Horizontal Pod Autoscalers (HPAs) were configured to respond to Prometheus metrics, scaling services based on concurrent request volumes and CPU usage, thus maintaining performance during traffic spikes.

- **Visualization and Reporting:** Grafana dashboards enabled real-time monitoring of key metrics, utilizing time-series plots and alert panels to present clear operational status.

```
{
  "title": "Service Health Dashboard",
  "panels": [
    {
      "title": "HTTP Request Latency",
      "type": "graph",
      "targets": [
        {
          "expr": "histogram_quantile(0.90, sum(rate(
              http_request_duration_seconds_bucket[5m])) by (le))",
          "legendFormat": "Latency - 90th percentile"
        }
      ]
    },
    {
      "title": "Autoscaling Trigger Events",
      "type": "stat",
      "targets": [
        {
          "expr": "increase(hpa_scale_replicas_total[1h])"
        }
      ]
    }
  ]
}
```

Outcome: The capabilities provided by integrated monitoring tools allowed for real-time alerts and dynamic resource scaling. The system maintained uptime during high-demand periods, significantly reducing user-perceived latency and preventing service crashes. Incident response times decreased by 50% compared to prior seasons due to the advanced alerting and visualization techniques implemented.

Case Study 2: Financial Services Firm's Regulatory Compliance Monitoring

253

Background: A financial services enterprise required its Knative-powered trading platform to adhere strictly to regulatory compliance and enhanced security monitoring, ensuring all transactions are traceable and conform to prescribed laws.

Challenges:

- Ensuring end-to-end traceability of transactions.

- Real-time anomaly detection for suspicious activities.

- Compliance with financial regulations like Basel III.

Solution: Through integration with third-party monitoring and observability software, New Relic, the firm gained robust transaction monitoring capabilities, using distributed tracing and AI-powered anomaly detection to secure operations.

Implementation Steps:

- **Agent Deployment:** Installed New Relic APM agents across all Knative microservices, deploying distributed tracing automatically to monitor each transaction's life cycle.

- **Fraud Detection:** Established anomaly detection patterns within New Relic, identifying atypical transaction behaviors, such as large transaction values or unusual transaction times.

- **Compliance Dashboards:** Created dashboards specific to compliance reporting, providing real-time visibility into transaction metrics aligned with financial regulatory requirements.

```
{
  "title": "Regulatory Compliance Dashboard",
  "widgets": [
    {
      "title": "Transaction Volumes",
      "visual": "line",
      "query": "SELECT rate(count(*), 1 minute) FROM Transaction WHERE
          appName='trading-service'"
    },
    {
      "title": "Anomaly Alerts",
      "visual": "alerts",
      "query": "SELECT * FROM AnomalyDetection WHERE category='transaction'"
    }
  ]
}
```

Outcome: The financial firm achieved a robust monitoring architecture capable of ensuring compliance mandates. New Relic's advanced analytics detected and reported anomalies flagging questionable activities promptly, maintaining transactional transparency and security. Regulatory audits reported compliance satisfaction, and incident response protocols showed a 60% improvement in efficiency.

Case Study 3: Healthcare Application's SLA Management

Background: A healthcare provider leveraging Knative for their patient management software must ensure strict adherence to service level agreements (SLAs) amidst a sprawling application backend integrated with numerous third-party services for ongoing operations.

Challenges:

- Managing downtime minimization to meet healthcare uptime standards.

- Accurate root cause analysis of SLA breaches.

- Efficient communication of performance metrics to clients.

Solution: The provider utilized Datadog's full spectrum monitoring capabilities to track performance against SLA targets and facilitate rapid incident response.

```
:-
description: "Simulated SLA Monitoring Example"
services:
  - name: "patient-api"
    sla: "99.99%"
    monitors:
      latency: "max:0.3"
      uptime: "min:99.99"
  - name: "appointment-scheduler"
    sla: "99.95%"
    monitors:
      error_rate: "max:1%"
```

Implementation Steps:

- **Latency Analysis:** Set up latency and degradation monitors through Datadog to automatically alert teams when SLA-defined thresholds were breached.

- **Outage Simulation:** Conducted simulated outage scenarios to test alerting and response protocols, ensuring SLA adherence even in unforeseen circumstances.

- **Stakeholder Reporting:** Developed automated reports and dashboards summarizing SLA status, incident occurrences, and root cause analyses, distributed to stakeholders on a scheduled basis.

Outcome: The deployment and integration of Datadog substantially reduced SLA violations, with defined alert policies ensuring uptime and performance met healthcare commitments. In essence, these improvements conferred reliability and transparency in the delivery of critical healthcare services, fostering trust within the client base.

Learnings and Conclusion

Each case study underscores the importance of a tailored approach to monitoring, factoring in organizational requirements, business objectives, and compliance mandates. A robust monitoring strategy reveals performance insights, enables rapid incident response, and aligns operations with broader business goals.

The successful integration of observability tools also highlights how well-educated teams, equipped with sophisticated visualization and analytics capabilities, can enhance service delivery and operational resilience. By building upon these frameworks, businesses operating within cloud-native paradigms like Knative can continue to navigate an ever-changing digital landscape, and convert observability into a strategic asset that drives sustained growth and innovation.

Chapter 9

Security and Best Practices in Knative Applications

This chapter addresses the security framework of Knative, identifying potential risks inherent in serverless architectures. It outlines strategies for implementing robust identity and access management to safeguard resources. Techniques for securing network communications, including the use of HTTPS and service mesh security features, are discussed. The chapter provides best practices for ensuring data protection and confidentiality in Knative applications, along with methods for safely managing secrets and configurations. Compliance requirements and the importance of audit logging in security maintenance are explored. Additionally, the chapter offers guidance on evaluating and mitigating security vulnerabilities specific to Knative environments.

9.1   Understanding Security in Knative

The architecture of Knative, a Kubernetes-based platform for deploying and managing serverless functions, brings unique security considerations. Understanding the security model of Knative involves analyzing how its components interact with one another and understanding the specific risks associated with serverless architectures. Knative extends Kubernetes with features such as serving and eventing, which require careful security analysis.

A fundamental aspect of security in Knative involves securing the components that handle code execution, network traffic, and data storage. This section explores these components' inherent vulnerabilities and the implications of operating Knative in dynamic environments.

Knative Security Architecture

Knative leverages Kubernetes' inherent security model and builds upon it by providing frameworks for automated scaling and event-driven processing. The modular design of Knative consists of components with distinct roles:

- **Knative Serving**: Manages the deployment of serverless services, autoscaling, and network routing.

- **Knative Eventing**: Facilitates the creation and consumption of events, enabling event-driven application architectures.

- **Knative Build**: (Note: As of Knative version 0.8, this component has been deprecated in favor of Tekton Pipelines for CI/CD tasks.)

Security challenges in these components pertain to authentication, authorization, data integrity, and protection against potential threats such as unauthorized access and injection attacks.

Authentication and Authorization in Knative

Authentication in Knative ensures that only verified entities can access or modify services. Knative typically relies on underlying Kubernetes authentication mechanisms, which may include mechanisms such as API tokens, OAuth, OpenID, and client certificates. To configure authentication in Knative, it is recommended to implement mutual TLS

258

(mTLS) and leverage Kubernetes' native Role-Based Access Control (RBAC) to define fine-grained access policies.

Enabling mTLS in Knative

To establish a secure channel using mTLS for a Knative service, it is essential to configure the appropriate Ingress settings. Below is an example configuration using Istio for enabling mTLS in a Knative service:

```
apiVersion: networking.istio.io/v1alpha3
kind: DestinationRule
metadata:
  name: example-rule
spec:
  host: example-service.default.svc.cluster.local
  trafficPolicy:
    tls:
      mode: ISTIO_MUTUAL
```

In this example, the destination rule specifies mutual authentication for the example-service in the default namespace using Istio's mutual TLS mode.

Potential Risks in Serverless Architectures

Operating in a serverless environment poses specific risks related to the ephemeral nature of function instances. Common risks include:

- **Function Misconfiguration**: Inadvertent misconfigurations can lead to vulnerabilities, such as overly permissive access or exposure of sensitive environment variables.

- **Data Exfiltration**: Improper handling of data and insufficient encryption mechanisms can result in unauthorized data access.

- **Execution Isolation Flaws**: Shared runtimes may expose attack vectors allowing container breakout and inter-function interference.

Ensuring separation between functions and strict network policies helps mitigate these risks. It's advisable to follow the principle of least privilege and to utilize network policies to restrict communication only to necessary services.

Knative and Network Security

In Knative, securing network communications involves leveraging service mesh capabilities to secure traffic at the application layer. Istio is commonly deployed alongside Knative to manage ingress and egress traffic with traffic control rules.

Traffic Control with Istio

Traffic management in Knative should ensure that only authorized traffic reaches the deployed services. Here is an example of a VirtualService configuration using Istio:

```
apiVersion: networking.istio.io/v1alpha3
kind: VirtualService
metadata:
  name: example-route
spec:
  hosts:
  - example-service.example-ns.svc.cluster.local
  http:
  - match:
    - uri:
        prefix: "/secure-path"
    route:
    - destination:
        host: example-service.example-ns.svc.cluster.local
```

This configuration directs traffic to the example-service service only when the request URI matches a specific pattern, enhancing security by using precise routing rules.

Vulnerabilities in Event-Driven Systems

Knative Eventing introduces additional vectors for security within event-driven architectures. Event data loads must be sanitized to prevent injection attacks and secure against denial-of-service scenarios. Employing content validation techniques and rate limiting can reduce the risk associated with untrusted data sources.

Consider an example of employing rate limiting in Knative to protect against floods of events:

```
apiVersion: networking.istio.io/v1alpha3
kind: EnvoyFilter
metadata:
  name: example-rate-limit
spec:
  workloadSelector:
    labels:
      app: example-service
  configPatches:
  - applyTo: HTTP_FILTER
```

```
match:
  context: SIDECAR_INBOUND
  listener:
    portNumber: 8080
    filterChain:
      filter:
        name: "envoy.filters.network.http_connection_manager"
patch:
  operation: INSERT_BEFORE
  value:
    name: envoy.filters.http.ratelimit
    typed_config:
      "@type": type.googleapis.com/envoy.extensions.filters.http.ratelimit.v3.
        RateLimit
      domain: "example-service"
      failure_mode_deny: true
```

This configuration applies rate limiting by using the envoy.filters.http.ratelimit for services annotated with the label app: example-service, ensuring that the service is not overwhelmed by excessive requests.

Understanding security in Knative involves integrating Kubernetes security principles with enhanced configurations specific to Knative's capabilities, such as autoscaling and event-driven processing. Leveraging robust authentication and authorization schemes, securing inter-service communications, and addressing potential vulnerabilities in serverless environments are critical considerations. By employing best practices for securing Knative components and components' interactions within the broader ecosystem, it is possible to mitigate risks and maintain secure, efficient serverless applications.

9.2 Identity and Access Management

Identity and Access Management (IAM) is a critical component of ensuring the security and reliability of applications deployed with Knative. Effective IAM strategies help prevent unauthorized access to sensitive resources and services by enforcing rigorous verification and access control measures. Maintaining robust IAM in Knative involves utilizing Kubernetes' native capabilities augmented with policies that align with business objectives and regulatory requirements.

Overview of IAM in Knative

IAM involves two primary components: authentication and authorization. Authentication verifies the identity of users or services attempting to interact with the Knative environment, while authorization determines the scope of actions that authenticated identities are allowed to perform.

In the Knative ecosystem, IAM is inherently dependent on Kubernetes since Knative operates as an extension of Kubernetes. IAM implementations leverage several Kubernetes constructs, such as Role-Based Access Control (RBAC), policies, and service accounts, integrated with Knative-specific configurations to achieve precise control over identities and permissions.

Authenticating in Knative

Authentication in Knative often relies on existing Kubernetes authentication mechanisms. This means integrating external identity providers or Kubernetes' built-in authentication methods to authenticate users or services interacting with Knative components.

External Identity Providers

Using external identity providers allows organizations to manage user identities in a centralized manner. Common providers include LDAP, OAuth2, OpenID Connect (OIDC), and SAML. Kubernetes clusters can be configured to delegate authentication to these providers, aligning with organizational standards.

To set up authentication using OpenID Connect with a Kubernetes cluster:

```
kubectl config set-credentials oidc-user --auth-provider=oidc \
--auth-provider-arg=idp-issuer-url=https://accounts.google.com \
--auth-provider-arg=client-id=client_id_here \
--auth-provider-arg=client-secret=client_secret_here \
--auth-provider-arg=refresh-token=refresh_token_here
```

This example configures a Kubernetes context to authenticate using OpenID Connect against Google's identity platform.

Service-to-Service Authentication

For authenticating services within Knative, mutual TLS (mTLS) is leveraged to ensure secure service-to-service communication. The use of service mesh solutions, such as Istio, provides easy management and implementation of mTLS.

Here is a sample configuration to enable mTLS between Knative services:

```
apiVersion: networking.istio.io/v1beta1
kind: PeerAuthentication
metadata:
  name: default
spec:
  mtls:
    mode: STRICT
```

This example configures a strict mTLS mode, ensuring that all service communications are encrypted and require mutual authentication.

Authorization in Knative

Authorization in Knative largely relies on Kubernetes Role-Based Access Control (RBAC). RBAC allows administrators to specify who can perform what actions on which resources. In Knative, it is crucial to secure access to services, routes, and configurations carefully, given that these are critical for application logic.

Implementing RBAC in Knative

Consider a scenario where we need to define specific access for a Knative service. Here's an example of creating a role with limited permissions:

```
apiVersion: rbac.authorization.k8s.io/v1
kind: Role
metadata:
  namespace: example-namespace
  name: knative-service-reader
rules:
- apiGroups: ["serving.knative.dev"]
  resources: ["services"]
  verbs: ["get", "list"]
```

Next, bind the role to a specific user or system account:

```
apiVersion: rbac.authorization.k8s.io/v1
kind: RoleBinding
metadata:
  name: read-services
  namespace: example-namespace
subjects:
- kind: ServiceAccount
  name: specific-user
  namespace: example-namespace
roleRef:
  kind: Role
  name: knative-service-reader
```

```
apiGroup: rbac.authorization.k8s.io
```

In this configuration, the role knative-service-reader is bound to a service account named specific-user, granting get and list permissions on Knative services within example-namespace.

Fine-Grained Access Control

Beyond RBAC, more granular access can be implemented using policies such as Pod Security Policies (PSPs), Network Policies, and Custom Resource Definitions (CRDs). These can be crafted to enforce specific security constraints within a Knative deployment, such as requiring specific labels on resources or controlling egress traffic from pods.

Here is an example of a network policy to restrict access:

```
apiVersion: networking.k8s.io/v1
kind: NetworkPolicy
metadata:
  name: restrict-egress
  namespace: example-namespace
spec:
  podSelector:
    matchLabels:
      app: knative-app
  policyTypes:
  - Ingress
  - Egress
  egress:
  - to:
    - ipBlock:
        cidr: 10.0.0.0/24
```

This policy restricts egress traffic for pods labeled with app: knative-app to a specified CIDR range, enhancing security by limiting outgoing traffic.

Multi-Tenancy Considerations

In environments where multiple tenants operate within the same Knative cluster, ensuring isolation becomes paramount. Besides using namespaces to segregate tenant resources, careful configuration of IAM policies is necessary to prevent resource cross-access among tenants.

Robust Identity and Access Management within Knative environments is essential to prevent unauthorized access and ensure the integrity of serverless applications. Leveraging Kubernetes' RBAC, integrating with external identity providers, employing mTLS for secure communications, and implementing fine-grained policies contribute to a comprehensive IAM strategy adapted for the dynamic nature of serverless computing with Knative.

9.3 Securing Network Communications

Securing network communications is a vital aspect of deploying and managing applications in Knative, as it ensures data integrity, confidentiality, and authentication of entities interacting within and outside the cluster. The dynamic and distributed nature of serverless architectures like Knative mandates a comprehensive approach to securing communication paths, both intra-cluster and external.

Network security in Knative encompasses the implementation of encryption protocols, authentication mechanisms, and access controls. It involves utilizing Kubernetes network policies and service mesh technologies to enhance security at multiple levels.

Transport Layer Security (TLS)

TLS is fundamental to securing communications in Knative environments. TLS provides confidentiality and integrity by encrypting data transmitted over networks and verifying the authenticity of communicating parties. Configuring TLS in Knative involves setting up secure ingress configurations and using service meshes to automatically manage certificate issuance and renewal.

Securing Ingress Traffic with HTTPS

Setting up secure ingress traffic with HTTPS ensures that communications from external clients to Knative services are encrypted. It involves configuring Kubernetes Ingress resources with TLS certificates, typically managed with solutions like Cert-Manager, which automates the issuance and renewal of certificates.

Below is an example of securing ingress traffic using HTTPS in Knative by setting up an Ingress resource with Cert-Manager:

```
apiVersion: networking.k8s.io/v1
kind: Ingress
metadata:
  name: example-https-ingress
```

```
  annotations:
    cert-manager.io/issuer: "letsencrypt-prod"
spec:
  rules:
  - host: knative.example.com
    http:
      paths:
      - path: /
        pathType: Prefix
        backend:
          service:
            name: example-service
            port:
              number: 80
  tls:
  - hosts:
    - knative.example.com
    secretName: example-tls-secret
```

This configuration ensures that traffic to knative.example.com is encrypted using TLS, with certificates managed by Cert-Manager via Let's Encrypt.

Service Mesh Security with Istio

Istio, a popular service mesh, enhances Knative's network security by providing functionality for mutual TLS, traffic encryption, and access policies. It facilitates end-to-end communication security without requiring changes to application code.

Implementing mTLS with Istio in Knative enforces secure communication between services, ensuring that all data transmitted within the cluster is encrypted and that services authenticate each other.

To enable mTLS for all services in a namespace, use the following Peer-Authentication configuration:

```
apiVersion: security.istio.io/v1beta1
kind: PeerAuthentication
metadata:
  name: default
  namespace: example-namespace
spec:
  mtls:
    mode: STRICT
```

This configuration ensures that any traffic within the example-namespace is required to use mTLS, thereby assuring both ends of the communication are authenticated and trusted.

Ingress Gateway Configuration in Istio

The Istio Ingress Gateway is an entry point for external traffic into the service mesh. Configuring secure ingress through the Istio Ingress Gateway involves defining secure Gateway and VirtualService resources:

```
apiVersion: networking.istio.io/v1beta1
kind: Gateway
metadata:
  name: https-gateway
spec:
  selector:
    istio: ingressgateway
  servers:
  - port:
      number: 443
      name: https
      protocol: HTTPS
    tls:
      mode: SIMPLE
      credentialName: example-credential
    hosts:
    - "knative.example.com"
---
apiVersion: networking.istio.io/v1beta1
kind: VirtualService
metadata:
  name: example-service-vs
spec:
  hosts:
  - "knative.example.com"
  gateways:
  - https-gateway
  http:
  - match:
    - uri:
        prefix: "/"
    route:
    - destination:
        host: example-service
        port:
          number: 80
```

The gateway listens for HTTPS traffic on port 443 and routes it according to the VirtualService definition, ensuring secure routes to the intended services using configured credentials.

Network Policies and Access Control

Network policies in Kubernetes provide a way to enforce rules about which pods can communicate with each other and with external services. By default, Kubernetes allows unrestricted communication between pods; however, implementing network policies allows cluster administrators to restrict unnecessary communications, thereby improving security.

Here is an example of a NetworkPolicy that restricts pod access based on labels:

```
apiVersion: networking.k8s.io/v1
kind: NetworkPolicy
metadata:
  name: deny-all-except-frontend
  namespace: example-namespace
spec:
  podSelector: {}
  policyTypes:
  - Ingress
  ingress:
  - from:
    - podSelector:
        matchLabels:
          role: frontend
```

This policy restricts pod ingress traffic to only those with the role: frontend label, thereby enforcing controlled access paths within the network.

Best Practices for Securing Network Communications

Effective network security in Knative requires a layered approach by integrating multiple technologies and practices:

- **Use Strong Encryption Protocols**: Always employ the latest cryptographic standards to protect data in transit. Regularly update and manage certificates appropriately.

- **Implement Zero Trust Policies**: Mandate authentication and authorization checks for all communications, both internal and external.

- **Regularly Audit Security Configurations**: Continuously monitor and audit network configurations to detect anomalies or unauthorized changes.

- **Leverage Automation Tools**: Employ tools like Istio and Cert-Manager to automatically manage and renew certificates, thereby reducing manual errors and ensuring consistent security states.

268

By adopting these practices, organizations can efficiently secure network communications in Knative environments, protecting sensitive data flows and maintaining robust application security.

Network communication security in Knative, built upon Kubernetes, requires comprehensive planning and execution. Implementing TLS, utilizing service meshes like Istio, enforcing network policies, and adopting best practices ensures secure and reliable communications, critical for protecting modern serverless applications.

9.4 Protecting Application and User Data

In serverless architectures, ensuring the protection of application and user data is a key security concern. Knative, as a platform for managing serverless deployments on Kubernetes, must incorporate comprehensive data protection strategies to guard against data breaches, unauthorized access, and ensure compliance with data privacy regulations. This section explores best practices and mechanisms to secure both application and user data within Knative environments.

Data Encryption

Data encryption is fundamental to protecting sensitive data, both in transit and at rest. Encrypting data ensures that even if it is intercepted or accessed without authorization, it cannot be easily read or misused. Encryption in Knative extends across multiple layers including network communication, data storage, and application-level data processing.

1. Encryption in Transit

Encryption in transit safeguards data as it moves across networks. Utilizing HTTPS and TLS protocols ensures that data exchanged between clients and services, as well as between services within the cluster, is encrypted. Configuring HTTPS for ingress using certificates and leveraging service mesh technologies like Istio facilitates transport-level encryption with minimal impact on application code.

```
apiVersion: networking.k8s.io/v1
kind: Ingress
```

```
metadata:
  name: app-ingress
  annotations:
    cert-manager.io/cluster-issuer: "letsencrypt-prod"
spec:
  tls:
  - hosts:
    - app.example.com
    secretName: app-tls
  rules:
  - host: app.example.com
    http:
      paths:
      - path: /
        pathType: Prefix
        backend:
          service:
            name: app-service
            port:
              number: 80
```

This configuration facilitates secure communication by enforcing HTTPS through a TLS secret managed by Cert-Manager and Let's Encrypt.

2. Encryption at Rest

Securing data at rest involves encrypting data stored in databases, object storage, or within persistent volumes used by applications. Deploying encryption mechanisms offered by cloud service providers or integrating libraries and tools for encryption ensures that data remains secure when not in motion.

For instance, Kubernetes supports encrypting secrets data at rest using encryption keys managed by a provider like AWS KMS, GCP Cloud KMS, or Azure Key Vault. Here's a simplified example of configuring at-rest encryption:

```
apiVersion: apiserver.config.k8s.io/v1
kind: EncryptionConfiguration
resources:
- resources:
  - secrets
  providers:
  - kms:
      name: example-kms
      endpoint: unix:///var/lib/kms-provider.sock
  - identity: {}
```

This configuration encrypts Kubernetes secrets using an external Key Management Service (KMS) provider.

Access Control and Authentication

Restricting access to sensitive data is crucial for maintaining data security. Implementing robust authentication and authorization mechanisms ensures that only authorized entities can access or manipulate data.

1. OAuth and OpenID Connect for Authentication

Implementing OAuth2 and OpenID Connect protocols allows Knative services to authenticate users using external identity providers, effectively managing user identity and access control. These protocols facilitate highly secure user authentication and can be integrated into microservices architecture within Knative deployments.

```
apiVersion: apps/v1
kind: Deployment
metadata:
  name: oauth2-proxy
spec:
  replicas: 1
  selector:
    matchLabels:
      app: oauth2-proxy
  template:
    metadata:
      labels:
        app: oauth2-proxy
    spec:
      containers:
      - image: quay.io/oauth2-proxy/oauth2-proxy:v7.1.3
        name: oauth2-proxy
        args:
        - --provider=google
        - --email-domain=example.com
        - --upstream=http://127.0.0.1:8080
```

This setup ensures that the application only allows access to authenticated users through the OAuth2 proxy.

2. Role-Based Access Control (RBAC)

Kubernetes RBAC allows precise definition of users' and services' access to APIs and resources, effectively enforcing the least privilege principle. In Knative, this requires setting roles and bindings that align with application security requirements.

```
apiVersion: rbac.authorization.k8s.io/v1
kind: Role
metadata:
  namespace: app-namespace
```

271

```
  name: app-role
rules:
- apiGroups: [""]
  resources: ["pods", "services"]
  verbs: ["get", "list", "watch"]

---

kind: RoleBinding
apiVersion: rbac.authorization.k8s.io/v1
metadata:
  name: app-role-binding
  namespace: app-namespace
subjects:
- kind: ServiceAccount
  name: app-service-account
  namespace: app-namespace
roleRef:
  kind: Role
  name: app-role
  apiGroup: rbac.authorization.k8s.io
```

This example binds a role with permissions to list and watch pods and services to a specific application service account, limiting its access scope to what is necessary.

Data Integrity and Validation

Ensuring data integrity involves implementing strategies for validation, error-checking, and using cryptographic hash functions to verify data.

1. Input Validation and Sanitization

Validation of data inputs at all layers, from user interfaces to service interfaces, is critical. This prevents external entities from injecting malicious data. Use validation libraries and sanitize inputs to mitigate risks of SQL injection, cross-site scripting (XSS), and other common vulnerabilities.

```python
import re

def validate_input(user_input):
    if not re.match("^[a-zA-Z0-9_]*$", user_input):
        raise ValueError("Invalid input!")

user_input = "test123"
validate_input(user_input)
```

This Python function validates input, preventing non-alphanumeric characters to safeguard against injection attacks.

2. Integrity Checks

Implement digital signatures and hash functions to verify data integrity and detect unauthorized modifications.

```
import hmac
import hashlib

message = b"Trust this message"
secret = b'secret_key'

h = hmac.new(secret, message, digestmod=hashlib.sha256)
signature = h.hexdigest()
```

This uses HMAC to ensure message authenticity and integrity. If the data or the secret changes, the signature will not match, indicating a potential breach in integrity.

Compliance and Data Privacy

Data privacy regulations such as GDPR impose stringent requirements on how user data is collected, processed, and stored. Ensuring compliance necessitates implementing appropriate technical and organizational measures within Knative ecosystems.

Organizations should adopt privacy-by-design principles and ensure transparent data practices. This includes obtaining explicit consent from users for data collection, providing options for data modification or deletion, and maintaining up-to-date records of data processing activities.

Dynamic data masking, tokenization, and anonymization are techniques commonly employed to protect personal identifiable information (PII) within applications, minimizing risk exposure and supporting compliance with regulations.

Protecting application and user data in Knative focuses on implementing encryption, access controls, validation mechanisms, and compliance strategies. Ensuring robust security for data at rest, in transit, and during processing helps safeguard against breaches, ensures user trust, and meets regulatory requirements. Organizations must continuously adapt and refine their data protection strategies to address evolving cybersecurity landscapes and maintain the integrity and confidentiality of their systems.

9.5 Managing Secrets and Configuration

Effective management of secrets and configuration in Knative applications is crucial for maintaining security and operational efficiency. Secrets typically include sensitive information such as passwords, API keys, and encryption keys, while configuration encompasses settings and parameters that can change without requiring changes to application code. This section delves into approaches and tools for securely handling secrets and configuration within Knative deployments.

Understanding Secrets and Configuration Management

Secrets management focuses on securing sensitive data needed by applications, ensuring they're not exposed inadvertently or unauthorized users gain access. Configuration management involves handling non-sensitive data that dictates application behavior and environment-specific settings.

Traditional approaches that involve hardcoding or embedding such information directly in application code or configuration files pose significant security risks. Instead, by employing dynamic secret and configuration management strategies, these risks can be mitigated.

Kubernetes Secrets

Kubernetes provides a native mechanism for managing sensitive information through Secret objects that allow storage and management of sensitive data in base64-encoded format. These secret objects can then be mounted as volumes or exposed as environment variables to Knative applications.

```
apiVersion: v1
kind: Secret
metadata:
  name: db-secret
  namespace: example-namespace
type: Opaque
data:
  username: c2VjdXJlVXNlcg==
  password: c2VjdXJlUGFzcw==
```

In this example, db-secret contains a base64-encoded username and password that can be used by a Knative application to authenticate with an external database.

Using Secrets in Knative Services

Knative services can securely access Kubernetes secrets by configuring the service's environment variables or volumes to reference secret data. When using environment variables, the secrets are consumed by the application, while maintaining the modularity and agility of the system.

```
apiVersion: serving.knative.dev/v1
kind: Service
metadata:
  name: secure-service
  namespace: example-namespace
spec:
  template:
    spec:
      containers:
      - image: gcr.io/example/secure-app
        env:
        - name: DB_USERNAME
          valueFrom:
            secretKeyRef:
              name: db-secret
              key: username
        - name: DB_PASSWORD
          valueFrom:
            secretKeyRef:
              name: db-secret
              key: password
```

The above Knative service configuration securely accesses the db-secret to set environment variables DB_USERNAME and DB_PASSWORD.

Security Best Practices for Kubernetes Secrets

To further enhance the security of secrets managed by Kubernetes, several best practices should be adhered to:

- **Encryption at Rest**: Use an encryption provider to encrypt secrets stored in etcd. This can be configured through Kubernetes' EncryptionConfiguration, ensuring secrets are safeguarded even from administrative access to the underlying storage.

- **Least Privilege Access**: Apply the least privilege principle by restricting access to secrets using Kubernetes' RBAC, ensuring only authorized service accounts have access.

- **Regular Rotation**: Perform regular secret rotation to minimize the risk arising from secret compromise. Use automation tools to

275

update deployed applications with new secrets seamlessly.

- **Audit and Monitoring**: Continuously audit access and usage of secrets. Implement monitoring tools alerting on unexpected access patterns.

Advanced Secret Management with External Tools

While Kubernetes Secrets provides a convenient way to manage application secrets, additional security layers can be achieved by integrating with external secret management solutions like HashiCorp Vault, AWS Secrets Manager, Azure Key Vault, or Google Cloud Secret Manager.

Integrating HashiCorp Vault with Knative

Vault provides a centralized, secure way to handle dynamic secrets, encrypt data, and control access. Integrating Vault with Knative involves setting up a Vault server, creating policies, and configuring applications to access secrets through Vault's API.

To use Vault with a Knative application, configure the Vault injector to automatically fetch secrets at runtime:

```
apiVersion: serving.knative.dev/v1
kind: Service
metadata:
  name: vault-enabled-service
  namespace: example-namespace
  annotations:
    vault.hashicorp.com/agent-inject: "true"
    vault.hashicorp.com/role: "example-role"
    vault.hashicorp.com/secret-path: "secret/data/db"
spec:
  template:
    metadata:
      annotations:
        vault.hashicorp.com/agent-inject-secret-info: "secret/data/db"
    spec:
      containers:
      - image: gcr.io/example/vault-app
```

In this setup, the Vault Injector Pod utility automatically injects secrets into the application, obviating the need for manual secret handling.

Configuration Management for Knative Services

Handling configuration in Knative involves separating configuration data from application logic to facilitate flexibility and scalability. Kubernetes' ConfigMaps are utilized to manage non-sensitive configura-

276

tion data.

```
apiVersion: v1
kind: ConfigMap
metadata:
  name: app-config
  namespace: example-namespace
data:
  log_level: "debug"
  feature_enabled: "true"
```

This ConfigMap contains configuration settings used to influence application behavior.

Using ConfigMaps in Knative Applications

Knative applications can access configuration data stored in ConfigMaps either directly through environment variables or by mounting configuration files.

```
apiVersion: serving.knative.dev/v1
kind: Service
metadata:
  name: config-service
  namespace: example-namespace
spec:
  template:
    spec:
      containers:
      - image: gcr.io/example/config-app
        env:
        - name: LOG_LEVEL
          valueFrom:
            configMapKeyRef:
              name: app-config
              key: log_level
        - name: FEATURE_ENABLED
          valueFrom:
            configMapKeyRef:
              name: app-config
              key: feature_enabled
```

This approach allows the application to dynamically adjust its operations based on configurations injected at runtime.

Configuration Management Best Practices

Similar to secrets, managing configuration data securely and efficiently requires certain best practices:

- **Version Control**: Version control is crucial for maintaining the history of configuration changes. Tools like Git ensure reversible

277

and auditable changes to configuration settings.

- **Environment-Specific Configurations**: Maintain separate configurations for different environments (e.g., development, testing, production) to avoid accidental configurations in unsuitable contexts.

- **Dynamic Reloading**: Enable applications to reload configuration changes at runtime without downtime, improving agility.

- **Centralized Configuration Management**: Use centralized tools and services to manage distributed configurations, adjusting them rapidly across environments and deployments.

Managing secrets and configurations in Knative requires leveraging Kubernetes native capabilities and integrating advanced external tools to enhance security and operational flexibility. Securely managing this information ensures that applications operate efficiently and reduce the risk of unauthorized access or accidental leaks. Organizations must adopt structured strategies around secret rotation, least privilege principles, and continuous monitoring to maintain their secure and agile application environments effectively.

9.6 Compliance and Audit Logging

Compliance and audit logging are critical components in the management of Knative applications, particularly in environments governed by stringent regulatory requirements such as GDPR, HIPAA, or PCI-DSS. Implementing robust logging strategies not only aids in compliance but also enhances security monitoring and operational transparency. This section explores how to effectively implement compliance and audit logging within Knative.

Understanding Compliance Requirements

Compliance regulations often mandate organizations to maintain detailed logs of system activities, access patterns, and data usage to ensure accountability and detect any anomalies promptly. In serverless environments like Knative, compliance logging should capture every interaction within the platform, including user actions, workload activities, and system events.

- **GDPR (General Data Protection Regulation)**: GDPR emphasizes data privacy and protection for individuals within the EU. Compliance requires maintaining logs that track data processing activities, storing logs securely, and ensuring access logging.

- **HIPAA (Health Insurance Portability and Accountability Act)**: For healthcare sectors, HIPAA compliance involves logging access to protected health information (PHI) and ensuring the confidentiality, integrity, and availability of electronic PHI.

- **PCI-DSS (Payment Card Industry Data Security Standard)**: PCI-DSS mandates comprehensive logging of all access to network resources and cardholder data, requiring storage and retrieval capabilities for audit purposes.

Ensuring compliance within Knative involves configuring logging mechanisms at both Kubernetes and Knative layers to capture the necessary details.

Audit Logging in Kubernetes

Kubernetes provides native support for audit logging, capturing critical data about operations on the cluster. It includes details such as "who did what" on the platform, enabling detailed tracking of API requests.

To enable audit logging, configure a policy file specifying the events to capture:

```
apiVersion: audit.k8s.io/v1
kind: Policy
rules:
- level: Metadata
  resources:
  - group: ""
    resources: ["pods", "services"]
    verbs: ["create", "delete", "update"]
```

This policy logs metadata-level information for 'create', 'delete', and 'update' operations on pods and services, providing sufficient detail for audit purposes while minimizing resource consumption.

279

Audit logs are typically written to files or external logging solutions for easy storage and retrieval:

```
--audit-policy-file=/etc/kubernetes/audit-policy.yaml
--audit-log-path=/var/log/kubernetes/apiserver/audit.log
--audit-log-maxage=30
--audit-log-maxbackup=10
--audit-log-maxsize=100
```

These flags configure where audit logs are saved, their retention policy, and the log rotation strategy.

Implementing Audit Logging in Knative

Knative itself doesn't directly provide auditing features; however, it relies on Kubernetes capabilities in conjunction with logging add-ons. Incorporating a service mesh like Istio can enhance visibility by logging network traffic, making it possible to capture communication patterns and access logs.

Integrating Logging Add-ons

Tools such as Fluentd, Prometheus, and Loki are often used to gather, process, and analyze logs generated from Kubernetes and Knative applications.

- **Fluentd**: Fluentd aggregates logs from containerized applications, forwarding them to external storage or analysis systems.

- **Prometheus**: While primarily a monitoring tool, Prometheus gathers metrics data that can be useful in understanding operation logs.

- **Loki**: A log aggregation system that integrates seamlessly with Prometheus, providing a query language for searching logs.

Here's an example of configuring Fluentd within a Knative environment:

```
<source>
  @type tail
  path /var/log/containers/*.log
  pos_file /var/log/fluentd-containers.log.pos
  tag kubernetes.*
  <parse>
    @type json
    time_key time
```

```
    time_format %Y-%m-%dT%H:%M:%S
  </parse>
</source>

<match kubernetes.**>
  @type forward
  <server>
    host logs.example.org
    port 24224
  </server>
</match>
```

This configuration reads container logs and forwards them to a centralized logging service, facilitating comprehensive log storage and monitoring.

Compliance Logging Best Practices

Adhering to best practices ensures that compliance and audit logging effectively meet regulatory requirements and organizational needs:

- **Log Location and Access**: Store logs in secure and tamper-proof systems to prevent unauthorized access. Implement access controls to ensure only authorized users can view and analyze logs.

- **Log Retention and Purging**: Retain logs for a period mandated by compliance regulations. Implement automated purging strategies to maintain a manageable log storage footprint.

- **Real-time Monitoring and Alerts**: Utilize data analytics to monitor logs in real-time and configure alerts for any suspicious activity. Implement tools that provide insights into usage patterns and unusual behaviors.

- **Regular Log Audits**: Schedule routine audits of logs to ensure they conform to compliance standards and verify the integrity and completeness of logs.

- **Distributed Log Collection**: Deploy logging agents across all nodes and services to ensure comprehensive log collection from every area of the cluster.

Implementing these practices minimizes the likelihood of untracked security incidents, ensuring that logs serve not only compliance needs but are also an integral part of the organization's security posture.

Building a Compliance and Security Culture

Successfully embedding compliance and audit logging into the operational framework of Knative requires cultivating a culture of security and compliance within the organization. This can be achieved through:

- **Policy Development**: Develop and disseminate clear policies highlighting the importance of logging and compliance. Include specific guidelines and protocols to be followed by personnel at all levels.

- **Training and Awareness Programs**: Conduct regular training sessions and awareness campaigns to ensure that staff understands logging practices, compliance requirements, and how to respond to audit findings.

- **Cross-Department Collaboration**: Engage multiple departments, including IT, compliance, and legal teams, in logging and audit activities to maintain standards compliance holistically.

- **Continuous Improvement**: Strive for continuous improvement of logging capabilities by leveraging new technologies and methodologies, and learning from past audits and incidents.

Compliance and audit logging are indispensable for Knative environments, enabling organizations to maintain transparency, meet regulatory requirements, and maintain a robust security infrastructure. By implementing comprehensive logging mechanisms and adopting best practices, organizations not only safeguard their serverless applications but also build a resilient and trustworthy digital ecosystem.

9.7 Evaluating and Mitigating Security Vulnerabilities

In the rapidly evolving landscape of cloud-native applications and serverless architectures like Knative, evaluating and mitigating security vulnerabilities is critical for maintaining the integrity and reliability of applications. This section delves into strategies and methodologies for identifying, assessing, and addressing security vulnerabilities specific to Knative environments, providing a comprehensive understanding for effectively managing security risks.

Understanding Security Vulnerabilities in Knative

Before delving into mitigation strategies, it is essential to recognize the different types of vulnerabilities that may affect Knative systems:

- **Application Vulnerabilities**: Refers to flaws within the application code, such as injection vulnerabilities (SQL, NoSQL), cross-site scripting (XSS), and insecure deserialization.

- **Infrastructure Vulnerabilities**: Arises from misconfigurations or outdated components in the infrastructure stack, such as Kubernetes misconfigurations, unpatched nodes, or vulnerable Docker images.

- **Network Vulnerabilities**: Related to unsecured communication paths, such as lack of encryption, inadequate access controls, and exposure to DNS attacks.

- **Configuration Vulnerabilities**: Result from incorrect settings or improper handling of secrets and sensitive data, leading to potential leaks or unauthorized access.

Evaluating Vulnerabilities

Effective evaluation involves systematically identifying and assessing vulnerabilities to prioritize them based on impact and exploitability.

1. **Vulnerability Scanning**: Use automated scanning tools to detect known vulnerabilities in application code, container images, and configurations. Tools such as Trivy, Clair, and Anchore are commonly employed for container image vulnerability scanning.

```
trivy image gcr.io/example/secure-app:latest
```

The command above scans the specified Docker image for vulnerabilities, providing detailed information on discovered issues and their severities.

2. **Penetration Testing**: Performing manual or automated penetration testing identifies weaknesses that automated tools might

overlook, assessing an attacker's potential paths to compromise the system.

3. **Security Audits**: Engage in regular audits using comprehensive checklists that cover areas such as code quality, access controls, network configurations, and compliance measures.

4. **Threat Modeling**: Conduct threat modeling exercises during the design phase to anticipate potential attack vectors and identify weaknesses in architecture and design patterns.

Mitigating Vulnerabilities

Mitigation strategies are necessary to address and remedy identified vulnerabilities to reduce or eliminate risks. Robust security practices in Knative environments include:

- **Patch Management**: Regularly update and patch all components, from application libraries to infrastructure services, to close existing vulnerabilities. Implement automated systems to apply patches promptly.

- **Code Security Practices**: Adopt secure coding practices including input validation, output encoding, and use of safety functions and libraries. Use static and dynamic code analysis tools like SonarQube or Checkmarx to identify and rectify vulnerabilities in code.

- **Container Hardening**: Minimize the attack surface of container images by using only essential components, verifying image security, and employing tools like Docker Bench for Security for best practices.

```
docker run -it --net host --pid host --cap-add audit_control \
-v /var/lib:/var/lib \
-v /var/run/docker.sock:/var/run/docker.sock \
-v /usr/lib/systemd:/usr/lib/systemd -v /etc:/etc --label
      docker_bench_security \
docker/docker-bench-security
```

- **Configuration Management**: Implement Infrastructure as Code (IaC) using tools like Terraform or Ansible to maintain consistent security configurations and automatically provision necessary components.

284

- **Network Security Enforcements**: Use Service Mesh technologies like Istio to enforce encryption, authentication, and network policies that protect communication channels.

```
apiVersion: security.istio.io/v1beta1
kind: PeerAuthentication
metadata:
  name: service-mtls
spec:
  mtls:
    mode: STRICT
  selector:
    matchLabels:
      app: critical-app
```

- **Access Control Practices**: Leverage Kubernetes RBAC to enforce the principle of least privilege, carefully defining roles and binding them to service accounts or user groups to limit access to only necessary permissions.

- **Secrets Management**: Use secure secret management systems like HashiCorp Vault or AWS Secrets Manager to store and retrieve sensitive data, ensuring encryption both at rest and in transit.

- **Intrusion Monitoring and Incident Response**: Employ monitoring tools like Prometheus, Prometheus AlertManager, and centralized logging systems to detect suspicious activities and activate response protocols.

```
groups:
- name: security_alerts
  rules:
  - alert: UnauthorizedAccessAttempt
    expr: rate(http_requests{status_code="401"}[5m]) > 5
    for: 5m
    labels:
      severity: critical
    annotations:
      summary: "Unauthorized access attempts detected"
      description: "More than 5 unauthorized access attempts in the last 5
        minutes."
```

Policy Development and Adherence

Developing and maintaining security policies are foundational to ensuring consistent security protocols across the organization. Policies should be comprehensive, regularly reviewed, and clearly communicated to enforce secure practices.

- **Security Training**: Conduct ongoing training and awareness programs for developers, operators, and users, fostering a culture of security vigilance and responsibility.

- **Regular Policy Reviews**: Conduct regular risk assessments and audits to review policies' effectiveness, making adjustments as technology evolves and new threats emerge.

- **Documented Procedures**: Maintain up-to-date documentation on security procedures, incident response plans, and mitigation techniques to ensure rapid response and recovery.

Continuously evaluating and mitigating security vulnerabilities within Knative environments ensures the resilience and trustworthiness of applications. By integrating robust scanning tools, applying timely patches, enforcing security policies, and cultivating a security-centric culture, organizations can significantly diminish potential risks, ensuring efficient and reliable serverless operations.

Chapter 10

Case Studies and Real-World Applications of Knative

This chapter presents a series of case studies and real-world applications that highlight the versatility and effectiveness of Knative across various industries. It examines how e-commerce platforms leverage Knative for scaling during peak periods, and explores its role in real-time data processing for financial services. The chapter details the migration of legacy systems to microservices architectures using Knative and its innovative applications within IoT environments. Additionally, it showcases the automation of DevOps pipelines and the reduction of manual deployment processes through Knative. Key lessons learned and potential future trends in Knative adoption are also discussed, providing valuable insights for leveraging Knative in diverse contexts.

10.1 Overview of Knative Use Cases

Knative, an open-source platform based on Kubernetes, has revolution-ized the domain of serverless computing by providing a seamless envi-ronment for deploying and managing microservices. Its dynamic scal-ability, ease of deployment, and efficient resource management have made Knative an attractive option across various industries. In this section, we delve into the diverse use cases where Knative has been ef-fectively employed, highlighting its unique capabilities and advantages in real-world scenarios.

Knative's fundamental architecture combines two primary components: Knative Serving and Knative Eventing. Knative Serving is responsible for deploying and managing serverless workloads, while Knative Eventing allows for handling and scaling event-driven applications. The synergy between these components offers a robust platform for building scalable and event-driven applications.

In e-commerce, Knative has been pivotal in addressing the challenges of handling variable traffic patterns, especially during peak sales peri-ods. E-commerce platforms utilize Knative for its auto-scaling capabil-ities and seamless integration with existing Kubernetes-based infras-tructure. This ensures that resources are optimally allocated and man-aged, significantly enhancing the user experience during high-traffic events.

Consider a typical scenario where an e-commerce platform anticipates a surge in traffic during a holiday sale. With Knative, the platform can automatically scale its services up or down based on real-time traffic data, all without requiring manual intervention. The following code snippet illustrates how a simple Knative service might be configured to handle such scenarios. Note the use of the autoscaling.knative.dev annotation, enabling the service to dynamically adapt to traffic fluctu-ations.

```
apiVersion: serving.knative.dev/v1
kind: Service
metadata:
  name: e-commerce-service
  namespace: ecommerce
spec:
  template:
    metadata:
```

```
annotations:
  autoscaling.knative.dev/target: "50"
spec:
  containers:
  - image: docker.io/ecommerce/app:latest
    resources:
      limits:
        cpu: "1000m"
        memory: "512Mi"
```

Real-time data processing is another domain where Knative's capabilities shine, particularly in industries such as financial services that rely on timely and accurate data streams. By utilizing Knative Eventing, organizations can build sophisticated data pipelines that efficiently process streaming data, responding to events as they occur.

A financial services company might employ Knative to analyze market data streams for detecting anomalies or executing trades. Using Knative Eventing, such a system can be configured to listen to specific events, process them using microservices, and trigger further actions based on the outcomes. Here, an example configuration illustrates event source and broker setup:

```
apiVersion: sources.knative.dev/v1alpha1
kind: ApiServerSource
metadata:
  name: market-data-source
  namespace: finance
spec:
  serviceAccountName: data-reader
  mode: Reference
  sink:
    ref:
      apiVersion: eventing.knative.dev/v1
      kind: Broker
      name: default
```

Knative also supports the migration of legacy systems to modern microservices architectures. This transition is critical for organizations looking to enhance their agility and reduce deployment times. By adopting Knative, businesses can refactor their existing monolithic applications into flexible microservices, which can be developed, deployed, and scaled independently.

A legacy application, for instance, could be broken down into a set of interconnected services, each performing a specific function. Knative enables developers to manage these services easily through its Serving component, maintaining high availability and performance. Additionally, with built-in support for canary deployments, Knative simplifies the process of testing new service versions before rolling them out to production environments, as shown in the following example:

```
apiVersion: serving.knative.dev/v1
kind: Service
metadata:
  name: legacy-service
  namespace: refactor
spec:
  template:
    metadata:
      name: legacy-service-v1
      annotations:
        serving.knative.dev/rollout-duration: "15m"
    spec:
      containers:
      - image: docker.io/legacy/app:v2
      - image: docker.io/legacy/app:v1
  traffic:
  - latestRevision: true
    percent: 10
  - latestRevision: false
    percent: 90
```

In the Internet of Things (IoT) landscape, Knative's capability to manage serverless functions aligns perfectly with the need for efficient resource management in IoT solutions. Devices generating sporadic data streams necessitate a platform that can respond to a wide range of events while minimizing resource consumption. Knative addresses this need by reducing the overhead associated with maintaining idle instances and providing an elastic infrastructure that activates functions in response to demand.

Enterprises deploying IoT applications leverage Knative to process sensor data, trigger workflows, and dynamically allocate computational resources. For instance, an agricultural IoT system might use Knative to collect environmental data from a network of sensors, addressing real-time analytics requirements in energy-efficient ways.

Moreover, automation within DevOps pipelines is another key area where Knative has been advantageous. By integrating Knative with continuous integration and continuous deployment (CI/CD) tools, organizations can automate their deployment processes, ensure consistency across environments, and reduce manual errors. This automation contributes to achieving a truly agile development ecosystem, where code changes are tested, deployed, and validated seamlessly.

Developers might create Knative pipelines to automatically deploy new application versions when code changes are committed. The following example demonstrates a simple pipeline that automates the deployment and testing of a Knative service:

```
apiVersion: tekton.dev/v1beta1
kind: Pipeline
metadata:
  name: knative-deploy-pipeline
  namespace: ci-cd
spec:
  tasks:
  - name: build-image
    taskRef:
      name: kaniko
    resources:
      inputs:
        - name: source
          resource: git-repo
      outputs:
        - name: image
          resource: docker-image
  - name: deploy-knative-service
    taskRef:
      name: knative-deploy
    runAfter:
    - build-image
```

Through meticulously orchestrated pipelines, DevOps teams are empowered to focus on innovation and performance improvements, leaving the stability and reliability of the deployment process to automated systems. The operational efficiency renders substantial long-term benefits, enabling rapid adaptation to market changes and enhanced customer satisfaction.

Knative's capabilities are not limited to production-centric use cases; it also proves invaluable for research and experimental domains. Researchers in academia, for example, leverage Knative's serverless framework to conduct experiments and simulations without worrying about underlying infrastructure constraints. By allowing seamless scaling and resource allocation, Knative facilitates computation-heavy experiments in fields like computational biology or climate modeling.

As enterprises and organizations continually seek innovative solutions to modern technological challenges, Knative's flexible and powerful features continue to support diverse applications. From dynamic scaling in e-commerce to efficient process automation in DevOps, the versatility of Knative lays a solid foundation for building the next generation of cloud-native applications.

10.2 Case Study: E-commerce Platform Scaling

E-commerce platforms face unique challenges, particularly those related to significant fluctuations in traffic volumes. The demand for such platforms can be highly variable, peaking during holiday seasons, sales events, or promotional campaigns. Traditional infrastructure can struggle to handle these spikes efficiently, leading to performance degradation or even downtime, which can severely affect customer experience and business revenue. This case study explores how one e-commerce platform deployed Knative to effectively manage scaling demands, ensuring seamless operations and robust user engagement during peak periods.

The e-commerce platform in question experienced a traditional problem: it had a fixed infrastructure capacity that could not elastically adjust to varying traffic loads. This resulted in under-utilization during off-peak periods and a risk of overload when demand surged unexpectedly. Incorporating Knative into their architecture enabled the platform to leverage Kubernetes' orchestration capabilities while introducing serverless functions for enhanced scalability.

Knative's Serving component played a crucial role in managing and deploying containerized applications. It enabled automatic scaling of services based on real-time demand, optimizing the use of resources. When idle, services utilized minimal resources, and during high demand, Knative scaled instances proportionally, ensuring availability and performance.

To implement Knative, the platform's team first containerized their primary applications, preparing them for deployment on a Kubernetes cluster. Each service was defined using a Knative Service configuration, ensuring that services could scale dynamically. Below is an example of a basic Knative Service definition used by the team to manage their product catalog service:

```
apiVersion: serving.knative.dev/v1
kind: Service
metadata:
  name: product-catalog
  namespace: ecommerce
spec:
  template:
    metadata:
      annotations:
        autoscaling.knative.dev/min-scale: "1"
        autoscaling.knative.dev/max-scale: "20"
        autoscaling.knative.dev/target: "80"
    spec:
      containers:
      - image: docker.io/ecommerce/catalog:v1
        resources:
          limits:
            memory: "512Mi"
            cpu: "500m"
```

In this configuration, annotations were used to set scaling parameters—such as the minimum and maximum number of replicas. By configuring these parameters, the team aligned resource usage with anticipated demand, while allowing flexibility for unexpected spikes.

During the initial integration of Knative, the platform's team focused on two core objectives: reducing latency and maintaining quality of service during peak loads. They conducted rigorous load testing prior to deployment, using tools such as Apache JMeter to simulate heavy traffic and measure system responsiveness. The results were promising: compared to their traditional setup, the response time improved by up to 40% under heavy load conditions due to Knative's efficient auto-scaling algorithms.

The implementation of Knative did present challenges, primarily related to adaptation and learning curve issues that typically accompany new technologies. The platform's DevOps team needed to familiarize themselves with Kubernetes and container orchestration concepts, as these were foundational to effectively leveraging Knative's capabilities. Overcoming these challenges involved strategic training sessions and the use of detailed documentation.

Furthermore, Knative's integration required adjustments in the platform's continuous integration and deployment (CI/CD) processes. The team utilized Tekton, a Kubernetes-native tool, to automate their

CI/CD pipelines. This integration allowed the platform to automate building, testing, and deploying code changes, channeling code through a streamlined workflow. An example of a Tekton pipeline used for the product catalog service is shown below:

```
apiVersion: tekton.dev/v1beta1
kind: Pipeline
metadata:
  name: catalog-deploy-pipeline
  namespace: ecommerce
spec:
  tasks:
  - name: build-catalog-image
    taskRef:
      name: kaniko
    resources:
      inputs:
        - name: source
          resource: git-repo
      outputs:
        - name: image
          resource: docker-image
  - name: deploy-catalog-service
    taskRef:
      name: knative-deploy
    runAfter: [build-catalog-image]
```

This pipeline demonstrates automation of tedious deployment processes, significantly reducing human errors and ensuring consistent updates across environments. By minimizing manual intervention, the platform achieved a more reliable and responsive system, improving overall operational efficiency.

Beyond the technical challenges, implementing Knative offered several business advantages. The platform observed a reduction in infrastructure costs, attributed to more efficient resource utilization. Idle resources were minimized, which directly correlated with financial savings, as resources were only consumed based on current necessity rather than being perpetually active. Additionally, the platform improved its agility in responding to customer needs — rapid provisioning and de-provisioning of resources allowed for prompt adaptation to market conditions.

Emphasizing security practices remained a priority post-Knative implementation. The team employed network policies within Kubernetes to secure service communications, SPF, and DKIM records to fortify email communications, and managed secure access with RBAC policies to restrict permissions appropriately. Ensuring that security was built into their DevOps pipeline helped safeguard sensitive customer data against potential breaches.

Complementing their scalable architecture, the platform leveraged Knative Eventing to integrate external event sources. They employed cloud event brokers to manage events from various origins (such as customer actions or third-party integrations) and routed them to designated Knative services for appropriate processing. This enabled a more versatile and responsive event-driven architecture that could respond proactively to events such as new customer registrations or inventory updates.

By adopting an event-driven approach, the platform could construct a continuity map across its services, linking different business operations in a cohesive, automated manner. An example of a broker configuration, managing cloud events within their infrastructure, is shown below:

```
apiVersion: eventing.knative.dev/v1
kind: Broker
metadata:
  name: ecommerce-broker
  namespace: ecommerce
spec:
  channelTemplate:
    apiVersion: messaging.knative.dev/v1
    kind: InMemoryChannel
```

While Knative significantly streamlined the platform's scaling capabilities, continual monitoring and optimization became essential practices. The team developed dashboards using Prometheus and Grafana to monitor performance metrics. These tools provided real-time insights into system health and allowed proactive adjustments to scaling parameters or resource allocations, based on changing patterns of traffic. Visualizing metrics such as latency, request throughput, and system load granted comprehensive control over their infrastructure.

Ultimately, the e-commerce platform successfully leveraged Knative to enhance their scaling capabilities, improve resource utilization, and maintain superior user engagement during high-traffic events. Knative provided a robust framework to overcome traditional scalability challenges, enabling the platform to deliver excellent service quality efficiently and economically. Further integration of advanced analytics, collaborative development processes, and enhanced customer interaction models will continue to provide strategic advantages to the platform, asserting its position in a highly competitive market.

10.3 Case Study: Real-Time Data Processing

The rapid advancement of technology in recent years has elevated the importance of real-time data processing within various industries, especially in sectors like financial services where time-sensitive data is pivotal for operational success. Financial institutions rely on the immediate processing of data streams to make informed decisions, manage risks, and optimize trading strategies. This case study examines the application of Knative in a financial services company to address their real-time data processing needs, highlighting the benefits and intricacies involved in implementing an event-driven architecture with Knative.

Within the financial services industry, timely and accurate data processing is critical. Streaming data, such as stock prices, financial transactions, and economic news, must be accessed and evaluated instantaneously to allow firms to execute trades, manage portfolios, and maintain regulatory compliance. Conventional data processing solutions often fall short due to their latency and inflexibility in handling real-time data velocity and volume. To counteract these limitations, the financial services company featured in this case study turned to Knative to develop a resilient architecture capable of processing high-throughput, low-latency data streams.

The cornerstone of their solution was Knative Eventing, which provided the company with seamless integration and orchestration of event-based processes. Knative Eventing offers a reliable framework for managing, routing, and processing events from a myriad of sources, enabling the company to swiftly react to real-time information.

They began by defining event sources from various data feeds, such as market data providers, news aggregators, and trading platforms. Using the Knative Eventing model, these sources were mapped as event streams that could be processed by Knative services in an elastic environment, ensuring that resources scaled with demand.

First, the setup involved creating and deploying a Knative Broker, which acted as an intermediary, receiving events and routing them to appropriate services. The following code snippet demonstrates the configuration for setting up an in-memory Broker within Knative:

```
apiVersion: eventing.knative.dev/v1
kind: Broker
metadata:
  name: finance-broker
  namespace: real-time-processing
spec:
  channelTemplate:
    apiVersion: messaging.knative.dev/v1
    kind: InMemoryChannel
```

The financial services team proceeded to design Knative Triggers—special constructs that linked the Broker and various services responsible for processing events. Triggers allowed them to define subscribing services that reacted to specific event types or payload attributes, promoting efficient routing and efficient resource usage.

For instance, a Trigger could pass stock price updates to a pricing service that calculates real-time moving averages or risk metrics. The following example showcases a basic Trigger configuration targeted at routing events of type finance.stock.update to the dedicated service:

```
apiVersion: eventing.knative.dev/v1
kind: Trigger
metadata:
  name: stock-update-trigger
  namespace: real-time-processing
spec:
  broker: finance-broker
  filter:
    attributes:
      type: finance.stock.update
  subscriber:
    ref:
      apiVersion: serving.knative.dev/v1
      kind: Service
      name: stock-pricing-service
```

Alongside Trigger configurations, the services themselves were defined using Knative Serving. To ensure responsiveness, the financial institution took advantage of various Kubernetes and Knative features, such as horizontal pod scaling, to automatically scale their services based on demand, maintaining a balance between performance and resource efficiency.

Below is an example configuration of a Knative pricing service that receives high-frequency pricing data and processes it in real-time:

```yaml
apiVersion: serving.knative.dev/v1
kind: Service
metadata:
  name: stock-pricing-service
  namespace: real-time-processing
spec:
  template:
    metadata:
      labels:
        security: stock-pricing
    spec:
      containers:
      - image: docker.io/financials/pricing:latest
        ports:
        - containerPort: 8080
        resources:
          limits:
            cpu: "1000m"
            memory: "1Gi"
```

To ensure comprehensive insight into service performance and system health, the team implemented monitoring and logging solutions using tools like Prometheus, Grafana, and Fluentd. These tools enabled them to set up detailed dashboards and alerts to monitor key performance indicators (KPIs), such as latency, throughput, and error rates—a critical aspect in maintaining real-time performance.

Knative's compatibility with existing Kubernetes infrastructure facilitated straightforward integration. Since the company already deployed mission-critical services on Kubernetes, extending their architecture with Knative components did not require a substantial shift in their technology stack, thus saving time and resources. The inbuilt flexibility of Knative allowed them to tailor event processing mechanisms to cater to their specific needs.

In transitioning to a Knative-powered architecture, the financial firm encountered a learning curve, as understanding and defining cloud-native patterns for event processing required adapting to new paradigms. To mitigate these challenges, the engineering team undertook dedicated training and engaged closely with the Knative community, drawing insights from case studies and best practice guidelines.

The shift to Knative brought tangible results in terms of reducing data processing latency and enhancing scalability. The platform's auto-scaling capabilities meant that it could dynamically allocate computing resources during market open periods when trading activity—and thus data volume—peaked, and scale down during quieter hours, leading to significant cost efficiencies.

The ability to leverage event-driven paradigms also streamlined business workflows, promoting improved decision-making and faster reaction times to market developments. This agility increased the organization's competitive edge by facilitating timely and informed trading decisions, thereby maximizing potential returns and minimizing risk.

Moreover, implementing security mechanisms, such as service mesh technologies (like Istio), within the Knative environment ensured end-to-end encryption and mutual TLS authentication, meeting compliance and regulatory requirements while safeguarding sensitive financial data.

In terms of future applications, the financial services company plans to extend its Knative-based architecture to support advanced analytics, comprising machine learning models that can predict market trends and provide real-time investment insights. Knative's flexibility and extensibility provide an ideal foundation for integrating these sophisticated, compute-intensive workloads into existing workflows.

This experience with Knative for real-time data processing not only satisfied immediate business needs but also established a robust, agile infrastructure framework capable of adapting to future innovations and demands. The company continues to explore refinements and optimizations to further exploit Knative's potential, looking at areas such as event replay mechanisms and multi-tenancy features to enhance utility and robustness in their operations.

Overall, this case study exemplifies how Knative can be employed within the financial services sector to address increasingly complex real-time data processing challenges, offering a scalable, efficient, and robust solution that leads to both strategic benefits and operational excellence.

10.4   Case Study: Microservices Migration

The migration from monolithic to microservices architectures represents a transformative shift for many organizations seeking to improve agility, scalability, and maintainability in their software systems. This migration, however, involves inherent challenges that demand careful planning and execution. This case study delves into the journey of a legacy application transitioning to a microservices architecture using Knative, a Kubernetes-based platform that streamlines and enhances scalable service deployment.

The organization in focus, a major enterprise software provider, originally operated a large monolithic application that served multiple business units. Over time, this monolithic system became increasingly difficult to manage as it grew in complexity, slowing down innovation and complicating deployment processes. The decision to transition to a microservices architecture stemmed from a need to decouple tightly integrated services, allowing independent development and deployment cycles.

Knative was identified as a key facilitator for this migration owing to its integration with Kubernetes, enabling serverless deployments with on-demand scaling and simplified operations. The pathway to a successful microservices-based system involved several phases:

Planning and DevOps Restructuring: The initial phase involved restructuring the DevOps processes to align with cloud-native patterns. This restructuring emphasized increased collaboration between development and operations teams and the adoption of continuous integration/continuous deployment (CI/CD) pipelines to automate building, testing, and deployment. By implementing a CI/CD pipeline with Tekton as shown below, the company ensured a seamless and error-free workflow for deploying new microservices:

```
apiVersion: tekton.dev/v1beta1
kind: Pipeline
metadata:
  name: microservice-deployment-pipeline
  namespace: migration-project
spec:
  tasks:
  - name: unit-tests
```

```
taskRef:
  name: run-tests
resources:
  inputs:
    - name: source
      resource: git-repo
- name: build-image
  taskRef:
    name: kaniko
  resources:
    inputs:
      - name: source
        resource: git-repo
    outputs:
      - name: image
        resource: docker-image
  runAfter: [unit-tests]
- name: deploy-service
  taskRef:
    name: knative-service-deploy
  runAfter: [build-image]
```

Service Identification and Decomposition: The next step involved identifying and extracting services from the monolithic application, a process known as decomposition. This entailed detailed analysis to define service boundaries—often influenced by business domains—and to ensure that extracted services were sufficiently autonomous. The objective was to create cohesive services that encapsulated related functionality, enabling developers to optimize them independent of one another.

Infrastructure Configuration and Knative Setup: Leveraging Knative's infrastructure, the organization set up a Kubernetes cluster that acted as the foundation for running containerized microservices. Knative Serving was employed to manage service deployments, autoscaling, and routing, while maintaining zero-downtime deployments. Below is an example of how a decomposed service was configured using Knative, illustrating the automatic scaling based on network request metrics:

```
apiVersion: serving.knative.dev/v1
kind: Service
metadata:
  name: customer-service
  namespace: business-segment
spec:
  template:
    metadata:
      annotations:
        autoscaling.knative.dev/target: "50"
```

301

```
      autoscaling.knative.dev/metric: "concurrency"
spec:
  containers:
  - image: docker.io/business/customer-service:v2
    ports:
    - containerPort: 8080
    resources:
      limits:
        memory: "512Mi"
        cpu: "500m"
```

Data Management and Service Communication: As services were decomposed, it was essential to address data dependencies and communication patterns. Knative Eventing enabled the organization to establish an event-driven architecture—promoting asynchronous communication via events and decoupling services further. This setup also allowed for the easy integration of new services and facilitated enhancements without hindering existing operations.

To ensure smooth communication between services, cloud event brokers were configured to manage the communication pathways. An example is demonstrated below where a broker is configured to link two services:

```
apiVersion: eventing.knative.dev/v1
kind: Broker
metadata:
  name: internal-broker
  namespace: business-segment
spec:
  channelTemplate:
    apiVersion: messaging.knative.dev/v1
    kind: InMemoryChannel
```

Monitoring, Observability, and Security: With a distributed architecture in place, effective monitoring and observability became critical. The organization capitalized on tools such as Prometheus and Grafana to collect metrics and visualize the performance of distributed services. In addition, leveraging a service mesh like Istio helped manage complex service communication while providing security features like mutual TLS authentication and request-level policies—a necessity for safeguarding data and ensuring compliance with industry regulations.

Progressive Migration and Canary Deployments: The migration was executed progressively, migrating services in phases to minimize disruption and allow for adjustments based on received feedback. As services were transitioned, canary deployments were utilized to test new services on a limited subset of users before full production roll-out. This enabled immediate detection and resolution of any issues with minimal impact on end users:

```
apiVersion: serving.knative.dev/v1
kind: Service
metadata:
  name: payment-service
  namespace: business-segment
spec:
  template:
    metadata:
      name: payment-service-v1
    spec:
      containers:
      - image: docker.io/business/payment-service:v2
  traffic:
  - latestRevision: true
    percent: 10
  - latestRevision: false
    revisionName: payment-service-v1
    percent: 90
```

The successful migration to a microservices architecture using Knative presented numerous advantages. An immediate gain was improved agility—the ability for multiple development teams to independently build, test, and deploy their services without conflicting with one another accelerated release cycles. Moreover, Knative's elasticity allowed the organization to handle varying workloads effectively, leading to optimized resource usage and substantial cost savings.

Challenges associated with microservices migration, such as data consistency and service coordination, were effectively managed through the use of event-driven patterns and robust service communication protocols. In addition, the comprehensive observability and monitoring solutions enabled the proactive identification of bottlenecks and potential service failures, ensuring minimal downtime and enhanced reliability.

The transition from a monolithic to microservices architecture also fostered an organizational culture shift. The restructuring necessitated a move from vertical teams managing specific components of the monolith to horizontal, cross-functional teams responsible for end-to-end service delivery. This shift, although initially challenging, fostered innovation, cooperation, and continuous improvement.

Looking forward, the organization plans to explore advanced service mesh capabilities, such as traffic splitting for A/B testing and fault injection for resilient testing systems with Knative, to further enhance the robustness and flexibility of their microservices architecture. As they continue to assimilate microservices principles, the organization anticipates further opportunities to enrich their operational environment and meet evolving business requirements.

This case study illustrates Knative's efficacy in navigating microservices migration, underscoring its role as a catalyst for agility and scalability in modern software architectures. The strategic insights gained from this migration provide valuable lessons for other organizations embarking on similar transformation journeys, marking a significant milestone in the ongoing evolution of cloud-native infrastructure and services.

10.5   Innovative Applications in IoT

The Internet of Things (IoT) has emerged as a transformative technology paradigm, enabling the integration of the physical and digital worlds through devices capable of generating, processing, and exchanging data. IoT applications span diverse domains, including smart cities, healthcare, agriculture, and industrial automation, requiring efficient data management and cost-effective computational resources. This expansive array of varied applications presents an ideal landscape for leveraging the capabilities of Knative—a serverless platform based on Kubernetes—to build innovative solutions within the IoT sphere.

IoT environments inherently generate sporadic and bursty data streams, making traditional static server provisions insufficient and economically impractical. Instead, serverless computing, embodied by Knative, provides the on-demand scalability and resource efficiency necessary to process these intermittent workloads effectively. In this section, we delve into several innovative applications of Knative in the IoT domain, exploring its potential to optimize resource allocation, reduce latency, and enhance reliability.

- **Smart Agriculture**

In agriculture, IoT devices such as sensors, drones, and connected machinery collect critical data, including soil moisture, weather patterns, crop health, and equipment status. Such real-time insights enable precision farming practices, improving yield while minimizing resource use. Knative facilitates the development of applications capable of extracting immediate, actionable insights from IoT-generated data, leading to more responsive decision-making.

A typical smart agriculture application involves deploying Knative for processing sensor data streams within a field management system. As field conditions change, sensor data is processed through Knative Eventing to trigger automated irrigation based on predefined thresholds. Sensors publish data to an IoT broker, serving as an event source for Knative:

```
apiVersion: sources.knative.dev/v1alpha1
kind: ApiServerSource
metadata:
  name: field-sensor-source
  namespace: agri-system
spec:
  serviceAccountName: sensor-reader
  mode: Resource
  resources:
    - apiVersion: v1
      kind: SensorData
  sink:
    ref:
      apiVersion: eventing.knative.dev/v1
      kind: Broker
      name: default
```

Data is filtered and processed using specific Knative Event Triggers tied to the aforementioned broker. These Triggers activate services for performing functions such as irrigation control or alert notifications:

```
apiVersion: eventing.knative.dev/v1
kind: Trigger
metadata:
  name: irrigation-trigger
  namespace: agri-system
spec:
  broker: default
  filter:
    attributes:
      type: io.sensors.data
      threshold: "30"
  subscriber:
```

```
ref:
  apiVersion: serving.knative.dev/v1
  kind: Service
  name: irrigation-controller
```

- **Smart Cities**

In the context of smart cities, IoT solutions include various applications such as waste management, traffic control, and public safety. Knative enables these applications by providing a flexible platform that can scale based on real-time demand. A Knative-driven urban management system might integrate data from sources such as traffic cameras, public transport sensors, or waste bin sensors, dynamically scaling processing capabilities as data volume fluctuates throughout the day.

In a smart traffic and public safety system, for instance, Knative can facilitate events like road congestion updates or emergency response actions. Combining Knative Eventing with geographical information system (GIS) services, cities can visualize and react to unfolding scenarios in real-time, helping to streamline traffic flow or coordinate response units.

The following example sets up Knative Eventing to manage traffic events, where data from city traffic sensors is fed through an event source:

```
apiVersion: sources.knative.dev/v1
kind: PingSource
metadata:
  name: traffic-pingsource
  namespace: smart-city
spec:
  schedule: "*/5 * * * *"
  jsonData: '{"location": "42.3601,-71.0589"}'
  sink:
    ref:
      apiVersion: eventing.knative.dev/v1
      kind: Broker
      name: traffic-broker
```

Similarly, Triggers are configured to actuate traffic control services or enable adaptive signaling systems:

```
apiVersion: eventing.knative.dev/v1
kind: Trigger
metadata:
  name: traffic-control-trigger
```

```
    namespace: smart-city
spec:
  broker: traffic-broker
  filter:
    attributes:
      location: "42.3601,-71.0589"
  subscriber:
    ref:
      apiVersion: serving.knative.dev/v1
      kind: Service
      name: traffic-signal-service
```

- **Healthcare and Wearable Devices**

In healthcare, wearable devices continuously monitor vital signs, activity levels, and other health metrics, forwarding critical data to medical systems for review and analysis. The ability of Knative to handle these constant albeit bursty data streams proves vital in crafting agile healthcare applications that can react to physiological changes in near real-time.

A health monitoring system might deploy Knative to receive alerts from wearables or biosensors, analyzing real-time data to detect critical health events like irregular heartbeats or falling glucose levels. These events trigger interventions such as notifying healthcare personnel or adjusting medication dosages automatically.

A sample configuration illustrating the setup for processing alerts from wearable devices is presented below:

```
apiVersion: sources.knative.dev/v1
kind: ContainerSource
metadata:
  name: health-alert-source
  namespace: healthcare
spec:
  image: docker.io/healthcare/alertsource:latest
  sink:
    ref:
      apiVersion: eventing.knative.dev/v1
      kind: Broker
      name: health-broker
```

Healthcare services listening for these alerts react through a configured Trigger setup, activating necessary medical responses:

```
apiVersion: eventing.knative.dev/v1
kind: Trigger
```

```
metadata:
  name: alert-notification-trigger
  namespace: healthcare
spec:
  broker: health-broker
  filter:
    attributes:
      type: health.alert
  subscriber:
    ref:
      apiVersion: serving.knative.dev/v1
      kind: Service
      name: alert-notification-service
```

- **Industrial Automation**

In manufacturing, IoT applications span predictive maintenance, quality control, and production optimization. Knative provides flexibility in managing vast data volumes generated by connected industrial equipment and sensors, enabling real-time decision-making and operational agility.

A predictive maintenance system can utilize Knative to process telemetry data from machinery, identifying patterns indicative of wear and tear, thereby preempting mechanical failures. By leveraging Knative's ability to scale event processing services based on telemetry input, businesses achieve superior maintenance scheduling, minimize runtime disruptions, and optimize operational expenditure.

Configured event sources collect and route sensor alerts and equipment logs, integrating autonomously with maintenance management solutions via Knative Triggers and services:

```
apiVersion: eventing.knative.dev/v1
kind: Trigger
metadata:
  name: maintenance-schedule-trigger
  namespace: industry-automation
spec:
  broker: default
  filter:
    attributes:
      type: equipment.alert
  subscriber:
    ref:
      apiVersion: serving.knative.dev/v1
      kind: Service
      name: maintenance-planner-service
```

The adaptability of Knative also aligns with evolving Industry 4.0 standards, where interoperability, data transparency, and real-time architectures are prerequisites for advanced industrial systems.

- **Robustness and Security Considerations**

Innovative IoT solutions leveraging Knative must address resilience and security requirements. Deploying a service mesh like Istio not only enhances service discovery and routing but also provides robust security mechanisms such as mutual authentication using mTLS (mutual Transport Layer Security) and policy-driven access controls. Such integrations fortify IoT applications against data breaches and unauthorized access while maintaining compliance with industry regulations.

- **Conclusion**

Through these various applications, Knative underscores its utility across the IoT spectrum. It enables reactive, real-time solutions for managing sensor data and controlling IoT devices with a flexible, scalable architecture aligned with the demands of dynamic IoT environments. By migrating workloads to serverless models with Knative, organizations attain cost efficiencies, computational elasticity, and enhanced application resilience—fundamental attributes for thriving in the connected world of IoT.

10.6 Case Study: Automating DevOps Pipelines

The acceleration of software development lifecycles hinges on the efficacy of DevOps practices, where automation plays a critical role in bridging development and operations. To achieve continuous integration and delivery (CI/CD), many organizations seek robust, scalable solutions that streamline entire build-and-deploy workflows. Knative, with its Kubernetes-based serverless platform, offers promising capabilities to enhance CI/CD processes by seamlessly integrating automation into DevOps pipelines. This case study explores the implementation of Knative to automate CI/CD pipelines within an enterprise, spotlighting best practices, challenges, and benefits realized throughout the transformation.

Current State and Challenges

The enterprise's initial development and deployment process involved multiple manual steps, spanning code review, build, test, and deployment stages. Though functional, this system suffered from inefficiencies and exposed the business to several risks:

- **Inconsistent Environments**: Deployments across staging and production environments often encountered discrepancies, leading to disruptions.

- **Prolonged Release Cycles**: Manual interventions extended release cycles, delaying feature rollouts.

- **Error-Prone Processes**: Human errors, particularly during configuration and deployment, could result in faulty releases and service outages.

Recognizing the challenges, the enterprise aimed to transition to a highly automated DevOps pipeline that facilitated agility, improved reliability, and supported rapid scaling.

The Role of Knative

By leveraging Knative's event-driven architecture alongside Kubernetes orchestration, the company sought to automate its CI/CD processes. Knative's components, particularly Knative Serving and Eventing, provided a scaffold for building recurrent, reliable workflows that supported dynamic scaling and resilient operations across environments.

Key advantages anticipated with Knative integration included:

- **Elastic Scaling**: Knative dynamically adjusts resource allocation based on real-time demand, optimizing both cost and performance.

- **Event-Driven Automation**: The platform's event-driven model automates responses to code changes, build completions, or even test results without manual interjections.

- **Minimized Downtime**: Built-in blue/green deployment strategies can ensure zero-downtime updates, improving service availability.

Pipeline Design and Knative Integration

The new automated pipeline envisioned by the enterprise utilized Knative in tandem with Tekton, a Kubernetes-native CI/CD system, to perfect its software delivery cycle. The process involved several stages: detection of change, automated build, testing, deployment, and monitoring.

Detection of Change: CI triggers, originating from code repository changes, ignited the pipeline's execution. Integrating with version control systems such as GitHub or GitLab, automated WebHooks initiated the build process upon detecting code pushes to the repository:

```
apiVersion: tekton.dev/v1beta1
kind: PipelineRun
metadata:
  generateName: app-build-
  namespace: devops-automation
spec:
  pipelineRef:
    name: app-pipeline
  resources:
    - name: source-repo
      resourceRef:
        name: source-repo-git
```

Automated Build and Image Creation: Tekton pipelines utilized industry-standard builders like Kaniko to automate Docker image creation. The pipeline was designed to fetch changes, execute build scripts, and package application artifacts within container images:

```
apiVersion: tekton.dev/v1beta1
kind: Task
metadata:
  name: build-image
  namespace: devops-automation
spec:
  steps:
    - name: build-and-push
      image: gcr.io/kaniko-project/executor:latest
      args:
        - --dockerfile=/workspace/source/Dockerfile
        - --context=/workspace/source
        - --destination=gcr.io/project/image:${github.sha}
```

Automated Testing: Once image creation concluded, automated testing ensued, harnessing testing frameworks relevant to the application. Tekton tasks were configured to run test suites against the newly built images to identify regressions or compatibility issues:

```
apiVersion: tekton.dev/v1beta1
kind: Task
metadata:
  name: run-tests
  namespace: devops-automation
spec:
  steps:
    - name: test
      image: test-framework:latest
      args:
        - npm
        - run
        - test
```

Deployment Automation Using Knative: Following successful testing, applications transitioned to deployment states. Knative's Serving component empowered the deployment process with auto-scaling services, defined through YAML configurations setting service revisions, routes, and traffic rules:

```
apiVersion: serving.knative.dev/v1
kind: Service
metadata:
  name: app-service
  namespace: devops-automation
spec:
  template:
    metadata:
      annotations:
        autoscaling.knative.dev/min-scale: "2"
    spec:
      containers:
        - image: gcr.io/project/image:${github.sha}
```

Traffic splitting facilitated canary releases, reducing exposure to new deploys while validating performance with real users:

```
apiVersion: serving.knative.dev/v1
kind: Service
metadata:
  name: app-service
  namespace: devops-automation
spec:
  template:
    metadata:
      name: app-service-v2
    spec:
```

```
    containers:
    - image: gcr.io/project/image:new
  traffic:
  - latestRevision: true
    percent: 10
  - latestRevision: false
    revisionName: app-service-v1
    percent: 90
```

Monitoring and Feedback Loop: The final iteration loops back by closing a feedback cycle. Monitoring tools like Prometheus combined with Grafana delivered real-time insights and alerting capabilities to dev and ops teams about application health, performance, and readiness for scaling:

```
apiVersion: monitoring.coreos.com/v1
kind: ServiceMonitor
metadata:
  name: app-service-monitor
  namespace: monitoring
spec:
  selector:
    matchLabels:
      k8s-app: knative-app
  endpoints:
  - port: web
```

Benefits and Outcomes

The implementation of an automated CI/CD pipeline utilizing Knative delivered comprehensive improvements to the enterprise's software engineering ecosystem:

- **Accelerated Deployment Frequency**: Release cycles shortened substantively, facilitating rapid feature deliverance and iterative software development practices.

- **Reduced Human Error**: Automation drastically curtailed manual interventions, decreasing the potential for errors in configuration and deployment steps.

- **Cross-Environment Consistency**: Uniform deployments were assured across development, staging, and production environments, thanks to containerization coupled with Kubernetes orchestration.

- **Cost Efficiency**: Dynamically scaling resources aligned cloud expenditure with actual usage, presenting significant cost savings, particularly in non-peak periods.

Beyond the immediate technical advantages, the transition enforced a culture of continuous development and deployment, embracing lean methodologies and iterative improvements. Teams became more agile, adapting responsive strategies to business requirements and prompter stakeholder feedback.

Challenges Encountered and Overcome

Throughout the transition, the enterprise faced challenges inherent to adopting new technology and integrating it within legacy systems. Specific areas pose particular concern:

- **Learning Curve**: The shift to Kubernetes-native tools necessitated upfront tool knowledge acquisition and training.

- **Cultural Shift**: Embedded habits needed adjustment to fully embrace the automated paradigm, requiring active change management.

- **Integration Complexity**: Legacy systems interfaced with the new pipelines encountered compatibility and interfacing challenges, mitigated through comprehensive refactoring.

Ultimately, careful planning, progressive implementation, and iterative refinements cushioned these challenges, rendering the deployment successful and beneficial.

Concluding Remarks and Future Prospects

The evolution towards automated DevOps pipelines utilizing Knative stands as a paradigm shift, enabling teams to achieve significant productivity gains and heightened response capability. As the enterprise advances, extending their pipeline to harness artificial intelligence for predictive deployment decision-making and further optimizing testing and monitoring processes remain strategic pursuits.

Knative's role in automating DevOps processes belts out a resounding assertion of its capabilities, positioning it as a formidable ally for businesses invested in technological advancement, efficiency, and innovation. This foresighted adoption equips teams with a framework to anticipate, adapt, and evolve suitably in the fast-paced technology landscape.

10.7 Lessons Learned and Future Directions

The integration of Knative into various domains, as explored through our detailed case studies, offers a rich repository of insights that can guide future applications and innovations. As organizations worldwide adopt Knative to leverage its serverless capabilities and Kubernetes foundation, understanding the strategic lessons learned from these implementations is crucial. This section expands on key takeaways from the applications of Knative across diverse scenarios while exploring potential future directions in the landscape of serverless computing.

Key Lessons Learned

- **Effective Automation Enhances Agility and Efficiency:** Embracing automation through tools like Knative facilitates a streamlined orchestration of compute resources, contributing significantly to increased operational agility. Automation not only reduces manual intervention, minimizing associated errors but also accelerates time-to-market by promoting continuous integration, continuous deployment (CI/CD), and faster response times to market demands.

- **Scalability and Resource Efficiency Are Core Strengths:** The serverless nature of Knative, especially when combined with Kubernetes' orchestration, allows for scalable solutions that match workloads dynamically. This elasticity results in optimized resource allocation, ensuring applications are cost-effective, responsive, and aligned with varying demand patterns, as observed in the e-commerce and IoT domains.

- **Event-Driven Architecture is a Powerful Catalyst:** By enabling event-driven paradigms, Knative can automate workflows that respond to real-time events. This capability can decouple

315

systems, enhance responsiveness, and allow businesses to capitalize on real-time data streams effectively. The financial services and IoT applications stand as clear exemplars of this architectural approach, providing invaluable feedback that drove functional improvements.

- **Cultural Shifts Accompany Technological Changes:** The transition to Knative is not solely a technical undertaking; it necessitates a cultural shift within organizations towards embracing DevOps principles, collaborative development practices, and agile methodologies. Organizational readiness, training, and commitment to change management are critical for seamless transitions and maximum benefit realization.

- **Security and Compliance Must be Proactively Managed:** With increased autonomy and dynamic scaling, security practices encompassing service mesh implementations, Network policies, RBAC (role-based access control), and TLS encryption have become essential. Similarly, adhering to industry compliance standards throughout the adoption process is necessary to safeguard data integrity and confidentiality.

- **Monitoring and Observability Foster Resilient Systems:** The inherently dynamic nature of Kubernetes and Knative-driven architectures mandates continuous monitoring and observability. Implementing comprehensive observability establishes transparency in operations, aids anomaly detection, and provides actionable insights for performance tuning and troubleshooting, leveraging tools like Prometheus and Grafana.

Future Directions

Given the rapidly evolving technological ecosystem and the continued growth of cloud-native and serverless paradigms, several future directions present themselves for Knative and its application across different sectors:

- **Advanced AI/ML Integration:** As machine learning models and AI algorithms become increasingly integral to business operations, Knative's scalable infrastructure can support real-time model updates and inferencing workflows. Integrating ML models as event-driven services can provide enhanced predictions, anomaly detection, and automated decision-making capabilities, further enriching applications.

- **Edge Computing and IoT Expansion:** The convergence of Knative with edge computing has the potential to transform how IoT applications are deployed and managed. Running Knative at the edge would allow real-time processing of data close to its source, facilitating faster decision-making and reduced latency while alleviating data transfer loads to central cloud systems.

- **Improved Multi-Cloud and Hybrid Cloud Support:** Organizations increasingly explore multi-cloud strategies to avoid vendor lock-in and optimize costs. Knative's potential for seamless multi-cloud deployments could be enhanced by improving interoperability and orchestration capabilities across heterogeneous cloud environments, providing the flexibility to run applications across public, private, and hybrid clouds.

- **Enhanced Developer Experience:** As Knative matures, improving the developer experience through more intuitive interfaces, better tooling, and integration with developer-centric platforms will be crucial. Facilitating ease of use, debugging, and seamless migration paths from traditional server-based systems to serverless architectures will drive enhancements in adoption and productivity.

- **Evolving Security and Policy Automation:** Future iterations of Knative stand to benefit immensely from tighter integration with automated security policy management systems. Closing gaps in anomaly detection, security compliance, identity management, and access controls are imperative as applications expand in complexity and footprint within cloud environments.

- **Inter-service Communication and Data Management:** Further innovations are necessary in efficiently managing inter-service communications, especially over distributed systems. Optimizing data-sharing protocols and storage systems to support Knative's dynamic workloads will be pivotal in

317

achieving performance gains, reliability, and resource efficiency across microservices-dependent architectures.

- **Plug-and-Play Architectural Components:** The ability to rapidly define, compose, and deploy Knative components as reusable architectural modules can boost organizational agility and innovation. By fostering modular design practices and standardized patterns, organizations will ensure faster prototyping, reduced development cycles, and the flexibility to adapt swiftly to technological advancements.

Embracing such advancements will necessitate close collaboration between Knative's active open source community, enterprises, and cloud providers. The ability to meet evolving requirements while overcoming technological challenges will play a vital role in shaping how Knative—and indeed, serverless computing—will continue to evolve in the forthcoming years.

To summarize, the lessons learned from deploying Knative have already highlighted its profound impact on operational efficiency, scalability, and innovation. As the community explores future potential applications and integrates advanced capabilities, Knative stands ready to forge new pathways in existing and emerging domains, securing a pivotal role in the cloud-native technology narrative. Continued investment in people, processes, and technology will unequivocally enhance its robustness and broaden its appeal to a diverse array of use cases.